W9-DAE-422

COSMIC TRIGGER II

Down To Earth

What Critics Say About Robert Anton Wilson

A SUPER-GENIUS ... He has written everything I was afraid to write.
— Dr. John Lilly

One of the funniest, most incisive social critics around, and with a positive bent, thank Goddess.
— Riane Eisler, author of *The Chalice and the Blade*

A very funny man ... readers with open minds will like his books.
— Robin Robertson, *Psychological Perspectives*

Robert Anton Wilson is a dazzling barker hawking tickets to the most thrilling tilt-a-whirls and daring loop-o-planes on the midway of higher consciousness.
— Tom Robbins, author of *Even Cowgirls Get the Blues*

The man's either a genius or Jesus.
— SOUNDS (London)

A 21st Century Rennaisance Man ... funny, wise and optimistic... the Lenny Bruce of philosophers.
— *Denver Post*

One of the most important writers working in English today ... courageous, compassionate, optimistic and original.
— Elwyn Chamberling, author of *Gates of Fire*

Malicious, misguided fanaticism.
— Robert Sheaffer, CSICOP

Wilson managed to reverse every mental polarity in me, as if I had been dragged through infinity. I was astounded and delighted.
— Philip K. Dick, author of *Blade Runner*

One of the leading thinkers of the modern age
— Barbara Marx Hubbard, *World Future Society*

The most important philosopher of this centur ... scholarly, witty, hip and hopeful.
— Timothy Leary, Ph.D.

He does for quantum mechanics what Durrell's *Alexandria Quarteet* did for Relativity, *but Wilson is funnier.*
— John Gribbin, Physicist

The man's glittering intelligence won't let you rest. With each new book, I look forward to his wisdom, laced with crazy humor.
— Alan Harrington, author of *The Immortalist*

A master satirist who views history as an open question
— Brad Linaweaver, *Atlanta Constitution*

COSMIC TRIGGER II

Down To Earth

BY

Robert Anton Wilson

NEW FALCON PUBLICATIONS
TEMPE, AZ U.S.A.

Copyright © 1991 Robert Anton Wilson

All rights reserved. No part of this book, in part or in whole, may be reproduced, transmitted, or utilized, in any form or by any means, electronic or mechanical, including photocopying, recording, or by any information storage and retrieval system, without permission in writing from the publisher, except for brief quotations in critical articles, books and reviews.

International Standard Book Number: 1-56184-011-4
Library of Congress Number: 91-68040

First Printing 1991
Second Printing 1993
Third Printing 1995
Fourth Printing 1996 (Revised Second Edition)
Fifth Printing 1997
Sixth Printing 1999
Seventh Printing 2000
Eighth Printing 2002
Ninth Printing 2005

Cover by S. Jason Black
Cover design by Christopher S. Hyatt, Ph.D.

The paper used in this publication meets the minimum requirements of the American National Standard for Permanence of Paper for Printed Library Materials Z39.48-1984

Address all inquiries to:
NEW FALCON PUBLICATIONS
1739 East Broadway Road #1-277
Tempe, AZ 85282 U.S.A

(or)
320 East Charleston Blvd. #204-286
Las Vegas, NV 89104

website: http://www.newfalcon.com
email: info@newfalcon.com

You can only go half-way
into the darkest forest;
then you are coming out
the other side.

— Chinese proverb

DEDICATION

This book is FOR
R. Buckminster Fuller,
in memory

It is AGAINST
the makers of war,
in anathema

Mine eyes have seen Saddam Hussein
The *Koran* on his knee
A-typing out communiqués
For all the world to see:
"Our missiles just hit Tel Aviv
And God is full of glee,
Islam goes marching on!"

Onward, Christian soldiers,
Children of the Beast!
Kill! Kill! Kill! for Jeee-sus!
Fight till you're deceased!
PRRRRRRRFFFFFFFFFFT!

the bridge persists
more than symbol, more than sermon
the bridge persists

TABLE OF CONTENTS

WHEN DINOSAURS ROAMED THE EARTH

Tales of Savagery and Voodoo

I grew up in a barbaric, pre-historic age. My parents lived on a long island which the natives, simply and logically, called Long Island. My tribe consisted of Irish Catholics who had seized control of an area called Gerrison Beach because, evidently, nobody else wanted it.

Dinosaurs still roamed the earth, wreaking havoc upon human encampments.

The most monstrous dinosaurs had strange, un-Irish names: the worst were called Hitler and Mussolini. Others, named Stalin and Franco, were said to be man-eaters also. But they were all far away, across the ocean. When I was small, we were all convinced they would never come and bother us in America.

We were much more afraid of a more immediate Monster called The Depression. The Depression had thrown many men out of work and everybody with a job seemed to fear they might wake up at Christ O'Clock in the morning any day of the year and find their own jobs had vanished like fairy's gold.

I hadn't been born in Gerrison Beach. I had been expelled from a kind of lush and lavish Lilly Samadhi Tank — a warm, watery womb — into the Flatbush area of Brooklyn, in 1932. The Depression had already brought unemployment to many, but not to my family. My father had a good job somewhere — I haven't a gopher's notion of what he was working at, but I dimly remember a very early time when I felt that we were safe from the God-awful things the Depression was doing to some of our relatives.

Then suddenly the Depression turned around and dumped its Golden Turd of the Week on us, too. The company my father had been working for went out of business and he and hundreds of others found themselves without jobs. We moved to Gerrison Beach where rents were very low because only the poor Irish Catholics lived there.

I learned somehow, vaguely, that back in Brooklyn and Manhattan vast armies of homeless, nearly starving people were roaming the streets, begging — the consequence of ten years of Voodoo Economics* in the White House.

We are beginning to see some of the same medieval squalor again, as I write this memoir. We've just had another ten years of Voodoo Economics, and the streets once more are as full of human debris as any "backward" nation in the Third World. As Santayana said, those who do not learn from history are doomed to repeat it.

Listen. You can hear those Hoodoo Voodoo zombie drums every time President Bush opens his mouth. Don't read his lips: he lies. *Listen closely*, and you'll hear the beat-beat-beat of the tom-tom as the jungle shadows fall...

---

* A system named by George Herbert Walker Bush, later its most skilled practitioner. It consists of keeping the marks distracted with bright chatter while you empty their pockets — or their S&L accounts.

DEITY AFFRONTED BY IMPIETY

Woman Turned Into Frog

To be a man is to fear God.

— Saint John Chrysostomos

An old Irish story tells of a farm woman who set out on the road, walking at a brisk pace. "Where are you going, Maureen?" a neighbor woman asked.

"I'm going to Galway," said Maureen.

"Be careful," the neighbor warned. "You should say, 'I'm going to Galway, *God willing.*'"

"Stuff and nonsense," said Maureen. "I'm going to Galway and sure that's the whole of the matter."

God thereupon waxed sorely pissed. He turned the poor woman into a frog and deposited her in a swamp with a few thousand other frogs, and there he left her for seven long, long years. All she heard or said for those dreary years consisted of "Gribbit! Gribbit! Gribbit!" and an occasional more classical "Koax, koax, koax!" Everything she saw was dank and dark, like a scene from Poe, and all she had to eat were flies.

"It's enough to bother a body," she thought mournfully on many a miserable and rainy day.

At the end of seven years, God relented and allowed Maureen to resume a human form. She immediately climbed out of the swamp, washed her clothes, and hung them on a traditional hickory limb. When everything was dry, the good woman dressed herself again and started out on the road once more.

"Where are you going, Maureen?" asked another neighbor.

"To Galway," she said, "or back to that damned swamp with the frogs."

SYNCHRO-MESH

The day I was born in frosty, wintry Brooklyn on January 18, 1932, all the way across this homonguous geological grok of a continent in sunny-gold Hollywood, Archie Leach was celebrating his 28th birthday. Archie had been raised in poverty, like me, but on his 28th birthday that was behind him. He had recently co-starred with Marlene Dietrich in *Blonde Venus* and he had reason to think $ucce$$ was opening its doors. In fact, it was. The studio had already changed his name to Cary Grant and he soon became the most bodaceously popular movie star of all time.

Men admired him as much as women, because he managed to project the image of just about what every male on the planet would like to be. "Every time I see you in a movie," a young guy once told him, "I think, 'Gee, I wish I was Cary Grant.' "

"That's just what I think," said Archie Leach, who understood the Arts and Crafts by which he had created "Cary Grant" just as well as I understand the Arts and Crafts by which I daily re-create the Authorial Voice addressing you now.

As an actor Cary Grant was trusted to improvise because directors realized his off-the-wall ad libs always "worked" — they inspired the other actors, rather than confusing them. His most interesting ad lib, I think, occurs in Howard Hawks's *His Girl Friday,* where Cary plays a newspaper editor and Gene Lockhart, as a pompous sheriff, is trying to bully him.

"Be careful," said Cary. "The last man who threatened me that way was Archie Leach and he cut his throat two weeks later."

Archie Leach? Yes: he was talking about a self he had discarded or buried somewhere.

Every success is built on the corpse of the person we were born to be.

We all have to "kill" ourselves, often in the most gruesome manner possible, to become more than the bloke produced by the collision of History, Genetics and Accident on the day we were born.

A SOCIOLOGICAL HOROSCOPE

Time-Locked Trajectories

If Cary Grant and I have the same birthday (separated by 28 years) astrologers prick up their ears...and I sometimes wonder a bit, myself.

In all the arguments between astrologers and their critics, I have never seen anybody make the simple point that, even if astrology "is true" (i.e., even if the stars and planets have an influence on our lives), it still remains *only one factor among many.*

An "honest" or synergetic astrologer would have to be also a social psychologist, economist, ecologist, historian, sociologist, anthropologist etc. because not one of us lives alone in an artificial eco-system in outer space like a 21st Century Robinson Crusoe. We live on a planet with certain resources and limits and are influenced by every human who lived before us, and by all the humans who live contemporaneously with us, and by all human history, art and inventions.

However, a "down to Earth" socio-evolutionary horoscope of my natal year may reveal a great deal about the forces that shaped me. Let us look at the other forces, besides the stars and planets, that may have shaped my destiny.

In addition to Archie Leach's dark good luck that year — having his throat cut so Cary Grant could be born — a lot of other things were happening. The 92nd *and last* naturally occurring chemical element was discovered. This makes 1932 a turning point in human history, according to R. Buckminster Fuller, who points out that "for the first time, Terrans knew all the basic building blocks of Universe." Before that we were like grocers who were unable to inventory their stock. After 1932, we had the inventory and were ready to do business in a big way.

In England, Cockroft and Walton split the atom (a feat defined as impossible in the science of the previous century) and in California E.O. Lawrence built the first cyclotron. These two achievements, 5000 miles apart in space, began the process that

19

would destroy Hiroshima and Nagasaki 13 years later and plunge the world into Biblical "fear and trembling" ever since.

In the same year, 1932, Standard Oil struck oil in the British protectorate of Bahrain in the Persian Gulf and all the major powers began decades of covert and overt struggle to control that region, of which the current culmination, as I write, includes George Bush Jr. owning most of the oil in Bahrain and George Bush Sr. declaring that the U.S. has a "moral" imperative to police that area. Today, American missiles are raining on Iraq and Iraqi missiles are bombarding Israel. (The American missiles are "good" because they only kill "bad" people; the Iraqi missiles are "bad" because they kill "good" people. Understand? I am writing about the Planet of the Apes.)

The kingdom of Saudi Arabia was formed in '32; and Eamon de Valera, elected president of Ireland, began the "trade war" with England, in an attempt to force the English to relinquish Northern Ireland; that struggle is now carried on, more violently, by the Irish Republican Army.

In 1932, 1,616 banks failed in the U.S., 20,000 businesses went bankrupt, and there were 21,000 suicides. Average weekly wage fell to $17, down from $28 in 1929, and the Gross National Product sank to 50% of its 1929 level.

Unemployment reached 17 million in the U.S., 5.6 million in Germany, 2.6 million in England. In India, Gandhi began another "fast unto death" to protest English occupation. Dearborn police fired into a crowd of unarmed men and women demonstrating outside the Ford Motor plant, killing 4 and wounding 100. The wounded were handcuffed to their hospital beds and charged with "rioting."

World War I veterans marched on Washington, protesting the lack of promised veterans' benefits and the Army used tanks, machine guns and bayonets to disperse them. There were more than 100 casualties.

At the Democratic convention, the Hon. Franklin Delano Roosevelt, Governor of New York, denounced Republican policies in general, and specifically deplored erosion of land and other ecological damage. The delegates nominated him for President and forgot about the ecology.

King Kong was the most sensationally successful film produced that year (although not released until 1933) and introduced 18 new types of special effects to film technique.

All of this influenced my life at least as much as, and probably more than, the Zodiac did.

A NET OF JEWELS

On April 19, 1942, chemist Albert Hoffman of Sandoz Laboratories in Basel, Switzerland, mixed up a compound he hoped would be a new and better cure for headaches. Not knowing he had inhaled a great deal of the fumes, Hoffman got on his bicycle and started to peddle home for lunch. He began to notice strange sensations. *She had the eyes of a saint...*

A 10-dimensional universe cracked into a 6-dimensional universe and a 4-dimensional universe. There were gold ornaments and silk curtains and heavy incense: it hurt like a bastard. Wild technicolor Maui trees and shrubs everywhere as Mother Superior raised the steel yardstick again — Uncle Mick understood with the same mathematical certainty that an egg within an egg gave birth to a quantum jump, huge lumbering reptiles. These Sun-Kings walking across the Brooklyn Bridge, hiding behind a bush going **cluck-cluck-cluck** — the inertial system changes back to that damned swamp with the frogs — he could see every black-head, every wart, every bead of sweat. Art works considered "pagan" bowed to Rev. Yoshikami and came down the stairs to New York 1959..."He wears thick goggles and a kind of scuba-diving suit"...they help us to understand our hallucinations better.

Dr. Hoffman got off the bicycle, a Wilde surmise dawning upon him: Each man spills the drink he loves.

According to one school of thought, much in favor among practiced meditators, there is no beginning, no ending, no linear progression, only an unbounded net of jewels each of which reflects and contains the reflection of each of the others.

QUICK EXIT TO NIRVANA

A Leap From The Bridge

At 25, I was "going with" a Jewish girl named Bobbie, and everybody thought we made a nice couple. Bob and Bobbie — it almost sounded as if we were made for each other.

Then Bobbie went up to the Catskills with her parents for a vacation. Two weeks later I got a "Dear John" letter. She had met a "wonderful man" and they were engaged to be married.

I went to a bar to have a few drinks and think things over. Every relationship I had had with a woman had been frustrating or had ended up with rejection in one form or another. I was 25 fucking years old and nobody wanted to publish anything I wrote. I belted away a few more drinks, wallowing in the self-pity of the young

The government seemed so brain-damaged I was sure nuclear war would happen before the '50s were over. Everybody I knew seemed to live with a kind of low-grade panic or minor depression.

I had had psychotherapy (not the Reichian variety yet) but was still a miserable neurotic.

To hell with it. I belted down some more booze, and left the bar.

I took the BMT to City Hall and walked to the Brooklyn Bridge. It seemed to me a spectacular way to make an exit. Suicides love bridges: it is by far the most dramatic exit from this Stage of Fools. The Golden Gate Bridge has a record of leapers that almost equals the Brooklyn Bridge, even though it's not as old.

A swan dive into eternity. Or oblivion.

To hell with Bobbie. To hell with all women. To hell with humanity, which was going to blow itself up soon anyway.

I walked on in my gloom and only occasionally, involuntarily, noticed the beautiful view from way up there.

I was ready for the swan dive. The whole world seemed like a very bad joke. What the hell reason was there to continue this sinister comedy?

I would jump when I got to the middle.

GENETIC VECTORS

A Net of DNA

Can anything be more ridiculous than that a man should
have the right to kill me because he lives on the other
side of the water, and because his ruler has a quarrel
with mine, though I have none with him?　　— Pascal

I have spoken of Gerrison Beach, where I grew up, as an Irish
Catholic ghetto. That shows how linguistic categories deceive
and blur memory.

When I think again, I begin to recall that not everybody in
Gerrison Beach qualified as totally Irish Catholic. Even my
mother, for instance, had only a half-Irish genealogy: *her* mother,
Anna McVey, appears to have been Scotch-Irish, but my maternal grandfather, Anton Milli, hailed from Trieste — a city that
has gotten shifted back and forth so often in the gang-wars of the
senile delinquents who run this planet that it should have wheels
on it by now. Trieste has belonged to Italy, Austria and Yugosla-
via in this century, and was part of "the Austro-Hungarian
Empire" when Anton left in the last century.

Anyway, even if not Irish, old Anton qualified as Catholic,
although semi-lapsed (he once told my mother that he didn't
believe in Hell) and worked as a blacksmith.

I seem to have "inherited" two *memes* — bits of semantic or
cultural heritage — from Anton the Smithy. The first was a kind
of cynical pacifism, or what one might call an *unashamed* lack of
patriotism. The whole family knew Anton had left the Austro-
Hungarian Empire to avoid military service, and he was proud of
the fact, as a sign of his sagacity. The best thing about America,
he told my mother, was that we had no compulsory military
service here.

His other legacy to me was a bit of Austrian folk-poetry he had
taught my mother, who taught it to me:

Ein, zwei, drei, vier, funf, sechs, sieben:
Wo is meine Schatz geblieben?
Er ist nicht heir, er ist nicht da,
Er muss' steh' nach Amerika!

("One, two, three, four, five, six seven: where is my lover gone? He is not here, he is not there, he must be in America.")

Although I got my middle name from him, I don't know much more about Anton than what I have just written. He died before my birth. Still, it's nice to know the old guy was brave enough to be a draft-dodger and sail across the wild Atlantic in a crude wooden ship to try to find a free country. I wish there was still a free country here, for others like him.

On the other side of the family, my paternal grandmother qualified as pure Irish Catholic; she had the name Mary O'Lachlann and came from County Westmeath. Through the O'Lachlanns, a large clan, I seem related (distantly) to the actors Victor McLaglen and Charles Laughton — *Laglen* and *Laughton* and *Loughlin* and *Lawton* all having emerged out of Lachlann in the period when, under English domination, the Irish had their names forcibly "Anglicized."

When I got to be middle-aged I became interested in these genealogical matters, and learned also that the Lachlanns descend from a Danish pirate named Olav the Black, who seized the Isle of Man in the 7th Century and proclaimed himself king. One of Olav's grandsons, Lachlann Mor, became king of Kerry, in Ireland, and another, Lachlann Gunn, was a chieftain of a Danish-Scotch clan in Scotland. *Lachlann* in Gaelic means "Dane" and O'Lachlann and McLachlann both mean "son of the Dane."

Although my paternal grandfather, Alexander Wilson, came from Dublin, his parents before him came from Belfast, and as you might guess from the name "Alexander Wilson" they had a Scotch ancestry and followed the Presbyterian religion. My grandmother, Mary O'Lachlann, sometimes called Alexander "You Black Protestant" when she became peeved at him.

Through Alexander Wilson I seem related, *very* distantly, to two other American offsprouts of the Ulster Wilson clan, who both attained the Imperial Crown, the Royal Purple and the divine right to pee on poor people — Woodrow Wilson and Ronald Wilson Reagan.

Well, we can't choose our relatives. Further removed, I have some distant cousins who live in the trees and, way back, we all have an ancestor who had the intellect and good looks of an iguana.

FROM WARLORD TO WARTHOG

Everybody has heard that if you use every letter in RONALD WILSON REAGAN, permuted, you will obtain INSANE ANGLO WARLORD — but did you know that GEORGE HERBERT WALKER BUSH, similarly cracked open to reveal its hidden secret, gives us HUGE BERSERK REBEL WARTHOG?

We all know how to deal with an Insane Anglo Warlord; we've had lots of them in our history. But nobody is really prepared for a Huge Berserk Rebel Warthog. It's like living in a surrealist painting.

ENTER HARVEY

A Strange Loop in Logic

All that is, is metaphor.
— Norman O. Brown, *Closing Time*

One day while I was living in Ireland in the 1980s I heard a radio show about the legends of County Kerry. Because of my own past history, I was especially intrigued by one portion of the broadcast, concerning the *pookah.* The *pookah* takes many forms, but is most famous when he appears as a giant, six-foot white rabbit — which is the form most Americans know from the play and film, *Harvey.* Whatever form the *pookah* takes, he retains the special ability of his species, which is like that of Thoth in Egyptian legend, Coyote in Native American myth or Hanuman the Divine Monkey in Hindu lore — he can move us from one universe, or Belief System, into another, and he likes to play games with our ideas about "reality."

One old farmer being interviewed knew lots of legends about the *pookah* and I was fascinated by the resemblance to some of my own weird experiences, in which I think I have moved myself, with great effort, into many "realities" (or reality-tunnels) that most people never enter. Sometimes, however, I wonder if I moved myself or if I *was moved by unknown forces.*

Finally, the interviewer asked, "But do you believe in the *pookah* yourself?"

"That I do not," said the farmer with exquisite Kerry logic, "and I doubt much that he believes in me either."

BARBARIC AGE RECALLED

Poverty And Disease Rampant

> Don't you know that if people could bottle the air they
> would? Don't you know that there would be an
> American Air-Bottling Association? And don't you
> know they would allow thousands and millions to die if
> they could not pay for air? I am not blaming anybody. I
> am just telling how it is.
> — Robert Ingersoll, *A Lay Sermon*

Gerrison Beach consisted, in my childhood, of a few hundred
bungalows and a mile or so of gently rolling sand dunes and
beaches; I have heard that now — nearly 60 years later — it contains huge and expensive condominiums full of retired Mafiosi
with ulcers, Rolls-Royces, good Catholic wives and prehensile
mistresses in Far Rockaway. They no doubt enjoy the view of
the Atlantic, from up there on their Imperial patios. I enjoyed it
every time I climbed a dune high enough to let me see it.

During my early years, the children all believed that quicksand
traps lurked somewhere among the dunes, and we had a deep
fear of accidentally stepping into the quicksand and getting
sucked down. Nobody ever actually encountered the quicksand,
but the legend lived on, at least among the kids. It probably still
survives, if there are any houses with kids left uncrushed between the nooks and ingles of Mondo Condo.

I don't think any of the adults ever believed in the quicksand.

When I remember life in Gerrison Beach in those days, I
define it chiefly in negatives. Most readers born since 1945 cannot imagine the ignorance and brutality of those days. Many
middle-aged women had goiter, a disease creating an ugly lump
in the neck, which looked like a cancer. (The cure was found
sometime in the 1940s and goiter disappeared from America.)
People regularly died of tuberculosis, which is now normally
cured in its early stages, and children had dozens of diseases now
abolished. I myself survived measles, German measles, mumps,

flu (still a major killer in those days)*, rheumatic fever, whooping cough, diphtheria and polio.

The community had no paved roads and nobody had central heating, wall-to-wall carpeting or tile bathrooms; inconceivably to most of my readers, TV had not yet come to squat like a pot-bellied idol spouting surrealist *kitch* in every American living room. Even worse, we didn't own a radio.

The bungalows were heated with coal, when we could afford it, but more often with driftwood we picked up on the beach in the summer and stacked in the yard to dry until we used it in the winter. Only the center of the house (living room/kitchen) got heated that way, and a trip to the bathroom in January or February was like a journey to the Pole with Scott of the Antarctic and twenty dog-sleds.

People were always dying of influenza and pneumonia and other diseases related to lack of heat in winter. Every head cold created minor panic because it might develop into one of these killer diseases.

Knowledge of medicine was primitive. I was told on good authority, by the adults of the tribe, that wearing galoshes in the house causes deafness, that masturbation causes blindness and that if you drank milk right after eating pickles you would die. It was also believed that if anybody ever said the words "cancer" or "tuberculosis" aloud somebody in the family would immediately catch one of those diseases. Relatives who had those ailments were "sick, very sick," and no further description was spoken, lest the evil spirits hear it and decide the afflict the family with more of the same. People were always expecting the worst because all they had known in all their lives were deadly diseases and grinding poverty.

Optimism was a sign of insanity.

One year after my birth, President Roosevelt declared that "one third of the nation" lived in conditions as bad as, or worse than, what I have described. When ecologists like Gary Snyder talk about "going back to the way things were in the 1920s," I think they must be a few gallons shy of a full tank. The '20s were even

---

* More American men died in the flu epidemic of 1919 than in the whole of World War I.

worse for poor people than the '30s; the Depression merely spread the misery around a little more generously, letting all but the very rich taste a little of it.*

In our tribe, nobody doubted that the local priests knew the correct answer to every question, and nobody had ever heard a symphony or seen an art museum. I don't think anybody had ever read a novel or a poem. The only things I remember the men reading were newspapers; the women also read True Confession magazines and movie magazines, which told the latest gossip about the stars.

All the men read the New York *Daily News,* because it had big headlines, short sentences and lots of photographs of murders and women with big pointy hooters. Once they printed a picture of a woman being electrocuted in Sing-Sing and got into a lot of trouble with the Law. Their reporter had hidden the camera under his coat. Lots of people rushed out to buy that issue of the *News.* I guess they had never had a chance to see a woman being charbroiled before.

I never saw a copy of the New York *Times* until I entered High School and my parents moved to Bay Ridge.

My father had relatives in Brooklyn Heights who actually owned a big two-story house, instead of renting a bungalow, and I think they had central heating, too. We referred to them as "lace curtain Irish." Only when I was much older did I discover that they called us "shanty Irish." But none of us knew any of the half-fabulous "cut glass Irish," who existed only as a romantic rumor...people who, even though Irish, lived as well as the Protestants. These semi-mythic beings, the cut glass Irish, lived in New England and drank cognac.

Down among the shanty Irish, where we lived, most of the men of the tribe had no jobs because of The Depression, which was dragging on, year after weary year. Almost everybody believed that the victims of The Depression were "responsible" for it (just as it is still believed, in some circles, that the victims of rape "are responsible" for it.) The men felt very ashamed of

---

* (Footnote, 1996) Bob Dole recently described that hellish epoch as a wonderful age which he would like to restore. Some folks want to put him in the White House. I think they should put him in a rest home.

themselves because of The Depression, which made it impossible to support their families even at the level of poverty familiar to the shanty Irish.

This forced them to live on government charity, at a level of poverty lower than they had ever known, which further shamed and humiliated them, especially since the small government dole always got spent before the fourth week of the month. This made them drink more, which in turn made them become more Irish and less Catholic, and, of course, that meant that sometimes there was no money left by the *third* week of the month.

They didn't drink cognac. They drank boiler-makers — beer with whiskey on the side. Later, when I lived in Dublin, I discovered this was a traditional Irish combination — except that the Dubliners don't drink weak American beers but no-nonsense Guiness Extra Stout, which has a kick like a berserk kung fu master. Generally, in both Dublin and Gerrison Beach, the beer would be sipped slowly and the whiskey swallowed in a gulp, with three whiskeys lasting as long as one beer. After three or four rounds, everybody became totally Irish and no longer Catholic at all, at all.

Some malcontents, including my father, said the unemployed men did not bear any personal responsibility for The Depression, but they sounded defensive, as if they still suspected that they *were* responsible after all. These timid rebels were divided into two hostile camps. The first group said The Depression resulted from the machinations of the Wicked Jews, but the other group said it resulted from the selfish scheming of the Wicked Republicans. My father was in the second group. Despite their ideological differences, both groups of heretics voted for Roosevelt religiously, just like everybody else.

In those days, Irish Catholics voted Democratic no matter who the Party nominated. We all believed that the Democratic Party was controlled by Irish Catholics like National Chairman Jim Farley and would "take care of its own."

It wasn't until I grew up that I learned that this was only true in the territory between New York and Boston, and that in other parts of the country there were Democrats who were neither Irish nor Catholic.

We all knew that President Roosevelt was a rich Protestant, but that didn't disillusion us. We believed that he never did anything that wasn't approved by Jim Farley.

My uncle Mick said Roosevelt was worse than a rich Protestant: he was actually a rich Jew, who had changed his name from Rosenfelt. But Uncle Mick was strange anyway. He had chest problems and didn't trust either political party and was generally cranky. He spent most of his time in bed, coughing, or in bars, smoking and drinking and coughing even more.

He had a pension because he was a War Hero.

Uncle Mick didn't like Black people any more than Jews. He said they were all getting good jobs in the post office while white men were unemployed.

He also hated squirrels. He called them "tree-rats."

WE ONCE AGAIN FLASH FORWARD 50+ YEARS

The enemy aggressor is always pursuing a course of larceny, murder, rapine and barbarism. We are always moving forward with high mission, a destiny imposed by the Deity to regenerate our victims while incidentally capturing their markets, to civilize savage and senile and paranoidal peoples while blundering accidentally into their oil wells or metal mines.
— John T. Flynn, *As We Go Marching*

All the time I am working on this book the humanoid robot named Huge Berserk Rebel Warthog a.k.a. George Herbert Walker Bush (whose designers seem to have used Uriah Heep as their model) and another android named Sodom Hussein or Goddam Insane or something like that (who seemingly was fashioned after The Godfather) are blowing the hell out of the Mid-East. This high-tech gang rumble is fought by dumb people with "smart" bombs and is causing my wife Arlen great anxiety and depression.

She always feels that way when hordes of males set out to murder one another, which she finds ugly and stupid. She finds it even uglier when, as in all modern warfare, these berserker males also murder a lot of innocent women and children.

The final estimate of the International Red Cross was that this latest rumble killed at least 70,000 children.

"In all other animals," Arlen says, "the females not only have a maternal instinct to defend their young but also the smarts to do the job. The human woman alone doesn't know how to defend her offspring." As other Feminists do, she blames this on women having been neurologically crippled by "patriarchal civilization," but she sees a special intent to repress or destroy female instinct-and-intelligence in what she calls "the three great He-God religions" — Judaism, Christianity and Islam, all of which have a misogynistic metaphysic, have been making increasingly omni-

35

lethal wars throughout their careers and are intimately involved in the genesis of the present blood-and-bombs orgy.

These feminine views are needed now and then, I think, to prevent me from remaining trapped in a male reality-tunnel all the time. Without Arlen's exegesis, I would regress to my characteristic view that this swinish war, along with most of the sub-human things government do, results from the fact that *"people"* like Bush and Hussein are a little bit retarded and not fully house-trained. A feminine eye observes that 90% of the *"people"* who fight wars and 99.9999% of the *"people"* who start the wars are **male people.**

I am gradually coming around to Arlen's idea that war-making is a characteristically male disease, just as cervical cancer is characteristically female.

Indeed, cross-cultural studies quoted in Michael Hutchison's *The Anatomy of Sex and Power* (Morrow & Co., 1990) show that in every culture around the world little boys are more violent than little girls. Laboratory research, also quoted by Hutchison, reveals that when both boys and girls are given testosterone, their violent behavior increases, but the boys still remain more violent than the girls.

Testosterone is the hormone that provokes male sexuality, and apparently, as this recent research indicates, also provokes violence. Kinsey noted that males are most sexually "active" (orgasmic, with or without a partner) in the years between 17 and 24, and those are the peak years for violent crimes by males. It seems likely that most violent crime results from excessive testosterone *plus bad environment.* Some studies show that extra testosterone in a good environment tends to flow into artistic or scientific creativity, rather than into criminality.

Nobody has explained scientifically why wars — the biggest of all violent crimes — are usually started by males over 60, when testosterone levels are not excessive but are, on the contrary, declining.

This is puzzling, but maybe there's an answer to it.

Some of the research quoted by Hutchison shows that winning at sports causes a temporary increase in testosterone. (This has been noted in tests on both wrestlers and tennis-players.) Some aging males may know this without having seen the scientific data, by sheer intuition. They have a gut-sense that conflict and victory will turn them on sexually.

This booster effect may be what Henry Kissinger had in mind when he said, "Power is the ultimate aphrodisiac."

Considering the scale of the war in the mid-East, Huge Berserk Rebel Warthog must require a lot of stimulation to get it up.

LESSER BREEDS WITHOUT THE LAW

(Horrors! Bigotry Found Rampant
Among the Poor and Ignorant!)

There were some Protestants in Gerrison Beach, and they all went to a church which we kids called the "piss-in-the-pail-ian" church. Many years passed and I was developing pimples and horniness — symptoms of the increase of testosterone at puberty — before I learned that the correct name was "Episcopalian."

The only Jews I knew anything about lived in Brooklyn, on Ocean Boulevard. Whether they had caused The Depression or not, everybody knew they had killed Christ.*

The only time I saw any Black people in those years was when we took a bus to visit our "lace curtain" relatives in South Brooklyn. I stared at the Black people until my mother told me that staring was impolite and would make them self-conscious. But she also told me, on another occasion, not to put a penny in my mouth because "a nigger might have had it in his hands."

Once I saw an Oriental family on the bus and stared at them, too, until my mother reminded me that was impolite. Then she and my father got into a whispered argument about whether these exotic creatures were Chinese or Japanese. My father agreed with my mother that, Chinese or Japanese, they were "beautiful, like dolls," compared to white people.

Nobody in our tribe knew that some Orientals were neither Chinese nor Japanese. Nothing in my childhood ever led me to suspect that the overwhelming majority of the human race was non-white, non-Irish, non-male and living in conditions far more deplorable than the Shanty Irish in Gerrison Beach.

---

* I was about 30 when I heard Lenny Bruce explain this: "All my life goys have asked me why we killed Christ. What can I say? Maybe he wouldn't become a doctor. Maybe it was just one of those wild parties that got out of hand."

I did know that there were people in far distant lands who did not belong to the True Church, but that was because they were savages and ignorant.

I doubt that these "Catholic" views are exclusively Catholic; most of them seem to be shared by most Protestants, too. All through my life the U.S. has been at war more of the time than it has been at peace, and virtually all the wars are directed at colored peoples far, far way who pose absolutely no threat to our soil. The only threats most of them pose are that they are non-white, non-Christian and no longer willing to be governed by "our" corporations.

THE MAN WHO WAS
ABSOLUTELY RIGHT

Mad Bill Casey, director of the Central Intelligence Agency, once explained the science of ethics in a speech,

"Some things are wrong," Mad Bill stated, "and some things are right — absolutely wrong and absolutely right."

You know in your heart that a man who can say that is capable of anything. Mad Bill had a deep involvement in Iran-Contra and assorted acts of conspiracy, perjury, illegal gun-running, assassination, terrorism, torture and dope smuggling. He lied continually to the Senate Intelligence Committee, even though the law of the land and his oath of office obliged him to inform them in accurate detail about what his Agency was doing. (See Bob Woodward's *Veil: The Secret Wars of the C.I.A.* for some of the details*.) This was all "absolutely right" in his judgment because he did it to all to serve God and America.

Catholic intellectuals are like that; even Saint Thomas Aquinas, "the angelic doctor," believed it was logically correct to burn "heretics."

The people I grew up among were Catholics, but not intellectuals. They tried to act decently, insofar as the Church would permit them.

---

* Further details appear later in this book. As we go to press, new details unearthed by the San Jose *Mercury News* seem likely to inspire a congressional investigation, at last, and a popular bumper-sticker says "DARE to keep the C.I.A. off drugs."

Coprophilia Among Swine Alleged By Dissidents

Wilson Tastes Tear-Gas

How many does it take to metamorphose wickedness into righteousness? One man must not kill. If he does it is murder. But a state or nation may kill as many as they please, and it is not murder... Only get enough people to agree to it, and the butchery of myriads of human beings is perfectly innocent. But how many does it take?
— Adin Ballou, 1845

"She had the eyes of a saint..."

"Zen is for samurais and neurotics."

Mother Superior raises the yardstick and brings it down again, hard, on a trembling hand.

The tear-gas bombs started to explode, spreading a smog of corrosive conjunctivitis among indignant, outraged eyes. The police fixed their Baby-Blue riot helmets, took out their clubs and, with the honest joy of simple men who love their work, began cracking Peacenik skulls. Bob Shea and I ran down the street, escaping. It was Chicago, 1968.

I was there to protest the war-mongering of the Democratic Party which had dragged our country into one war after another ever since 1937. Shea was more recently disillusioned with the Democrats than I was, but by 1968 he was fed up, too.

We looked back and saw the cops clubbing some demonstrators who couldn't run as fast as we did, and some who were Gandhians and/or masochists — the Holy Madmen who "put their bodies on the line" for peace. Neither Shea nor I were quite that religious.

"Motherfucker," somebody howled as a cop bashed him. I could tell from the tone of voice that this was not an insult directed at the cop. It was an exclamation of outraged pain, just as "Son of a bitch!" may often be an exclamation of surprise or even joy.

41

Most of the demonstrators — except the Weathermen[*] — were genuinely shocked at the violence of the police. They were college kids and middle-aged liberals who had no knowledge of the bloody saga of American radicalism. Like the Weathermen, I was neither shocked nor outraged. I had read enough about the history of labor unions to know that, whenever the Establishment is annoyed, they send the cops to beat the shit out of people.

The Concerned Clergymen started singing "We Shall Overcome" again, but were drowned out by the Weathermen chanting "ONE TWO THREE FOUR WE DON'T WANT YOUR FUCKING WAR."

...Deep in my heart
I do believe
We shall overcome
Some da-aay

WE DON'T WANT YOUR FUCKING WAR

"Commie bastards..."

"The Feast of Pure Reason," I said to Shea as we huffed and puffed along.

We ducked into a bar on Michigan Avenue and grabbed a table. I ordered two Bloody Marys. The plush leather and the technicolor bottles of booze on the wall all looked wonderfully normal and reassuring after what we had been through. I looked at the silvery mirrors with me and Shea and a room full of strangers in them: a net of jewels, each of which reflects and is reflected in each of the others.

Our eyes were still running slightly. On the TV, we could see cops clubbing demonstrators. Voices were chanting, "THE WHOLE WORLD IS WATCHING, THE WHOLE WORLD IS WATCHING." The camera cut to the Hon. Senator Abraham Ribicoff, inside the convention, denouncing the Hon. Mayor Richard Daly for allowing the police to attack nonviolent protesters. The Hon. Mr. Daly, of the family Suidea, shouted something back, greenly empurpled, but the mike didn't pick it

---

[*] Who only became Weather People after two years of Feminist polemic about "implicit sexism in language," later abbreviated to simple "sexism."

up; from the look on the Hon. Daly's face the network probably would have bleeped his words if they had picked them up.

Shea and I drank, thoughtfully, wiping our burning eyes. We knew we were going back out again, in a little while. Our commitment was undefined verbally but we both understood it. We would go out there into the streets and risk getting clubbed but we would not stand still and submit to the clubbing if we could escape. I think almost everybody, except the Hard Core Pacifists, had that attitude.

Eight hours before, at the Playboy Club, I had had lunch with Allen Ginsberg and William S. Burroughs, who had both come to Chicago to join the protests against the Vietnam war. I was a Playboy editor then and enjoyed ordering lunch for two of my favorite living writers and putting the tab on my gold Playboy V.I.P. card. The three of us had talked mostly about the poetry of Ezra Pound and very little about the risks we were going to run that night. That was when Ginsberg told me about his remarkable meeting with Pound, in Rapollo, Italy. The old man, bent and guilty and looking like Remorse in an allegory, listened to Allen cordially but refused to talk himself, except to issue one bitter self-condemnation for the "stupid, suburban anti-semitism" of his middle years.

*I had asked what Allen said to that. Allen told me he quoted **I Ching:** "No blame." Pound, still morose, had said nothing in reply.*

Shea and I finished our drinks and gingerly stepped out into Chaos and Mother Night again. A horde of Weathermen were lined up in Grant Park, looking like cowboys too poor to have their jeans cleaned. I suspected that, like everybody else from SDS I had ever met, they were from well-to-do families. In accord with the Marxist texts they had memorized, they systematically taunted the police — trying to provoke another attack.

"PIGS EAT SHIT, PIGS EAT SHIT," they chanted, over and over. **"PIGS EAT SHIT PIGS EAT SHIT PIGS EAT SHIT..."**

I thought of poor old Pound, driven bonkers by his hatred of war, so that eventually it degenerated into hatred of Jews in his blind, helpless fury, just because he needed a target more localized and tangible than human folly. The Weathermen went on chanting, and I realized, in a shock like a Jocyean epiphany, that when opposition to violence becomes hatred of violence it immediately gestates its own violence.

The cops fired more tear-gas canisters and the Weathermen retreated, still chanting, **"PIGS EAT SHIT...*PIGS EAT SHIT..."***

The gassing and clubbing went on for hours...but by now it is as effectively erased from national memory as the much worse police brutality and flagrant bloodshed when the cops broke the unions in Flint, Michigan, and Harlan County, Kentucky, and Paterson, New Jersey, and other places in the early '30s. It is the business of the schools, and the media, to see that such episodes are not remembered (except by the embittered survivors, who cannot be persuaded to forget.) The next gang of peaceful protesters will be just as shocked and outraged when the cops are let loose upon them.

Almost everybody believes "those things don't happen in America."

Before Dr. Salk & His Vaccine

> Practically speaking, no government knows any limits
> to its power except the endurance of the people.
> — Lysander Spooner, *Trial by Jury*

The bungalows in Gerrison Beach had large yards around them, so everybody had a vegetable garden. My father sold his car during a particularly bad month, and used the money to buy about a hundred chickens, which we kept in the garage, so we had fresh meat and eggs as well as fresh vegetables.

I enjoyed the chickens, because they were the funniest animals I ever saw. Our dog, Sparky, had a definite personality, which I found lovable, but the chickens seemed to have no individuality at all. They reminded me of mechanical toys.

Bucky Fuller says all infants are born "naked, hungry and intensely curious." I was not in school yet, so my curiosity had not been stifled. I listened to everything the grown-ups said and remembered it, although much of it was misinformation. For instance, I heard that Dinah Shore once had a Black baby but gave it away, that if you dug a deep enough hole in the back yard you'd come out in China, and that there were real live Communists across the river in Manhattan — but nobody I knew had ever gone there and actually seen one of them. The Communists were terrible people who carried bombs and had no respect for The Church. Some of the men said the Communists weren't really that bad, but they were the same men who said the Wicked Republicans had caused the Depression. It was suspected that they actually read books and only went to church because their wives made them do it.

My father didn't go to church at all, and my mother went seldom. I didn't find out why until I was an adolescent.

Few in our tribe had cars, anymore than they could afford to eat in restaurants like the rich Protestants in Bay Ridge. We stored food in an ice-box and an Italian "ice-man" delivered ice once a week; he came door to door in a cart pulled by a horse.

My mother said she knew the Italian ice man was an Italian nice man because he treated his horse well and talked to it.

She talked to all animals. Eventually, she found personalities even in some of the chickens — to my astonishment — and then my father couldn't kill those birds for Sunday dinner. Fortunately, Mom didn't find that much individuality in many of the chickens.

I tried talking to the chickens a few times, and I can assure you it is easier to get an intelligent response out of a post office clerk. I then tried talking to the n/ice man's horse. That was much more rewarding, but I still prefer dogs as companions.

Later, when Arlen and I and the kids lived in Ohio, I kept chickens again. This time I had to do my own slaughtering. The chickens still reminded me of mechanical toys. Any other animal, knowing itself in danger, will hide behind a bush and *keep quiet;* chickens hide behind a bush and go **cluck-cluck-cluck** loudly, so you know exactly which bush they are behind. Their wild ancestors must have had some intelligence, but by now they have been domesticated to the point of idiocy, like most American voters.

(On the other hand, I sometimes suspect that pigeons are not birds at all. Birds, like other animals, vanish like lightning when they see a car coming, but pigeons casually stroll to the side, or laconically flutter a few feet at the last minute. I swear they can calculate how fast a car is coming. Perhaps they are extraterrestrial invaders, observing us, looking for our vulnerabilities...)

We didn't get our first refrigerator until The Depression ended. (I didn't even know it was called a refrigerator until I became adult. My mother always called it "the fridge.")

I limped occasionally, when I was tired. Although children are, as everybody knows, inordinately cruel to one another, I only remember one case where somebody — a girl actually — made fun of me for limping. If a boy had said something similar about my limp, I would have punched him in the mouth; but we were taught that it was improper to punch girls. This encouraged the girls to be much nastier, verbally, than the boys. They knew nobody would punch them in the mouth for it.

(I sometimes have suspected that this explains the rhetoric of the more vicious Radical Feminists — they know nobody will punch them in the mouth for it. But then Arlen told me some things she had heard at Feminist meetings, and I realized those ladies are so verbally nasty because they have already been punched in the mouth. And elsewhere. Frequently. Most men, it appears, do not share my distaste for violence.)

Once a month I went to a doctor's office for mysterious manipulations which were supposed to help the limp. I liked the ride on the trolley car, because it made my penis tingle; somehow, I knew, even at that age, not to mention the tingling to my mother or the doctor.

The limp was a result of the polio I mentioned earlier. I had been cured of that disease, which left most of its victims permanently paralyzed. The cure was considered a miracle, and had been accomplished by the Blessed Virgin Mary and something called the Sister Kenny Method. The manipulations I was still receiving were part of the Sister Kenny Method.

MONEY & MIRACLES

How The Vatican Bank Acquires Capital

When I was diagnosed as having polio at age two the doctors told my parents I would never walk again. (And I was 42 years old before I had an experience of suddenly empathizing with the shock and grief Mom and Dad must have experienced; by then I had been a parent long enough to know what parents suffer.)

My mother fought back against the medical Verdict, the only way she knew how to fight. She lit candles before a statue of the Blessed Virgin Mary in the local church for nine weeks, said various prayers, and put enough money in the candle box to attract Divine attention. This was called "doing a novena." Only after I reached adulthood did I realize that "novena" comes from the Latin root for "nine" — hence, the nine weeks of the ritual — and relates back directly to the ninefold form of the Great Goddess as the Nine Muses. (And "the nightmare and her ninefold" in *King Lear* — the ancient Celtic horse-goddess.)

The novena, everybody knew, would not work unless you paid for the candles by putting a few coins in the candle box. It is a firm axiom of the poor everywhere that the deities, just like land-lords and other superhuman beings, want all the **MONEY** they can get and won't give a fried fart for you until they are well paid. The priests made this abundantly clear when my mother began taking me to Mass occasionally. God wanted **MONEY** even more fervently than the BVM or the land-lord did, and He wanted it in regular installments, every Sunday. Jesus wanted **MONEY**, too. All the Catholic demigods want **MONEY**. I didn't discover until I was living in Ireland and researching the Roberto Calvi case that most of the **MONEY** goes to the Vatican Bank where it finances high living by the clever chaps who run this lovely racket and helps support various fascist regimes in Latin America by laundering their drug money.

The Sister Kenny Method was used to treat my polio by lucky accident — or *perhaps* by intervention of the BVM, who *might* have been bribed sufficiently by my mother's pitiful dimes during the nine weeks of the novena. On the surface, my parents, after giving up on the doctor who said I'd be paralyzed for life, then — right after the novena and just by *blind chance* — found one of the few doctors in the United States who thought the Kenny Method was worth trying.

The A.M.A. and the whole organized medical profession at that time had denounced Kenny and all her works. She was only a nurse and therefore couldn't discover anything of importance; she was only a woman, also, and therefore could not understand medicine, which requires male brains; her technique of treating polio, we were told, was dangerous nonsense and hogwash and "witchcraft."

Thus, the major event of my early childhood consisted of being cured of a major crippling illness which left most of its victims permanently confined to wheelchairs, *by a method which all recognized Experts denounced as unscientific and useless.* This instilled me with certain doubts about Experts. Those doubts have lingered, and even increased, over the years — especially since large corporations have demonstrated in recent decades that Experts can be hired to testify to the safety of *anything,* from a poisonous pesticide to a nuclear power plant, no matter how many people "coincidentally" drop dead after using it or living near it. (Some readers are naive enough to consider me an "Expert" in certain fields, which adds to my doubts, since I know all-too-well what a damned fool I can be at times.)

When I got to high school I encountered among my teachers other Experts who said we could never send a rocket to the moon, and still other Experts who denied this and said that we *could* do it, but it would take at least a hundred years. When we landed Neil Armstrong on the moon in 1969, I became even more dubious about Experts.

ATTACK OF THE KILLER SPIDER

The first time I entered Virtual Reality involved a Giant Spider. I don't know how old I was at the time, but it must have been somewhere around age four because I was already talking a great deal. Indeed, a neighbor had told my parents they should send me to law school because I could "talk any judge off the bench," an Irish metaphor I do not quite understand. (Of course, the thought that my parents could afford law school was absolutely ridiculous at the time, but such dreams are typically Irish. The Celtic temperament, when not sunk in Beckett-like despair, always leaps to the other extreme and believes, whatever the evidence, that tomorrow will be better.)

One day in our backyard, between the tomatoes and the potatoes, I saw a Monstrous Giant Spider, about the size of a large doll-house or an Australian sheep hound — in other words, almost as big as I was. It scared the screaming blue Jesus out of me and I ran, weeping, to my mother, howling about this Monster.

She slapped my face and told me not to invent lies.

I was so shocked and hurt that I remember that experience better than anything else that happened before I entered school.

This was over half a century ago, and my mother has been dead for more than ten years, so I have no resentment left as I write this. The poor woman had no way of dealing with such an event and shut me up the only way she knew how.

Of course, over the years I have often wondered about this experience. Since nobody else in Gerrison Beach ever reported that Monster lurking in their garden, and books on spiders have never described a species that large, I guess there was no Giant Spider in our yard. On the other hand, I have never had any "psychotic episodes" (unlike many writers I could mention...) and nobody qualified to pass judgment has ever diagnosed me as schizophrenic. I can only conclude, as many anthropologists and social scientists have also concluded, that every tribe *teaches* its children how to see — that **"seeing" is not a function of the eyes alone but of the eyes-and-brain working together.** I saw something unknown — something for which the tribal reality-tunnel had no category — so in my child's brain I classified it as best as I could, as a bodaceously large member of the spider family, and shocked the hell out of my mother in the process.

Brooding over this process by which every tribe teaches its children to "see" the world in terms of the local reality-tunnel led me to take a degree in perception psychology in later years. Some think it has even made a philosopher of me. In short, whatever the deuce was in that garden that day, it eventually set me adrift in the wild oceans of speculation, far from the comfy little islands of dogma in which most people happily spend their entire sheep-like lives...

By now I am so far gone in the stormy waters of gonzo ontology that I am willing to entertain the possibility that the Thing in the Garden *was* an unknown species of spider, after all — a critter which is too elusive to be cataloged by biologists, like the Loch Ness monster or Bigfoot — or the Killer Rabbit that once attacked President Jimmy Carter — Don't understand me too quickly — I just said I was willing to entertain that idea. I didn't say I believe it.

Like one of my novels or an Orson Welles film, this book intends to show different *angles of perspective,* not to convert you to a new Religion or Ideology.

BUCKY & SYNERGY

It was 1956. I was 24 years old, working as an engineering aide, and I had come to a seminar on General Semantics at Bard College in Annandale-on-the-Hudson. There were several brilliant speakers — Dr. Marge Swanson, talking about the biochemistry of the brain, Dr. Russell Meyers, talking about conditioned and conditional reflexes in cats and humans, Dr. Ray Bontrager, talking about the role of neurolinguistic reactions in psychology — and others I have, alas, forgotten over the years.

The speaker who I had most wanted to hear and who bowled me over was Richard Buckminster Fuller, talking about mathematics and architecture and city planning and global planning and chemistry and metallurgy and semantics and poetry and a few dozen other topics. Fuller was a short man, overweight in those days (he later dieted) and shaped like a pear. Everybody called him Bucky.

Bucky said that, like the other scientists at the seminar, he had been shaken up by Alfred Korzybski's neurolinguistic theory that words literally can hypnotize us.* He had tried the experiment of not talking for a year, in 1928, and had emerged with a whole new way of perceiving the world.

Korzybski always stressed that as science advances, we discover, in one field after another, that "non-elementalistic" or "non-linear" *structural* relationships explain more than simple additive relationships. (On the daily level, husband + wife + mother-in-law produces a less stable, more explosive household than ordinary arithmetic would lead you to suppose. In metallurgy, the discovery that tin + copper + heat produces something completely new — namely, bronze — revolutionized humanity, as we shall see.) Bucky generalized Korzybski's insight into synergetic geometry, the geometry of non-additive structural relationships.

---

* Since writing this, I have cooperated in presenting my version of Korzybski in workshops along with the First Institute of Neurolinguistic Programming; I now see the hypnosis in vivid detail around me.

Synergetic geometry allowed Bucky to build houses that weighed 1/100th or even less than 1/1000th of the weight of similar houses, enclosing the same space. This allowed him to ship "houses" or buildings of various sorts around the world. He also showed us, that day, how this new geometry simplified our understanding of organic chemistry. (Organic molecules have Fuller geodesic structures.)

I had read about some of that in *Mechanix Illustrated* and similar publications, and it was part of what I expected from Bucky. But then he went on to ideas the Popular Science journals had not yet written up.

Synergetic thinking, generalized, led Fuller to the concept of *ephemeralization* — "doing more with less." The tendency of technology, he showed us with graphs of various historical stages of machinery, always moved steadily toward greater and greater ephemeralization. Every step forward in information allowed us to do more and more with less and less energy. Economists, he said, were still thinking in terms of scarcity while science was inexorably moving the world toward abundance and super-abundance.

Bucky then spoke about the 92 natural chemical elements, and I got a tingly feeling of strange intuition or "predestination" when he mentioned that the last of them was discovered the year I was born. These elements occurred at random around our planet, he said. Universe — a term he used the way theologians use "God" — would eventually force us to make a choice, as technology advanced, between two ways of getting maximum benefit out of these elements. We could follow traditional mammalian politics, in which one nation would try to dominate the others in order to access all 92 elements, which we now call a zero-sum game. Or we could choose a new synergetic path, a non-zero-sum game, in which all Terrans cooperate to "advantage all without disadvantaging any."

Since war will continue to become more and more "omni-lethal," Bucky said, humanity would have to choose the latter cooperative path eventually, because "we always do the intelligent thing after we have tried every stupid alternative and none of them works."

Everybody at the seminar seemed as overwhelmed by Bucky as I was.

"He puts you into a trance," somebody said.

"No," somebody else said. "He wakes you out of your trance."

THE BIG BANG ...
AND ITS CONSEQUENCES

When I was born in 1932, I carried the genes of millions of Northern and Southern Europeans (and some North Africans) who had at one time or another lived in or near Trieste and/or Dublin.

When the atom was split that same year, it signaled not only a *prelude* to Hiroshima but also the *resultant* of all scientific research until that date. Most directly, it resulted from the development of quantum mechanics in the 1920s by such towering geniuses as Schrödinger, Bohr, Dirac and Heisenberg — but that work, in turn, derived from the pioneering papers on quantum theory by Plank (1900) and Einstein (1904) — which were based on all the thermodynamic and electromagnetic discoveries of the 19th Century by Boltzman and Maxwell and Faraday *et al.* — which followed from the scientific revolutions of Galileo and Newton — which would have been impossible without ancient engineering and philosophy...

And all of that Egyptian-Greek-Roman speculation and design science was rooted in all the discoveries of humans and hominids from the time the first stone ax was carved in Africa about 4,000,000 years ago.

Which would never have happened if life had not, somehow, formed on this planet around 4,000,000,000 years ago...and this planet would not exist if a 10-dimensional universe had not split apart, in a Big Bang, around 18,000,000,000 years ago, into a 6-dimensional universe which shrank to invisibility in a few nanoseconds and our 4-dimensional universe which has been expanding steadily ever since.

Without getting lost in the mysteries of cosmology, affixing our attention to just this planet, life evolved for 3,396,000,000 years before that first tool appeared in Africa. The most popular life-form was (and remains) the six-legged winged or wingless insect. (The great biologist Haldane, asked what dominant trait he would attribute to the Mind behind evolution — if he admitted such a Mind — replied at once, "An inordinate fondness for beetles.")

Around 230,000,000 years ago the highly complex reptiles appeared — a quantum jump in both size and organization — and 150,000,000 years ago they had evolved into giant dinosaurs.

75,000,000 years ago, the dinosaurs disappeared. They did their best, but — "We're all in this alone," as Lily Tomlin says.

65,000,000 years ago the mammals appeared and 4,000,000 years ago (more or less) that first tool was created by a clever mammal distantly related to you and me and the Queen of England.

100,000 years ago, some hominids in Hungary made amulets and other artifacts suggesting they had some kind of "religion."

38,000 years ago Homo Sapiens and Femina Sapiens had evolved in Europe, Asia and Australia.

Around 5,000 years ago, somebody in Thailand or Cambodia (an area naturally rich in tin and copper) discovered by lucky accident or brilliantly designed experiment that tin + copper + heat = bronze.

This triggered a total mutation in human society. As Riane Eisler has pointed out, previous human groups ("tribes") had been based on partnership models (or as mathematical game theory would say, non-zero-sum games). Post bronze society was based on Authority and Submission (zero-sum games.)

Concretely, Bronze Age civilization — called The First Wave by Alvin Toffler — created an Elite of warriors with bronze spears and their Leader, a high testosterone "alpha" male of the type that usually leads huge mammalian herds. These alpha males almost always called themselves sons of the Sun-God, and their huge agricultural civilizations are often termed "sun-kingdoms."

These agricultural sun-king civilizations spread "westward and mildly northward" (as Bucky says). Almost always they had the primal Sun King structure: the "divine" alpha male at the top, the nobles below, and women and slaves at the bottom. The whole world had changed. You could not mistake a citizen of one of these Sun Kingdoms for a tribal human anymore than you'd mistake a canary for a Gila Monster.

It took thousands of years, but eventually the largest part of humanity had been conquered, domesticated, de-tribalized and incorporated into one Sun-Kingdom or another. As late as the 18th Century, Louis XIV was still called "the Sun King," although the metaphor was no longer taken literally. In Japan, the Mikado remained a sun-god until 1945.

In 1 AD, the largest of all sun-kingdoms, owning more slaves than any previous despotism, was the Roman Empire.

If you use a computer and know the correct algorithms, you can convert anything into binary notation. You can then estimate the information in a mathematical theorem, a painting, a book, or any human product. In this way, in 1974, statistician George Anderla estimated how much information humanity had accumulated between that African stone ax of 4,000,000 BC and the beginning of the Christian calendar in 1 AD when Rome was the biggest slave-state yet organized.

Naturally, 4,000,000 years worth of information gives you a rather large number. Anderla, however, took that as his basic unit, and then calculated how long it took to *double* that amount of binary units of information.

It only took 1500 years. By then power had shifted northward and mildly westward to the great Italian city-states ruled by bankers like the Medici.

SHE HAD THE EYES OF A SAINT

Arlen and I arrived in Dublin during the celebrations of Blooms-day (June 16, 1982) and everything seemed "high-lighted," luminous, "psychedelic," *more real than real,* because I already knew all the store names and streets from Joyce's novels — and because I couldn't stop thinking that *statistically* I must have been walking at least part of the time in the *exact* footsteps of my grandfather, Alexander Wilson, who had left there and gone to Brooklyn one hundred years earlier in 1882.

That was the year Jesus James the Joyce was born...and the Invincibles, headed by Joe Brady, murdered two English officials in Phoenix Park, on the West of Dublin. Curiously, it was also the year when the French Scientific Academy announced that it would no longer examine attempts to "square the circle."

But in 1982, the Invincibles were not commemorated. June 16 was Joyce's Day in Dublin. RTE (*Radio Telefis hEirann*) was broadcasting its monumental 30-hour dramatic reading of *Ulysses,* Siobhon McKenna was doing another dramatic perfor-mance of several of Joyce's women that evening at the Abbey Theatre, Eamon Morissey was doing a performance of several of Joyce's men around the corner at the Peacock Theatre, a new statue of Joyce was unveiled in Stephen's Green (with the Lord Mayor of Dublin and the President of Ireland in attendance) and, at 3-to-4 p.m. a hundred or so actors performed the "Wandering Rocks" chapter of *Ulysses* on the sites of the 19 different streets in Dublin where Joyce set these scenes.

That Wandering Rocks performance was the most Joycean event of the day, since nobody but God could see all of it, just as nobody but God can understand *all* of a Joyce novel. The actions of the 19 mini-episodes all overlap in time, being organized by synchronicity, and it was impossible for a mere human to see more than a few of them. Meanwhile, to add to the merriment, hundreds of people — including Arlen and me — were carrying radios and listening to the reading of the novel, which intercut with the live action very amusingly.

The unveiling of yet another statue of Joyce, in Stephen's Green, with so many government dignitaries present, especially delighted me. I had recently read the long-suppressed erotic letters Joyce wrote to Nora Barnacle when they were separated in 1909 (he had returned to Dublin temporarily, to try to start the first movie theatre in Ireland, and she had remained in Trieste with their children)* and the letters reveal exactly why Joyce had picked June 16, 1904, as the date to be immortalized in his epoch-making psychological novel.

On June 16, 1904, Joyce and Nora had sex, of a sort, for the first time. A 20-year-old virgin from Galway, Nora had been afraid to "go all the way" to coitus, but she masturbated him ("...with the eyes of a saint," he says in the letter recalling this.)

Ireland remains Catholic and very, very puritanical. It is Joyce's last and funniest joke that he has, by the sheer force of his genius and international reputation, tricked them into commemorating a Hand Job every year on June 16. Even if the truth ever gets published in the Irish press — which still prefers to say evasively that June 16, 1904 was the day Jim and Nora "first walked out together" — they couldn't stop Bloomsday now. The Joyce Industry is a large part of the tourist business and Ireland lives largely on tourism.

Which means, bedad, that they're all living partly on the legacy of a Hand Job.

---

* One of my grandfathers came from Dublin, the other from Trieste. Joyce spent his first 22 years in Dublin and the next 11 in Trieste. Funny coincidence.

SYNCHRO-MESH

One of the amusing by-products of war is its pricking of
the fundamental democratic delusion. For years *Homo
Boobus* stalks the earth vaingloriously, flapping his
wings over his God-given rights, his inalienable freedom, his sublime equality to his masters. Then of a
sudden he is thrust into a training camp and discovers
that he is a slave, after all — that even his life is not his
own.   — H. L. Mencken, *Minority Report*

If Cary Grant was celebrating his 28th birthday the very day I
was born (as mentioned before) then common arithmetic — or
counting on your fingers, for the current crop of college gradu-
ates — assures us that he had his 29th birthday party when I had
my first, and his 39th birthday party when I had my eleventh etc.

Through most of those years, while I was growing into and
then out of a Roman Catholic reality-tunnel, Cary was making a
series of wildly successful movies and becoming a very, very
rich man.

Marxists and other puritans will be glad to learn that Cary was
also a miserable man —as he later said in many interviews. No
matter how much cash he piled up, no matter how many spectacularly lovely women he bedded, no matter how many adoring
fans treated him like God On Wheels, he felt empty and dead
inside and full of hostilities he didn't understand. The corpse of
Archie Leach, with his throat cut, was buried somewhere
between Liverpool and Hollywood... *"O lost, lost and by the
wind grieved, ghost, you tread on my dreams..."*

It is hard to believe this inner torment when you see Cary in
his best work, especially in such great screwball comedies as
*Bringing Up Baby, His Girl Friday, My Favorite Wife, Arsenic
and Old Lace.* We all tend to confuse the artist with the art-work.

I'm sorry to disappoint the moralists but this story has a happy
ending: Cary finally found the answer to his problems, in the late
1950s. He told interviewers about it over and over again. He had
found the Stone of the Wise, the Medicine of Metals, the

Alchemical Gold, and it made him happy at last, confident enough to become a father for the first time at 60, and generally able to rewire all his neurological circuits.

He had found a shrink who used LSD psychotherapy...the product, intended only a head-ache cure, that had given Dr. Hoffman such an amusing bike ride in April 1942 when almost everybody outside Switzerland was trying to murder almost everybody else.

The more Cary talked about this Wonder Drug in interviews, the more people there were who wanted to get their hands on the Magick potion. I was one of them.

"AND HOW ARE YOU TONIGHT, MR. WILSON?"

> Obedience to the law is freedom.
> — Sign over the prison stockade at Fort Dix

Between 1969 and 1973 I was doing a lot more Acid than I admitted in the first *Cosmic Trigger*. At the time I wrote most of that book, Dr. Timothy Leary was still *in prison* for poor usage of the first amendment, Dr. Wilhelm Reich's **books had been burned** by government agents only a few years earlier, and I had an acute suspicion, heightened by Vietnam, that our Corporate Liberal Establishment was capable of turning fascist in a nanosecond if somebody challenged it seriously.

Now I am too old to be timid any longer.

So: I was doing a lot of Acid, and I was combining it with both Positive Thinking and traditional Cabalistic Magick. That is, for some Trips I would play a hypno-tape with positive suggestions on it ("I am at cause over my mind... I am at cause over my body... My mind abounds with beauty and power..."),* and for other Trips I would use the exercises in Aleister Crowley's *Magick in Theory and Practise* to enter Virtual Realities.

The major beneficial effect of these experiments was that I erased several (not all) the neurotic compulsions that have been with me since childhood. I lost my anxieties. I began developing an adult emotional life, instead of repressing emotions behind a Rationalist mask until they exploded periodically in their most childish form. I became so optimistic that it seriously annoyed

---

* Some people disapprove of this type of auto-suggestion. The same people often give themselves continuous *negative* suggestions all day long ("You can't win...the big boys have it all rigged against us...I always fuck up") and accordingly they live in misery. I have stolen Highly Positive programs from Christian Science, the Course in Miracles, How to be Popular, How to Get Rich etc. etc. and some of them worked wonderfully and some still need more effort. In general, I am much happier than before starting these experiments.

Ecologists, Marxists and other people who think we are only "moral" if we are deeply worried and habitually angry. Instead of regarding social problems as cancers that humanity could not survive, I began to see them as challenges to be surmounted.

Aside from these psychological benefits, the major "spiritual" effect of LSD may be considered either another benefit or a dire curse, depending on your viewpoint. I began to develop a strong suspicion that there was, somewhere in space-time, another Adept of Brain Change, or perhaps a School of Adepts, helping and guiding me. This is not at all unusual. In most human societies, historically, the shamans have used similar brain-change drugs and soon become convinced they have "allies" helping them. Even a man with such a long and orthodox scientific career as Dr. John Lilly confesses that he thought he had superhuman "Guides" on some of his LSD voyages.

My teachers seemed to have a damned peculiar sense of humor at times.

At one point I was almost totally convinced that my teachers were a school of extraterrestrial adepts resident in the double-star system of Sirius. Strange coincidences — or Jungian synchronicities — then accumulated around me, supporting this theory.

Later, a "psychic reader" told me I was "channeling" the spirit of an ancient Chinese sage. Coincidences or "omens" supporting this model then obligingly appeared.

Then, another "psychic" told me I was channeling a medieval Irish bard. More synchronicities followed.

This sort of thing always happens to people who mess around with Cabala (even if they don't use Acid.) The late Dr. Israel Regardie, a psychotherapist and Cabalist, often distinguished two ways of looking at this phenomenon, when it happens to you. The objective theory, as he called it, assumes an external reality to these "entities." The subjective theory, on the other hand, assumes the "entities" exist only in our brains, as anti-selves or Jungian archetypes or something of that sort. Dr. Regardie believed you will get the best results when you are not committed to either theory but just open yourself to whatever happens.

Somewhere along the way I got concerned with the direction all this was taking and decided to safeguard my sanity by choosing the subjective theory — *It's all in my head* — and ruthlessly repressing any tendency to speculate further about possible objective theories — *There are super-human forces at work here...)* In terms of the neurological model then current, I explained everything as my over-developed left brain learning to receive signals from the usually "silent" right brain.

(We now know that this left brain/right brain model does not quite explain everything, and Karl Pribram's hologram model of consciousness seems more inclusive. But I refer here to my state of ignorance in the mid 1970s, before I advanced to the more complex state of ignorance I now possess.)

Then one night I was looking at *Harvey,* the comedy about the *pookah,* on TV. One character in the story is a medical orderly named Wilson; since I was once a medical orderly and named Wilson, he attracted more of my interest than the major characters.

Wilson-in-the-TV was more "skeptical" about the giant rabbit than anybody else, and began to seem to me like a parody of my attempts to reduce everything to the right brain/left brain model.

The *pookah* refrains from playing any nasty tricks on the Unbeliever. Instead, he arranges that *just by accident* Wilson meets a young woman who falls in love with him — which is obviously just what he needs. Then, when Wilson learns that the giant white rabbit is called a *pookah,* he looks the word up in a dictionary and reads the definition aloud. It says:

"A Celtic elf or vegetation spirit, wise but mischievous, fond of rumpots, crackpots and how are you tonight, Mr. Wilson?"

Wilson-in-the-TV dropped the dictionary, his mouth hanging open.

Wilson-outside-the-TV (me) also had a startle reaction. Thinking it all over, I decided *Harvey* offered the best approach to Cabala and its entities. From then on when High Weirdness occurred, I would just file-and-index it as a six foot tall white rabbit from County Kerry, playing games with me.

I still prefer this model to all others, because there is no chance that I *or any sane person* will ever take it literally.

WE ARE BETTER AT BELIEVING

Generals are fascinating cases of arrested development.
After all, at five we all wanted to be generals.
— Peter Ustinov

Back to the Giant Spider —

A popular proverb says, "Seeing is believing," but as the philosopher Santayana once pointed out, humans are much better at believing than at seeing.

The feedback loop between our eyes and our brain, by which we *interpret and "project"* (in the Freudian sense) when we think we are merely *observing,* creates problems worse than *pookahs* or Giant Spiders — problems that neither psychology nor philosophy has yet solved. As Charles Fort once pointed out, if we had no concept for "horse," a man could parade a dozen horses down the street and everybody would see — something else.

I personally think this factor obviates most of the reasoning of both Believers and Debunkers in matters like the "reality" of the poltergeist, or Bigfoot, or the Face on Mars, or UFOs. In many anomalistic and "paranormal" cases, I suspect, people are looking at something like horses without having a concept of "horse" to explain to themselves what they are seeing.

In other books, I have mentioned an exercise I often perform in my seminars, in which the participants are asked to describe the hall they passed through outside the seminar room. There are never two people in the group who describe exactly the same hall — and I have done this experiment thousands of times now. Everybody thinks they are in "the same hall," but each is actually in her own or his own reality-tunnel.

Once, when I was just starting to use this exercise, I thought I would get a more interesting and dramatic response by "rigging" the hall a little. I tacked up the Playmate of the Month on the wall, thinking everybody would react to this so intensely that they would hardly notice anything else at all. To my astonishment nobody *saw* the Beautiful Naked Young Woman at all...

Honest. The men did not slaver over her. The women did complain about "sexism." She simply did not exist for them.

Questioning revealed that everybody in the group used that hall one or more times a day. They had simply stopped looking, because they "knew" what was there.

(This explains a lot of human behavior. The next time you notice conspicuous stupidity, try to see if the subject has simply **stopped looking** because she or he thinks they "know" what is here.)

If there had been a Giant Spider in the hall, maybe nobody but a very small child would have seen it.

You haven't gotten the point of this unless you connect it with two other important bits of data, to wit:

(1) Victorian doctors believed firmly that children have no sexual drives and were shocked and outraged when Freud "discovered" they do; most respectable physicians denounced him as a "pervert," a "charlatan" or even a "lunatic."

(2) We have absolutely no guarantee that equally important and obvious facts are not screened out of our perceptions by our current dogmas.

SOMEWHERE OVER THE RAINBOW

"Pay no attention to the man behind the curtain!"
— Oz the Omnipotent

You can see that I never forgot the Giant Spider — and I also
still remember the second time I entered Virtual Reality. I was
five or six years old at the time and my parents had taken me to
see a wonderful movie called *The Wizard of Oz*. Toward the end
of the film there was a scene in which the Wicked Witch of the
West, riding her broom, wrote in the sky like one of the mysterious sky-writing airplanes that I was accustomed to seeing. The
airplanes always wrote the same strange, inscrutable message, as
puzzling to me as any "inhuman" chant in a Lovecraft story —
I.J. FOX FINE FURS LOW PRICES — but the Wicked Witch
wrote something far different and absolutely terrifying. She
wrote:

SURRENDER

DOROTHY

I was so frightened that I burst into tears. My parents had a hell
of a job quieting me down, and I must have annoyed all the
adults in the theatre. Today, well over 50 years later, I understand better what had happened. Sitting in the dark, staring at the
movie screen, I had crossed the line between "reality" and
"fantasy" — a line that is not nearly as firm for a child as it is (or
seems to be) for an adult. Dorothy's danger, up there on the
screen, was more "real" than my safety, down in the dark audience. This may or may not qualify as an imprinting experience in
the Lorenzian sense, but it was traumatic in the Freudian sense.
Even today, as I keyboarded the terrible, blood-curdling words
"SURRENDER DOROTHY," I felt a reflex shudder pass
through me.

Well, a few years later I was able to distinguish movies from
"real" reality. I watched the Frankenstein monster wreak havoc
on the villagers, The Mummy stalk his victims among the pyramids, Lon Chaney Jr. turn into a werewolf, and none of it fooled

me. I was amused at the younger kids who screamed during these films, or closed their eyes "in the scary parts." Still — *only my conscious ego, or forebrain, was immune to the hypnosis.* I still jumped when the director pulled a shock scene.

Watching adult audiences these days, none of whom believe literally in Indiana Jones or the Temple of Doom, or even in Batman and Joker, I see that, whatever they *think* they know, parts of their old brain, and of their bodies, still enter hypnosis easily. That's why they gasp, and cringe, and breathe hard, and have similar adrenaline reactions, when things get rough up there on the white screen of sorcery. I can still see these neuro-chemical reactions in myself, too, of course.

Only a small part of our brains, or our "selves," is able to resist the illusions, or lies, of a good artist. Nobody can sit through *Alien,* I would wager, without at least one sound of fear or distress escaping their lips during that "ordeal"...which consists only of looking at pictures projected on a screen, pictures telling a story nobody literally believes...

A movie theatre is the best place to learn the true meaning of Plato's parable of the prisoners in the cave, who accept shadows as reality. Every artist who moves us, from a movie maker to Beethoven or Shakespeare, is a bit of a hypnotist.

In this sense, that seemingly stupid and mechanical contraption we call "society" must rank as the greatest artist (or hypnotist) on the planet. For instance, when I was attending school at last and feeling superior to the kids who closed their eyes "during the scary parts," I was entering a deep hypnoidal trance created by another Virtual Reality called language. This hypnosis was a worse nightmare than the Wicked Witch of the West or The Mummy or the Wolf-Man or any of their kith and kin, but it made me a "member of society" — and "a member of the Body of Christ" as well.

My parents had put me in a *Catholic* school. The first lesson I learned was that I was poor. The second lesson was that nuns could be a lot more frightening than the Wicked Witch of the West.

THE MUTED VOICE

Arlen once pointed out to me that the Victorian doctors before Freud, who believed children have no sex drives...were all male.

It seems improbable-to-impossible that *women* did not know about the sex-play of infants and children. Women spend a hell of a lot of time with children, both as mothers and as older daughters who get assigned to "watch the smaller children" when Mom is busy.

My mother, for instance, never heard of Freud (I can assure you of that) but she knew children have sex lives. I heard her discussing infant masturbation with some other mothers once, when she didn't know I was listening.

The only way Victorian doctors maintained their ignorance was by declaring women part of *the set of "all people who have nothing to say that we need to listen to."* Every society has such a set, and since the rise of Bronze Age Patriarchy, women have usually been part of it.

Those men who think they "are" "liberated" because they have started listening to women still have a large set of "all people who have nothing to say that we need to listen to."

Right now, for instance, almost everybody in America regards the Iraqis as part of that set. In fact, the reports from Iraq, on CNN, have been widely denounced, just because they contain information Americans do not want to hear — especially information about how other people feel about America when American bombs keep falling on them, hour after hour, day after day. The Iraqis, like residents of countless other nations who have had this educational experience of being under American bombs, belong to **the set of all people who have nothing to say that we need to listen to.**

Dr. James DeMeo of P. O. Box 1395, El Cerritos CA 94530 has a bibliography available listing over 400 papers by more than 100 scientists who have replicated some of the "orgone" experiments of Dr. Wilhelm Reich. All of those scientists belong to **the set of all people who have nothing to say that the American Medical Association feels it needs to listen to.**

GET OUT YOUR HANKIES

A Dickensian Interlude

Since my father was still unemployed in early 1937, I qualified for the school's free lunch program. My mother, somehow, got the wrong idea about how to certify me. She simply gave me a note to give to the Mother Superior, in which she declared the fact of Dad's unemployment and requested my inclusion in the free lunch program.

Well, that was not all that was required, after all; my mother — like Rick when he moved to Casablanca — had been misinformed. Some bureaucratic paper-work of some sort was also necessary (I don't remember the details) but the Mother Superior announced that, lacking the proper paper, I could not have lunch. I don't recall the exact words she used, but somehow I got the impression she was accusing my mother of lying.

At lunch time, I saw most of the kids, who qualified for the free lunch, file into one room, and then a few kids who brought their own lunches file into another room. I heard some remarks that made it perfectly clear to me that the kids who had their own lunches were mocking the free lunch kids. Being on the free lunch program meant you were poor, and this meant that the other kids could say nasty things about you.

Since I didn't even qualify for the free lunch program, I was the bottom of the pecking order — low man on the totem pole.

I went out on the sidewalk in front of the school, sat down and cried. It seems impossible that my actual hunger was extreme (my mother had undoubtedly given me a good breakfast). Rather, I was suffering the kind of acute humiliation and loss of self-esteem that only small children can experience, because, whatever adults suffer, they can always consider it unfair. Small children lack that much independence and don't know how to resist group condemnation.

My mother was suspected of lying. I was therefore so low that I didn't even have the "right" to join the despised free lunch kids. And, being a child, I couldn't even feel outraged: I only felt disgraced and dehumanized. My definition in that school, that day, was Piece of Shit, and that's what I felt like.

CLERICAL CAREER PROPOSED

Child Abuse Recorded

The problem got straightened out the next day, when my mother came into the school and screamed and hollered and generally raised flaming blue hell, and I got on the free lunch program — for a while.

My definition soon changed from Piece of Shit to Teacher's Pet, because I could read better than anybody (my mother had taught me when I was about four). I also had a great memory — which is all you need to seem very bright in a Catholic school, where "intelligence" is measured by your ability to repeat what you heard yesterday.

Being on free lunch antagonized the kids who brought their own lunches. Being Teacher's Pet antagonized all the other kids. Nonetheless, my high marks helped me to build up a fairly strong ego — up to a point, anyway.

Even though the nun who taught first grade thought I was "bright enough to become a priest" — high praise in that tribe — the Mother Superior had a grudge against me, over the free lunch hassle. She caught me one day at recess and decided that my hair wasn't properly combed, which was all the excuse she needed. I was marched to the front of the class after we reconvened, and punishment was administered. This consisted of being told to hold out my hand — I knew what was coming, having seen other boys punished, but I held the hand out anyway, since I had a nasty suspicion that something even worse would happen if I refused — and then she whacked me across the knuckles, as hard as she could, with a steel yardstick, five times.

I felt every eye in the class on me and did not allow myself to cry.

My hand cramped and hurt like a bastard for about a day after.

I now regard that as a most fortunate incident. I was no longer defined only as Teacher's Pet and I began to make friends. Since I managed to restrain my tears, I also earned the respect of the boys. I had learned the "muscular armoring" required of males in this society, and didn't cry again until I entered Reichian therapy 20 years later. (Actually restraining the tears during this minor form of child abuse seemed fairly easy to me; it seemed much, much harder to restrain the natural impulse to grab the yardstick and whack the sadistic old bitch back a few times.)

Of course, once I learned not to cry, I began to "leave my body" and live in my head. I eventually became a compulsive Rationalist.

Meanwhile, I was being brainwashed — or as the nuns called it "educated in the Mysteries of the Faith." This involved such metaphysical mystification as understanding how God could be three persons and yet remain one person. This was known as the Mystery of the Trinity.

Since the nuns didn't know about Multiple Personality Disorder, they had a hard job explaining that three-in-one business. Besides, they wouldn't really like having to admit that their God was, medically speaking, psychotic.

THE EIGHTH WONDER
OF THE WORLD

Around the time I went through this Initiation into sado-
masochism and Catholicism, RKO Studios re-released *King
Kong* and I saw it for the first time.

Naturally, I loved the dinosaurs and the next day went looking
for books in the Public Library about them. I passed through the
traditional period of making drawings of dinosaurs and hanging
them in my bedroom. It appears, from conversations I have had
over the years, that most boys go through this dinosaur bedaz-
zlement. My late friend, Bob Shea, said that secretly we were
trying, in an unconscious way, to perform a magick rite that
would bring the dinosaurs back from the dead. I don't know a
better explanation.

But the Epic of Kong made a more profound and long-lasting
imprint upon my tender young neurons. I went into Virtual
Reality again at the very end, when Carl Denham (Robert Armstrong) says, "It wasn't the airplanes. It was Beauty that killed
the Beast."

And this time Virtual Reality was deeper, less frightening and
more wonderful than it had been with the Witch and the Spider.
It was years and years before I learned the word "allegory" and
more years before I learned about "the unconscious" and
Freudian and Jungian symbolism, but the Giant Ape and the
White Virgin had opened me to the world of the *noumenon*.

I was left with a haunting suspicion that there was a "reality"
deeper and more "true" than ordinary "reality."

INFORMATION DOUBLES

The World Is Transformed

I never aimed at reality; I aimed at truth. Look at Cagney. Nothing he ever did on screen was realistic, but it was all *true*.　　　— Orson Welles

In 1500, the human race had twice as much information as the Romans in 1 AD, remember?

The center of power-and-information had shifted northwestward from Rome to the North Italian States with their huge banks and up-to-the-minute Universities. The bankers (e.g. the Medici family) lavishly patronized Art, and the painters in their employ left us a Disneyland of pagan classics.

But soon the Medici and their class would patronize Science even more, because a great artist in their employ only gave them Glory but a great scientist gave them gadgets to pry more wealth out of every square of Earth they owned.

Columbus had returned from the "New World" eight years before, with wild stories of what he had found. Vasco de Gama had made his voyages and Amerigo Vespucci (who would later have two continents named after him) had completed one voyage to Novus Mundo (as he called it)* and was about to embark on his second voyage. Leonardo da Vinci, still in his prime, was creating *those conventions we still tend to consider "realistic" art* and designing airplanes and other Futuristic wonders in his notebooks.

Any educated person could potentially learn twice as much as the most erudite Roman of 1 AD, and something called "the Renaissance" was challenging every dogma and orthodoxy of Europe. In China, the Confucian bureaucracy sought justice and fairness, as Confucius had taught them to do, and also, as he had taught them, piously studied the Ancient Classics and cautiously stifled anything new or innovative.

---

* The future would call it South America in his honor.

Within one breeding generation of the doubling of information — 17 years — in 1517 the first successful Protestant Revolution broke loose in Germany, because an anal-retentive named Martin Luther thought he had the right to think, and because Northern merchants were tired of being taxed to pay for the Pope's beautification of the Vatican with modernistic and "pagan-looking" art works.

Only one breeding generation later, in 1534, the second successful Protestant Revolution occurred in England.

The Papacy felt itself losing control of the Western world and fought back; the Protestants refused to lie down and die, so one religious war followed another for over 200 years. (By 1723, Swift observed mournfully that Christians "have enough religion to hate one another, but not enough to love one another.") In that 200 years, the *avant* minds of Europe increasingly turned away from the fanaticism of both the Catholic and Protestant reality-tunnels and moved, slowly and imperceptibly at first, toward "humanism," secularism and Objective Science.

It had taken around four million years to get from the first African stone ax to the Roman engineers and Roman law; but an even more total revolution had occurred by the time knowledge doubled again in 1500.

And as religious wars tore Europe apart again and again, science found more and more Unifying Principles on which all observers could agree. The world was going to continue to change... faster and faster...

TOWARD A GENERAL THEORY
OF B.S.

> A free government with an uncontrolled power of military conscription is the most ridiculous and abominable contradiction and nonsense that ever entered into the head of man.
>
> — Daniel Webster, Speech in the House of Representatives, January 14, 1814

My eventual Ph.D. dissertation (Paideia University, 1980) had the stentorian title, "The Evolution of Neuro-Sociological Circuits: A Contribution to the Sociobiology of Consciousness." (That really has the true academic stink, doesn't it, by God?)

My major theme in that paper, as in most of my books, consisted of trying to understand how something as complex as human society emerged out of ordinary primate packs — mammals only marginally more intelligent than wolves or Norway rats. My thesis held that *language and hypnosis form the foundation on which humans create worlds of consciousness and of fantasy* which no other animals seem able to achieve.

That is, however language appeared — and I think it represented the evolutionary equivalent of a quantum jump* — it allowed people to do what no other known animals seem to do, namely to visualize and/or verbally "contemplate" something that is not present before their senses. This fantasy or reflection or cogitation allows us, then, to compare the imagined with the experienced.

Animals only suffer physical pain; humans suffer both physical pain and an additional psychological pain from the thought (verbal construct), "I should not have to suffer this."

This causes us to struggle for social progress, better medicine etc. but it also causes us to feel the same bitter sense of "injus-

---

* A jump probably due to hominids stumbling upon psychedelic plants, I think. Of course, I did not express this view in this dissertation. I may be an idiot, but I am not a *blithering* idiot.

tice" or "wrongness" when there is nothing concretely that can be done to ease the pain.

In short, without language we'd have less suffering and no progress.

Remember also that the imagined contains a great deal of both the desirable and the terrifying — what we want and what we fear. Thus, unlike our relatives the chimpanzees and baboons, however clever one of them may be, humans alone can long for things that never existed outside their language-games (i.e., their "thinking") and can get very irritated at the world for being less pleasing than these fantasies. They can also scare the hell out of themselves, and one another, with other verbal constructs that have never appeared in sensory experience.

Thus, the state of "living in fantasy" or "being on a head trip" is by no means uncommon and is not typical *only* of well-fed intellectuals in academic Chairs. Everybody does it to a quite alarming extent. Humans never deal with raw experience as other animals do; they deal with experience filtered through what Dr. Timothy Leary calls a reality-tunnel and sociologists call a grid or gloss — a belief system. Every belief system (or BS)[*] *colors* experience in a different way, rosy-red or gloomy black or some unique personal flavor.

We can all see how other people's BS makes them blind and "stupid" at times, but we find it very hard to notice how our own BS is doing the same to us. This is what anthropologists call *acculturalization.*

Following Gurdjieff, I prefer to call it hypnosis. Every culture on the planet — from the Stone Age bushmen of Africa to the still-medieval peasants of County Kerry, from the Parisian art crowd to the Oxford agnostic crowd, from the Ohio Republicans to the Iranian Moslem Fundamentalists, from the science-fiction buffs to the neo-pagans and "witches," from the Tibetan Buddhists to the Committee for Scientific Investigation of Claims of the Paranormal — represents another case of group hypnosis by BS (belief systems.)

---

[*] I owe this delightful abbreviation to David Brown, author of *Brainchild* (New Falcon Publications, 1988)

That is, when I was sent to a "school" to be "educated," that meant I was to be hypnotized into the tunnel-reality of my tribe.

As indicated earlier, the emotional response to Indiana Jones movies shows that it is remarkably easy to induce at least partial hypnosis in domesticated primates.

Every politician knows how to induce hypnosis, and very damned few people on the whole planet know how to de-hypnotize themselves.

The world is not governed by facts or logic. It is governed by BS (belief systems.)

If you assemble in one room a group made up of Irish Catholics, German bankers, French intellectuals, Hindu priests, Orange County Republicans, Russian bureaucrats, nudists, Buddhists and Scientologists, none of them will be able to understand any of the others except in a dim and distorted way. Their BS will get into the brain-ear-eye system and warp all perception.

IMPORTANT!
READ THIS CAREFULLY!

What I have been saying — the important lesson of this book — can be put into two simple imperatives:

1. Never believe *totally* in anybody else's BS.
2. Never believe *totally* in your own BS.

These formulations are my own, but the basic idea here, of course, derives from Gotama Buddha.

If you do not retain some zeteticism* about all ideas, however appealing they may be, you have entered hypnosis, as I entered hypnosis when placed in a Catholic school to be "educated" by the nuns — a bunch of ignorant women who had been so deeply hypnotized themselves that they remained mentally crippled for life.

In a famous story, the Buddha was asked, "Are you a God?"
"No," he replied.
"Are you a Saint?"
"No."
"Then what are you?"
"I am awake."

He meant that he was able to see who he was, where he was, and what was going on around him, because he was no longer blinded by Belief Systems.

---

* A term from ancient Greek philosophy revived by Dr. Marcello Truzzi, because the similar term "skepticism" has been pre-empted by certain entrenched dogmatists. The modern so-called skeptic accepts the dogmas of the reigning Establishment and is cynical only about ideas that are new, original or Heretical. The zetetic is skeptical of *all* dogmas.

BURY MY HEART
AT WOUNDED KNEE

In the Spring of 1977, we were living in a big barn of a modernistic house in the Berkeley hills. The house had picture windows everywhere and decks and patios in odd places, and it tried awfully hard to pass itself as a Frank Lloyd Wright original. It was as convincing at that imposture as the Ayatollah Khoumeni would be posing as Playmate of the Month. Arlen and I shared this enormous, mansion-like place with our daughter, Alex, our son, Graham, and two bachelors who worked in the computer industry. Since the building had two stories (set akilter of each other, of course) and more than a dozen rooms, we were not crowded.

One evening Arlen and Alex and I had a date to meet Alex's boy friend, Mike, at the Empress of China in San Francisco, our favorite Chinese restaurant. I was sitting out on the veranda, at sunset, digging the view. (Some evenings I applauded a particularly gorgeous sunset and shouted, "Author! Author!" All of us Infidels have our own moments of piety and forget the real Identity of the artist who makes this world so weirdly lovely.) Inside, Arlen and Alex were busy as women always are when getting dressed for dinner at a fancy restaurant.

My daughter Luna had been murdered by a burglar six months before, and I thought I was finally over the worst of the grief. I didn't know yet that such grief never ends: you just get better at "handling" it.

I had arranged for cryonic preservation of Luna's genetic material. This seemed to me a scientific and rational decision. With the advances in genetic engineering and related technologies — together with the fact that cryonic freezing will preserve anything for literally billions of years — it seemed mathematically certain that at some future day, science could give Luna a chance to live again.

Still, like the Christians who weep even though they think they know the dead are now in heaven, I wept often in those first awful months.

I could never let my rage settle only on the murderer. This surprised me, mildly, but it appeared true, no matter how deep I looked inside. Sociology had so permeated my neurons that I could not think of any individual, including the murderer, as an entity isolated from historical processes. I perceived myself, for instance, as the resultant of genetic vectors (Irish-Austrian) and historical trajectories (America's evolution, in my lifetime, from a Depressed nation to a computerized, atomized, Futurized but still messianic Perpetual Warfare system.)

The murderer was a Sioux Indian and an alcoholic, who had been at Wounded Knee when, according to eye witnesses, the FBI opened fire on unarmed Native American demonstrators and killed several. I could not think of him without seeing him as the resultant of all the horrors and atrocities committed against the Native Americans since we whites first arrived here. My rage went through him and past him to include the whole structure of Christian bigotry, white racism and Capitalist greed that had made the genocide of the Native Americans inevitable — and made the high alcoholism and violence rate of the survivors equally inevitable.

I hated not the one man whose crime had hurt me most, but all the men whose crimes had perpetuated the mechanical and bloody cycle of injustice and revenge that we call History.

Suddenly, I began weeping there on the veranda, looking at that incredibly beautiful sunset. In all my weeping since Luna's death, I had never cried like this. It was an explosion of rage and despair, for all the murdered children everywhere. Arlen and Alex came out and hugged me. They didn't say much; maybe they didn't say anything. Somehow, they knew I had to go through this. They gave me warmth and noises of empathy.

The weeping went on and on and on. My whole body shook with the convulsions of it. I had suddenly lost my belief in the cryonic gamble. Mathematics crumbled into uncertain calculations of dubious probabilities. I saw the Cryonics Movement as most people see it: a bunch of screwball Technocrats. Luna was dead, and my cryonic attempt to evade that was as sad an exam-

ple of wishful thinking as religious doctrines of heaven and rein-
carnation. I was deluded again, as always.

It felt as if I might never stop weeping. Eventually Alex asked
if we should call off the dinner. I said no, and promised I'd be
"all right" shortly.

In a while we all went out and got in the car. I was still
weeping softly. Alex drove. We went down Grizzly Peak and
across Shattuck and passed the Emoryville Mud Flats with their
mad, surrealist sculptures. My sobs began to subside. We crossed
the East Bay Bridge and headed for Chinatown.

By the time we reached the restaurant I was okay again.

CRIME & PUNISHMENT

The penalty for laughing in a courtroom is six months
in jail; if it were not for this penalty, the jury would
never hear the evidence.   — H. L. Mencken

Of course, from what you already know of my attitudes, you
could reasonably expect that I would get arrested eventually,
right?

I was finally arrested in Yellow Springs, Ohio, in 1964. I
heartily recommend the experience to all young writers seeking a
quick way to learn how fast a reality-tunnel — a definition of
"my Self and my World" — can collapse.

Yellow Springs had a barber shop called Gegner's, which was
a reasonable name since the owner was named Mr. Gegner. This
barber shop was segregated — as all barber shops in that part of
the country were segregated when Mr. Gegner was young.* By
1964, however, most of the others had accepted the inevitable
and desegregated themselves. Gegner was a recalcitrant and in
many ways I admired his stubborn intransigence.

The City Council of Yellow Springs had passed a desegre-
gation law, but Gegner claimed he could not comply because he
simply did not know how to cut Negro hair. The case went to
court. Expert testimony was presented indicating that one white
man whose head had been barbered by Gegner had "kinkier" hair
than a Black man Gegner had refused to serve. By the time the
lawyers for both sides were finished with the precise criteria of
"kinkiness," it had become almost as impenetrable as Jacques
Lacan's neo-Freudian doctrine of Phallus as "signifier of signi-
fiers." The dispute was working its way through the appeals
courts when some of the "radical" students at Antioch College — all of them members of the newly-formed Students for a
Democratic Society, as I later learned — decided to accelerate
progress by staging a series of sit-ins at Gegner's barber shop.

---

* Southern Ohio borders Kentucky and the Confederacy, and it is even
hard to distinguish the Southern Ohio accent from a Kentucky accent.

This made a lot of problems for the Chief of Police, who was Black and did not really like the idea of arresting people who were demonstrating against segregation. Nonetheless, the sit-ins were illegal under the law, and the Chief had to arrest hordes of students on several occasions. I felt sorry for him, especially since I knew his sister-in-law (Yellow Springs is a very small town) and she assured me she was giving him the sharp edge of her tongue every time he arrested more of the protesters.

I was working as Assistant Sales Manager of the Antioch Bookplate Company, a local business. I sympathized with the students because I felt segregation was a running sore and needed strong medicine, but I also sympathized with old man Gegner because I always sympathize with Individualists, however ornery they may be.

Besides, the Gegner case presented a peculiar moral ambiguity, in my view of things. Yellow Springs had *two* barber shops, and the other one was desegregated. The walking time between the two was certainly less than three minutes for a healthy person and no more than ten minutes for somebody on crutches. I tend to like pluralistic, rather than totalitarian, solutions, so I thought the town might achieve a workable and symmetrical balance if somebody opened a shop that only cut Black hair. Then we'd have one all-white barber shop (Gegner's) for white segregationists, one all-Black shop for Black separatists, and one desegregated shop for liberals, which in my Rationalistic mind should have satisfied everybody. "You pays your money and you takes your cherce."

Whenever I presented this idea, people stared at me as if I had just killed a goat in the sacristy. This was only one of several occasions in my young adulthood in which it forcibly came home to me that abstractly rational ideas have no appeal at all in the emotional arena of hominid politics.

Things started to come to a head when Gegner's lawyers succeeded in getting an injunction against further sit-ins at his shop. The immediate response of the students, naturally, was to announce they would violate the injunction.

Before the students could organize a massive demonstration again, an elderly Quaker called a meeting of young business-people of liberal persuasion. I attended. It was proposed that *we* should stage the next sit-in, just to demonstrate that it was not just a bunch of "radical longhair students" who objected to segregation; that mature liberals were ready to Take a Stand.

That night, I went home after the meeting and talked with Arlen. Then I did a great deal of private philosophizing. Despite my rationalist compromise scheme above, the fact was that I actively hated segregation, which I considered genocide in slow motion. I had had an affair with a Black woman once (just before I met Arlen in fact). Some of my favorite writers and virtually all my favorite living musicians were Black. The climate of Racism was ugly, and getting uglier — while the police chief in Yellow Springs was gently and regretfully arresting civil rights activists, a few miles further south you entered territory where the activists were being murdered, castrated, tortured unspeakably.

I felt I had to Take a Stand. The whole country was becoming polarized and I could not sit on the fence offering rationalistic "solutions" that nobody on either side wanted to hear.

A few nights later, our "liberal" group* met again, to plan how we would handle the sit-in. Somebody had brought along a lawyer, a Black man who definitely did not want to preserve segregation but who also felt it his duty to make clear to us what was involved in violating a court injunction. Once we learned what "indefinite sentence" means, almost all of us dropped out of the project.

Including me.

Indefinite sentence means the judge can keep you locked up just as long as he damned pleases. It is the penalty in most States for "criminal insanity" and also for violating a judge's injunctions or otherwise expressing "contempt" for judicial authority.

I felt like a coward, but my kids were all under six years old and I could not bear the thought of being parted from them while they were in those crucial years. I could endure whatever jail might do to me, and I even thought I could endure being without "conjugal love" in the service of my Ideals, but I did not think I could or should "desert" my children at those tender ages.

---

* I was actually an anarchist but since I didn't throw bombs and had a responsible job and a wife and family the liberals considered me an eccentric member of their own clique.

Two days later I changed my mind. Nothing dramatic happened, no sudden Vision or divine voice; I just remembered that Medgar Evers and Chaney and Shirmer and Goodman and lots of others had died for this cause, and what I faced was not that terminal. Besides, the lawyer had pointed out that some authorities hold that "indefinite sentences" had to be within "reasonable and prudent" limits and then he went off into more legal gibberish, but what it all meant concretely was that the best guide to what the judge would consider reasonable was his previous record, and he was not a "hanging judge" or a racist.

Still — and the lawyer insisted on this — you could never know for sure, until you heard the verdict. If the judge had a real animus against people who do not respect judicial incantations, he had the right under the law to lock us up until zebras grow wings and fly loop-the-loops.

So, on the day of the sit-in, I had no idea whether I was risking 30 days in the town hoosegow or 30 years in the State pen. I didn't know if the fear I felt was the only sane response to this monstrous situation my language-games ("ideas and ideals") had led me into, or if it was something I would laugh about later.

Out of the group of over 20 who had planned this demonstration, there were six of us who walked into the barber shop — two Blacks and four Whites. I wondered if we were the six bravest men in town or the six biggest eejits.

We all took seats. Gegner, who was appraised that we were coming, looked at one of the white men (not me) and said, "Wanna hair-cut?"

The man addressed pointed to one of the Black men. "He's ahead of me," he said. This was in accord with the advice of the lawyer, who, like all his profession, wanted to create Byzantine ambiguities so he could try to get us off on a technicality. (I am convinced that law relates to common sense and logic about as closely as phrenology does.)

"I don't know how to cut Nigra hair," Gegner said.

"We'll wait," we all said in turn.

Gegner, no doubt in accord with the advice of his own lawyer, explained again, slowly and distinctly, that he did not know how to cut Nigra hair but would happily cut the hair of us white folks.

We all said we'd sit and wait until he cut the hair of our Black friends who were ahead of us coming in.

Gegner went to the door. The police chief entered, looking no cheerier than a man going to his own hanging, with two plain-clothes cops behind him. Naturally, the chief knew all of us, and we knew him — I told you Yellow Springs was a small town.

The chief explained that we were engaged in an illegal sit-in and he would have to arrest us if we didn't leave.

We explained that we just wanted hair-cuts.

The chief then addressed each of us in turn, explaining that we were in violation of the law and a court injunction and he would have to arrest us if we didn't leave. He asked us if we under-stood.

"I don't understand," I said. "I just want a hair-cut and I don't believe that's a crime." That wasn't the lawyer's idea; I was just being a wise-ass again.

The cops stood us up, turned us around, and cuffed our hands. I have heard that they can tighten the cuffs so it hurts like hell. They didn't do that. The chief might have reamed them out like Saniflush if they had. I knew he was going to catch fire and brimstone from his sister-in-law anyway. I felt sorry for him.

He probably felt sorry for me, too.

When we were properly cuffed, they led us out, and suddenly *I turned on.* You all know I have done my share of pot and acid and meditation and other Kwik-Brain-Change gimmicks, but this was unique. A mob of supporters and opponents of our action had gathered — the supporters from largely-Quaker Yellow Springs and the opponents from nearby redneck Xenia — and I could literally see every wart and black-head, every bead of sweat, on every face. Colors were like rainbows. Time not only s l o w e d and s l o w e d but then seemed to STOP. I was in Eternity in the middle of an emotional mob.

Some were singing WE SHALL OVERCOME and some were shouting GO BACK TO NEW YORK YOU COMMIE JEW QUEERS and it was all going on and on for hours and days and they could have built the pyramids and gotten bored with them and torn them down again in the millenniums as we crossed the sidewalk to the paddy wagon. I suddenly understood the High experienced by lion-hunters and mountain climbers. For the first time in my life, I had released enough adrenaline to be as tripped out as a shaman on magic mushrooms.

I realized with total clarity and no emotion at all that now I was a Prisoner of the State. The chief was a nice guy and hated this, but once he delivered us to the Greene County Jail in Xenia we were out of his jurisdiction. Anything could happen. My body did not belong to me. It belonged to men with guns who had badges that gave them the authority to do whatever they wished with me, as long as they had a plausible explanation later.

I was a Philosophical Anarchist before they put cuffs on me. I was rapidly becoming a Stone Paranoid Anarchist. Being totally helpless does that to you.

HYPNOSIS, VIRTUAL REALITY &
THE GROUND-GLASS SYNDROME

> There is no absurdity so palpable but that it may be
> firmly planted in the human head if only you begin to
> inculcate it before the age of five, by constantly repeat-
> ing it with an air of great solemnity.
>
> — Arthur Schopenhauer

Every day, school began with a prayer. After lunch, there was
another prayer. When lessons were finished for the day, before
they let us go, there was another prayer. Five days a week,
September to June every year, for eight years, these prayers
formed my consciousness into a Catholic mold. They were rein-
forced by Religious Knowledge class, in which we memorized
the catechism, containing all the dogmas of the church. We had
to pass examinations on that, just like we did in arithmetic, as if
the two subjects were equally valid.

Even today I can remember parts of the Baltimore Catechism,
the text in that Religious Knowledge class:

Why did God make me?
God made me to love Him and serve Him in this world, and to
be happy with Him forever in the next.

What is a sacrament?
A sacrament is the visible sign of an invisible grace.

Who killed our Lord, Jesus?
Jesus was killed by the Wicked Jews.*

We were systematically made more vulnerable to the hypnosis
by those vicious steel yardsticks that made your hands go numb
and hurt all day. Although we dared not think it explicitly, every
child knew they were in the hands of giant insane robots with no
human compunction about inflicting pain. The result of all these

---

* This passage was eliminated from the catechism in the 1960s, during
the reign of Pope John XXIII.

prayers and all that memorization and terrorism was that I came to dwell in a Virtual Reality in which a nasty old man living on a cloud a few miles above Earth was watching me all the time and would probably charbroil me or roast me or toast me or poach me or French Fry me if he ever caught me doing anything he didn't like. He was called God, and I have already mentioned his great demand for MONEY. He had a rival who oddly seemed to work for him part time, called Satan, who presided over the charbroiling and roasting and toasting and poaching and French Frying, in caverns that honeycomb the hollow Earth. Between the two of them, God and Satan, life was far more terrifying than any "horror movie."

God's singular passion for MONEY was the major topic of the sermons I heard at Mass on Sundays. (Although my father never went to Mass, and my mother only went on Easter and Christmas, they insisted that I should go.) The priests were very fond of the story of the Widow's Mite, in the New Testament, which teaches that God is just as happy to get a small coin from a poor woman as he is to get a million dollar donation from a Rockefeller. I think the original point of the story was that God doesn't draw class distinctions, but the way the priests told it, the moral was that you had to put something in the collection basket no matter how poor you were. My parents always gave me a dime to put in.

I learned eventually that some of the boys would stop at a candy store, buy a chocolate bar for a nickel and put the nickel change in the basket, but I was afraid to try that. I was sure God would find out and it would lead to eventual charbroiling.

A whole dime seemed a lot of money to kids in those days. For a dime, which my parents occasionally gave me on Saturdays as well as Sundays, I could go to the local theatre and see, not just a an hour-and-a-half feature movie, but also a second feature or "B" movie about an hour long with less famous actors in it, three animated cartoons, a newsreel and a chapter of one of the serials of the time — *Nyoka, Queen of the Jungle* or *Flash Gordon* or *The Lone Ranger.*

Sunday did not give me any of that entertainment. The priests did some rituals in Latin, a language none of us understood. Then the pastor gave another sermon about God's desperate need for more **MONEY.** The collection basket was a wickerwork gizmo on the end of a long pole. The ushers could stand at the end of a row of pews and pass it slowly past each person. That way, if you didn't put anything in, everybody would know you were cheating God. I'd put my dime in, secretly wishing I could go to the movies again instead.

If they had put the collection box in back of the church, some people could walk by without paying and nobody would notice. The collection basket guaranteed that God got more **MONEY.** I've often wondered which of the Blessed Saints thought up that scheme. It was probably the same guy who invented those paper towel dispensers that never let you get enough to dry your hands.

Besides those steel yardsticks that hurt like a bastard, I particularly remember one charming story we heard in Religious Knowledge class. Loss of faith is the worst thing that can happen to you, we had been told many times; but now the good nun who taught this class informed us that you could never be sure you wouldn't lose your faith.

Exemplar: a good and pious man who had loved and served God all his life inadvertently committed the Sin of Pride. That is, he allowed the thought to form: "I will never cease to love God and believe in Him." Satan picked this up via ESP and rushed to tattle to God at once (I guess God's ESP wasn't working that day), asking permission to put this man to the test. God, of course, consented. (This seems a condensed, Stephen King-ish version of the story of Job.) Satan then poured *ground glass* in the man's eyes as he slept at night, and when he awoke, the man was bloody all over and blind. Even so, he did not lose his faith, and Satan was frustrated.

The nun told this story with great relish and vivid Sam Peckinpah imagery. It haunted me for years afterward, especially when I was just about to doze off at night. I'd lie there, in the dark, thinking that Satan might be up there, near the ceiling, getting ready to pour the ground glass in my eyes.

This did not make for tranquil and restful nights. But, then, nobody gets through a Catholic education without acquiring some form of anxiety neurosis.

I still have more chronic eye problems than any other writer I know. It gives me a deeper sense of empathy with Joyce.

THE CALL OF THE WILD

Escape From The Planet Of The Apes

Worrying about that ground glass being dropped in my eyes led me to brood over the whole Catholic reality-tunnel. Somehow, in a way I don't understand, I had acquired the rudiments of a logical mind, or at least an analytical one. (That is what the neighbor meant when he told my parents I should be a lawyer when I grew up.) Church teaching insisted that we must love God and never lose our faith or He would send us to Hell for the aforementioned charbroiling, toasting etc.; this lovely story, however, warned us that if our faith became too sure of itself, God might allow Satan to "test" that faith by some horrible torture or other.

The nuns had convinced me to try very hard to have faith — that is, to believe everything they said, even if it sounded like blatant lunacy at first. I tried very hard to have faith, so I wouldn't go to Hell.

But the ground-glass story showed that the Catholic belief system (BS) had a Strange Loop in it. It was quite clear to me that faith could be as dangerous as the absence of faith. If your faith wasn't strong enough, God would let the devil torture you after you died; if your faith was too strong, He'd let the devil torture you right now, as a test. It was a "Choose this way and lose, or chose the other way and lose" situation — what Gregory Bateson later labeled a "double bind."

I gradually realized that the only way out of this was to be born non-Catholic, and I had missed that option. Once you were born Catholic, there was no way out, because you could not question anything the nuns told you. Questioning was "the sin of Pride" and absolutely guaranteed the most extreme forms of charbroiling and roasting and toasting and poaching and French Frying.

Like a lot of American writers (Leslie Fiedler has written a wonderful book examining this theme in our literature), I began fantasizing about being an Indian. Whatever provoked this in other writers (Fiedler blames it on Puritanism), in my case it was based on the wishful idea that if I had never heard of the Catholic

Church I would never have to worry about a demon dropping ground glass in my eyes or about all that roasting and toasting.

Many, many years later a Cherokee woman told me the Native American characters in my novels were so real that she had decided I must have been an Indian myself in a previous incarnation. She didn't know about my fantasies in childhood...

When I read *Huckleberry Finn* in high school, I immediately empathized with Huck's decision, at the end, to light out for the wilderness and escape forever from the Widow, a religious woman who wanted to "Sivilize" him. When I got a bit older that seemed as useless as Paul Gauguin's headlong flight to Tahiti: there was no place left on solid earth for the nonconformist. By the time I was in my '30s, I was preoccupied with various libertarian schemes to organize "free communities" of *ships in International Waters*. The criticisms of the more paranoid anarchists, who insisted that the governments of the world would find some excuse to bomb these "utopias," led to the fantasy of the submarine anarchist commune in *Illuminatus*.

The latest form of my desire to escape the lunacy of our race consists in ardent support for the L5 colony idea and the American Rocket Company, who are trying to make civilian space cities possible. Many other people support libertarian space colonization — Barbara Marx Hubbard, physicist Gerard O'Neill, Stuart Brand, Tim Leary etc. etc. — and all have their own reasons for thinking this is a worthwhile goal. My reasons are very simple and I have condensed them into three sentences:

1. I like peace, quiet afternoons, the prose of James Joyce, chess, and listening to the sonatas of Scarlatti with my eyes closed while stoned on marijuana.

2. Most people like booze, football, violent noisy movies full of gore, and increasingly frequent wars.

3. I have finally admitted that I can't change most people, so I want to get away from them and live with the minority who share my own eccentric tastes.

Escape from the Planet of the Apes... I think that is the secret dream that has fueled science-fiction and the great space pioneers like Goddard and Ley all along, although they knew it was undiplomatic to say it openly.

I don't mind being accused of being an "escapist." On a planet that increasingly resembles one huge Maximum Security prison, the only intelligent choice is to plan a jail break.

ACCIDENT & ESSENCE

Another profound lesson of Religious Knowledge class concerned the Mystical Presence of Christ in the hosts or eucharists — the pieces of bread blessed by priests during the Mass. To understand this, you had to understand the Thomist (or Aristotelian) concepts of "accident" and "essence." Anything you could sensorially or instrumentally experience about an object was an "accident." The true "essence" — the *whatness* or *whichness* of the thing, as it were — remained sensorially and instrumentally unavailable to us. That means, concretely, that the bread remained seemingly unchanged after the blessing — neither our sight nor taste nor microscopes nor other instruments could find any difference in it, because the "accidents" remained unaltered. The "essence," however, which we could never see or experience, had changed entirely into the body and blood of Jesus Christ.

It took me many years to figure out that this literally implied a species of spiritual cannibalism. It took even longer before I noted that an "essence" — *defined as something which we can never experience* — might be, or might be claimed to be, anything imaginable. Instead of the body and blood of Christ, it could be the hide of the Easter Bunny, or the liver and aorta of the Dong With The Luminous Nose, or the Sacred Mustache of Groucho Marx.

My remarks about hypnosis and language a while back may have sounded obscure or extreme. Please note that the demon with the ground grass, the old man called God living on the clouds, who liked to charbroil little boys, and the Mystical Presence of flesh and blood within something that tasted like bread had all become as *real* to me, due to the good nuns, as the Wicked Witch of the West was when I was sitting in the dark staring at the magic images on a movie screen.

If this bit of Catholic autobiography seems like a medieval aberration, I would like you to remember that, to many physicists today, Murray Gell-Mann's amazing "quarks," lifted right out of *Finnegans Wake,* have become equally "real," and they even have "color" and "charm." *Hypnosis exists on all levels of human society,* and very few scientists can remember that their favorite models started out as metaphors.

THE FRIENDS OF ROBERTO CALVI

> Every government is run by liars and nothing they say
> should be believed.   — I.F. Stone

On the morning of June 18, 1982 — when Arlen and I had been in Ireland only two days — a man was found hanging from Blackfriar's Bridge in London, where the rising tide had covered his dead body; oddly, his pockets were full of bricks. He was soon identified as Roberto Calvi, president of the Banco Ambrosiano in Milan — the man the European press called "God's Banker" because of his links with the Vatican Bank.

The Hon. Signor Calvi was also a member of the allegedly Freemasonic conspiracy named *Propaganda due* (usually called simply P2 in English). Being hanged where the rising tide will cover one's dead body is the punishment threatened to Freemasons who betray their Fellows in the Craft, so it seems likely that Calvi had been killed by a Masonic conspiracy, or by persons who ardently wish us to think he had been killed by a Masonic conspiracy.

The Irish newspapers covered the Calvi case and the subsequent investigations of P2 in great detail. This is because Irish newspapers are mostly staffed by ex-Catholics very alienated from Irish culture, who are delighted to print anything which reflects unfavorably on the Vatican. I read it all avidly, because the labyrinthine and spaghetti-like tangle of conspiracies surrounding Calvi was like one of my own absurdist novels. I was also curious to learn what became of all the dimes I had put in the collection plate as a child, after the Vatican Bank got its hands on them.

When books on the Italian trials began to appear, I bought them all and read them. In what follows, I am chiefly indebted to Foot and della Torre's *The Mysterious Death of God's Banker* (Orbis, London, 1984), Larry Gurwin's *The Calvi Affair* (Pan Books, London, 1984), Penny Lernoux's *In Banks We Trust* (Doubleday/Anchor, New York, 1984), Richard Hammer's *The Vatican Connection* (Penguin Books, New York, 1982), Stephen

Knight's *The Brotherhood* (Grenada, London, 1984) and David Yallops's *In God's Name* (Jonathan Cape, London, 1984)

The original coroner's jury ruled that Calvi had killed himself. This verdict was greeted with derision by most of the English press, which noted that Calvi was 62-years old, not given to exercise, distinctly out of shape, and thus very unlikely to have performed the acrobatic feats required in lowering himself over the railing of the bridge and somehow climbing or leaping to the middle of the bottom of the bridge where his body had been found hanging from an under-girder.

It was also pointed out, repeatedly, that Calvi was a fugitive from the Italian police, who had charged him with multiple conspiracies, and that his associates may have wanted to silence him before he could turn State's evidence. A second coroner's jury was eventually convened and they ruled that the evidence was not conclusive enough to decide if Calvi had killed himself or had been killed by persons unknown.

Clara Calvi, the dead banker's widow, came to England at the time of the second coroner's inquest and told the jury her husband had been planning to testify against his former colleagues and lived in terror that he would be killed by order of persons in the Vatican — "at the very top," Signora Calvi said, apparently accusing the Pope himself, unless there are two tops in the Catholic Church.

Scotland Yard was ordered to investigate further, but in the intervening years they say they have found no clues. Every time I go back to England I meet a few intense people who assure me that Scotland Yard is a nest of Masonry and has spent all this time covering up another Masonic crime. (This is, indeed, the thesis of *The Brotherhood* by Stephen Knight.)

Those who claim foul play in the Calvi hanging have all made much of a rather singular coincidence. The morning Calvi was found dangling with pockets full of bricks from that bridge in London, his secretary, Graziella Corrocher, plunged to her death from a window of Calvi's Banco Ambrosiano in Milan. Like Calvi's death, Corrocher's defenestration was originally pronounced suicide, but many have questioned that verdict.

Maybe suicide was contagious in that bank.

Maybe — but then again, as Stalin's henchman Beria once said, "Any damned fool can commit a murder. It takes an artist to arrange a suicide."

THE GREAT ONE WHO MAKES THE GRASS GREEN

One of the first *koans* (philosophical riddles) that Zen Buddhists give to students is, "Who is the Master who makes the grass green?"

Some say that "Master" is not quite an accurate translation. "Great Lord" or "Land-lord" have been proposed as more true to the original Japanese term. I think you will get the idea if you just remember that *lords* and *masters* of all sorts acquire their power due to game-rules or social conventions.

One Zen Master provided a Helpful Hint to those pondering this puzzle. "When you know that Great One," he said, "it will be like seeing your own father's face in a crowd. You will have absolutely no doubt about the matter."

EVERYBODY CELEBRATES

The Depression Ends And We Go to War

There is many a boy here who looks on war as all glory,
but, boys, it is all hell.
— General William T. Sherman

Back in Gerrison Beach: while I was acquiring the usual
Catholic anxiety and worrying about the demon who might drop
ground glass in my eyes, the world around me was changing.

For one thing, I escaped the degradation of the free lunch
program.

In 1938, for most of the men of our tribe, The Depression
ended as mysteriously as it had begun. The Navy Yard in
Brooklyn was hiring longshoremen again, in great droves, and
my father had work at better wages than he had before The
Depression. Of course, he was out in the cold weather in winter
and not in a snug office, and you don't know how cold "cold
weather" can be until you face it on the waterfront with a wind
blowing, but he was glad to get the money for it. He was around
50 by then, and maybe he was afraid he'd never get a job again.

Everybody knew this sudden good luck had its sinister side.
The Navy Yard was busy because the government was tooling
up for another war. I heard my father and his cronies talk about
this, in worried tones, over and over. Some of them were even
getting a little cynical about President Roosevelt and said he was
deliberately plotting to get us into a war with the dinosaurs in
Europe.

The war sounded like a splendid idea to me. I had seen several
war movies and they made shooting and bombing people seem
almost as wonderful and exciting as being a pirate like Errol
Flynn.

I remember expressing this view of war, in my own childish
way, to my father, and I clearly remember his sad eyes as he
tried to explain to me that real war wasn't like war in the movies.
His sick brother, Mick, the one with the chronic chest problem,

he said, was that way because of the last war, where poison gas was used, and there were many others even sicker, who never had gotten out of the hospital, even though the last war had been 20 years before. Some of them had lost their arms or legs. Some had lost *both* their arms and legs and were called "basket cases."

Roosevelt said he was not going to get us into the war. He promised he would keep us out of the war. My father said that Woodrow Wilson had made the same promises and then connived us into the first world war anyway.

My mother told me again about old Anton, her father, who believed that when the politicians start a war, the smart man goes to live in another country.

But, meanwhile, we got our refrigerator — "the fridge" — and then, much more marvelous to me, we got a radio. It was as big as a desk (I don't think they made small radios in those days) and it soon dominated the living room.

Every day when I came home from school for lunch, my mother was listening to a show called *Our Gal Sunday*. I still remember the opening of that show: "And now...*Our Gal Sunday*...the story that asks the question: Can a girl from a small mining town in the West find happiness as the wife of a wealthy and titled Englishman?" (She did, but she had a lot of hassles, too. Sunday's husband was named Lord Henry Winthrop. Isn't it amazing what trivia sticks in the mind over half a century?) After that, my mother turned on *The Romance of Helen Trent*, which asked the question, "Can a woman find Romance at 35, or even beyond?" (She did, but the guy was always in a wheelchair and wouldn't accept Helen's love because he thought it was pity, or he had amnesia or some damned thing. There was a lot of amnesia going around in those days, not only in the Soaps but in movies, too. I think Ronald Colman got it at least three times. Even Bogart caught it once.) Then lunch was finished and it was time for me to walk the mile back to school.

I also remember a commercial we heard every day. "Today is Monday! Today is Monday! What a day for Chicklet's Candy-Coated Chewing Gum!" No matter what show you tuned into on Monday, you'd hear that loonybird howl during the first commercial break. Then on Tuesday they'd change it: "Today is Tuesday! Today is Tuesday! What a day for Chicklet's Candy

Coated Chewing Gum!" And so on, through Wednesday etc. and on to Sunday. Then, on Monday, they would start over again.

Those who think B.F. Skinner has solved all the mysteries of psychology will be disappointed to learn that, even though that jingle got lodged in my brain and has stayed there all my life, I only tried Chicklets once, decided I didn't like them, and never bought them again.

I became a fan of Jack Armstrong The All-American Boy, Captain Midnight, Jack Benny, Colonel Stoopnagle and especially The Shadow, who was always warning, "The weed of crime bears bitter fruit" and asking "Who knows what evil lurks in the hearts of men?" The Shadow had a beautiful, resonant voice, and made me appreciate the "musical" or tonal qualities of the human larynx long before I heard any singers I liked.

Later on I found out The Shadow was an actor named Orson Welles. I began to recognize his voice on lots and lots of other radio shows, and I wondered how he managed to travel so fast.

Just last year, reading a biography of The Great Round One, I finally found the answer: Orson sped around Manhattan in an ambulance. He was doing all those radio shows to finance some experimental stage productions he was directing in Manhattan, which our tribe out in Gerrison Beach never heard of. Among them were a terrifying version of *Macbeth* with an all-Black cast and genuine Voodoo drummers, a modern-dress *Julius Caesar* with everybody in fascist uniforms and Caesar played by an actor who looked like Mussolini, and a production of Marlowe's *Dr. Faustus* using stage-magic tricks to produce shocks like the "special effects" in movies. These productions are still legendary with old-time New Yorkers, and I wish I had gotten to see them.

Soon awesome Orson had a radio show of his own, ORSON WELLES PRESENTS THE MERCURY THEATRE ON THE AIR. He started doing shows I found exciting, like *Dracula* and *Moby-Dick,* and shows I couldn't quite understand, like *Jane Eyre.* On October 31, 1938, Halloween night, he had something different to offer. At the beginning he told us it was a dramatization of *The War of the Worlds* by H.G. Wells, and then he began with a parody of the documentary style, sort of like the bogus newsreels he later used in *Citizen Kane* and *F For Fake.* I didn't even know the word "parody," but I knew he was making fun of news broadcasters and using that as a cute way of telling a story so weird that neither my parents nor I knew it belonged to the *genre* of science-fiction.

I found the show tremendously exciting. It reminded me of the goose bumps I felt at the end of *King Kong* when Carl Denham says, "It wasn't the airplanes... It was *beauty* that killed the beast." I knew something was going on that transcended entertainment, but I didn't know the name for it.

(I still don't know the name for it. It seems somewhere on the borderline between Art and Magic and whenever I encounter it — in poetry, music, literature, films or painting — I enter Virtual Reality again.)

The next day I found out that a considerable number of adults had been mentally out to lunch at the beginning of the show, didn't register Orson's voice announcing the title, and accepted the parody newscasts as real newscasts. These people had really entered Virtual Reality and went totally ape; some hid in their cellars and others took to the hills and hollows to escape the Martians. Now they were mad as hell and wanted the government to prosecute Orson for malicious mischief or something like that.

I found it all exhilarating. I experimented further with the radio and found more and more "weird" things — voices from outside the Irish Catholic reality-tunnel. Even a simple thriller like *The Shadow* had an evil glamour about it, because it suggested that Orientals might know things even the Pope didn't know, such as "the power to cloud men's minds" which made the Shadow *invisible.*

My uncle Mick, the one who had been poison-gassed, was a big fan of a priest named Father Charles Coughlin who had a radio show on Sunday afternoons. Father Coughlin said the Wicked Jews had indeed created The Depression and now they (and Roosevelt) were plotting to get us into a new war. Whenever uncle Mick visited on Sunday, we had to listen to Father Coughlin. My father preferred another Expert named Walter Winchell, who said the dinosaur Hitler was planning to attack us and we had to get ready to fight him. Winchell also said, or strongly implied, that people like Father Coughlin were working for Hitler and trying to turn America into a Nazi state.

My father didn't think we should get into any more wars — the first world war, in his opinion, had killed lots of people and did the world no good at all — but he liked Winchell better than Coughlin, and went on voting for Roosevelt. I never did figure that out. It had something to do with Roosevelt's support for labor unions and Father Coughlin's frequent claim that the unions were all run by Communist Jews.

Father Coughlin's show was finally taken off the air, because of protests by Jewish groups. Uncle Mick began bringing around pamphlets Father Coughlin wrote, telling all about the Jewish Banker's Conspiracy and how it worked together with the Jewish Communist Conspiracy. My father only disagreed with this mildly and infrequently, and I think I first noticed that adults could be even dumber than kids when I realized Dad was "humoring" Uncle Mick and Uncle Mick didn't even realize it.

Dad had joined the C.I.O., a new labor union even more "radical" than the old A.F. of L. Uncle Mick had a mocking song about the C.I.O. that he liked to sing, set to a tune from Walt Disney's *Snow White:*

> Hi-ho, hi-ho, I joined the C.I.O.
> I paid my dues to a bunch of Jews
> Hi-ho, hi-ho, hi-ho!

Adults never discussed any of these ideological differences with children — I owe my knowledge of all this to what I overheard — but my father did tell me personally where he stood on the subject of labor unions in general. "Some of the unions are crooked," he said "but remember this: I know what it was like before we had unions, and there was nothing the companies couldn't get away with in those days. *Nothing*," he repeated very vehemently. "They cheated us and robbed us every way they could."

My mother never talked about any of this, until the war started. Generally, all she talked about, beside family matters, were the alleged private lives of movie stars, which she read about in those magazines I mentioned.

After Pearl Harbor, my brother — who was 18 years older than me, and married already — received a draft notice. That night I woke up and went to the kitchen to get a drink of milk. I found my mother and my brother's wife, who normally did not get along well, drinking whiskey. Their faces were stained with tears and they were cursing President Roosevelt — I guess they were too drunk, by then, to remember that they had a rule about not using such language in front of children. They had no doubt that President Roosevelt had plotted Pearl Harbor and they were saying wild, crazy things, even threatening to vote Republican for the rest of their lives.

"It's men," my mother said. "They never grow up. They're all still boys. Playing with guns." She started to cry again.

INFORMATION DOUBLES AGAIN

Government is an association of men who do violence
to the rest of us.   — Leo Tolstoy

By 1750, the information larder of humanity had doubled again.

It took almost four million years after the first African tool to arrive at the information density of Rome 1 AD, but then only 1500 years to double that. The second doubling had taken *only 250 years,* during most of which Europe had been torn by crazy and fanatical religious wars.

In 1750 Julien de La Mettrie published the first book giving a completely mechanistic and materialistic account of human life and behavior. It raised so much fury that he had to flee France and live in Berlin. The same year, Bach completed *The Art of the Fugue* and died on July 28, age 65.

That was an advanced age for those days; most humans did not survive their first year, and those who did mostly died by the age of 30. But world population had now reached 750 million, up 50% from 500 million a century earlier in 1650, and three times what it was in 1 AD.

The center of information-and-power had continued to move north-westward and England now dominated the world — the first "Empire on which the sun never set" (because God wouldn't trust an Englishman in the dark, the Irish say.) As the Inquisition continued to rage in the Catholic South, most of the world's new knowledge was only available in the Protestant North, creating the pattern that still survives in Europe: the further South you go, the more primitive and impoverished everything looks, and the further North you go, the richer and more "modern" everything appears.

Within one year, all this new information gave Benjamin Franklin the ideas he needed to embark on his electrical experiments, which led David Hume and many others to consider him "the greatest scientist since Newton."

Within 15 years, in 1765, James Watt in Scotland invented his steam engine and the Industrial Revolution began.

Watt had set a time-bomb under Patriarchy: *The whole sun-king system which had held agricultural civilization together since the Bronze Age began to crumble.* Industrialism demanded, and got, a major transformation of humanity, as radical as that which had occurred when the sun-kings arose to conquer the "partnership societies" (tribes) around them.

The American Revolution began in 1776. The French Revolution in 1789. The United Irish uprising in 1798. The first Mexican Revolution in 1810. The ideas of democracy and the free market began to win converts, and following in their wake were wilder heresies like socialism, anarchism, feminism...

All of these Utopian ideas represent what my wife Arlen has called "Stone Age Backlash." As Western Man set out to explore and exploit the rest of the world, each contact with a preliterate partnership society brought more wealth to the Bankers and other elites, but also brought back news of human beings who lived without kings, without popes, without slavery, without the sub-jugation of women...

Rousseau enthused about the "noble savage" and the American founding fathers borrowed a lot of ideas from the Native Americans in forming our Constitution. In the next century, both Marx's State Socialism and Proudhon's libertarian socialism also showed the influence of Native American, Polynesian and African "partnership societies" in which sun-kings and submissive masses had never been invented.

This Second Wave Civilization (as Toffler calls it) moved *ten times faster* than the Revolution of the sun-kings, which took millenniums before it transformed humanity from cooperative partner-bands into huge clusters of enslaved masses taking orders from Divine Emperors. In only two centuries, Indust*reality* transformed us into democratic and Utopian peoples, keenly aware of the imperfections of each new stage of our evolution, and constantly seeking to make the world better.

The American Declaration of Independence invokes, not the Christian God, or Jewish God, or Islamic God, but Nature's God — a concept of the secular philosophers who arose after 1750.

Of course, due to nearly 5000 years of Sun Kings, humanity was so **domesticated** that many features of the old agricultural order remained in the new system — the subjugation of women, for instance. Similarly, although the U.S. Constitution gives us the right to speak, publish and demonstrate against the government in power, the domesticated masses still regard all that as blasphemy — just as they learned to do when the ruler was literally considered a Sun God. Every sociological survey in this century has shown that the majority of Americans do not like the Bill of Rights and would abolish it if they could.

Hitler understood this, and said that the masses are "feminine" and want a Strong Male to lead them. After 5000 years of Sun-Kings, most people cannot see the government as anything human, and still regard it as semi-divine.

The intelligentsia and all other minorities still have the right, under the Constitution, to oppose the government's decisions on anything, but even if the party in power is liberal enough to tolerate this, the masses will not tolerate it. They are just as shocked by such "blasphemy" as medieval Catholics were when people like Luther started to criticize the pope.

Of course, under the Sun King system, even deeper, we still keep some tribal "partnership" habits. Sociological studies show that the average city dweller has a circle of about 120 friends and acquaintances — the size of the average tribe. Within that "tribe," many Stone Age values survive. There are Alpha males and Alpha females, docile "followers," and at least one Shaman or Trickster. And there is always a deep tribal loyalty, which is why the average Catholic in Belfast, who sincerely opposes the terrorist tactics of the I.R.A., still will not help the Protestant police by telling them which way an I.R.A. gunman ran after shooting an English soldier.

CALVI AND THE
KNIGHTS OF MALTA

For Theirs Is The Kingdom Of Heaven

"You gotta save Christianity, Richard! You gotta!"
— Loretta Young, to Richard the Lion-Hearted,
The Crusaders (1935)

In researching P2 I have become fascinated by the little-known fact that Roberto Calvi — the banker hanging from Blackfriar's Bridge, remember? — was a Knight of Malta.

Who the hell, you may well ask, are the Knights of Malta? Didn't Dashiell Hammet invent them for a detective story?

Well, the "Knights of Malta" are a fabulously wealthy secret society of Catholic laypersons. Back in the 11th Century they were called the "Knights of St. John of Jerusalem." Later they became the "Knights of Rhodes," and then the "Knights of Malta," under which name they are still usually known. Their current correct name, however, is the Sovereign Military Order of Malta (often abbreviated to SMOM) since they now admit Dames as well as Knights. After they lost Malta to Napoleon in 1798, their actual world headquarters has been a small building in the Vatican. According to Catholic sources, they are a charitable order devoted to good works. Nobody else seems to believe that.

According to most secular humanist historians, and especially Freemasons, SMOM is the Vatican's secret police, and its members are all sworn to destroy Protestantism, liberalism, democracy and everything else that has interfered with Papal Omnipotence in the last 400 years. All 32nd degree Freemasons vow solemnly to oppose "the Knights of Malta" and "all other agents of tyranny and superstition." This is the most intriguing mystery in the Calvi affair: how could "God's Banker" be a Knight of Malta and a Mason sworn to oppose the Knights of Malta at the same time?

According to English journalist Gordon Thomas, members of SMOM in the early '80s acted as couriers between the Pope and Mad Bill Casey, the Director of the CIA According to Mae Brussel, the late conspiracy researcher (who was often more passionate than accurate, but was accurate enough when it didn't interfere with her prejudices) members of SMOM are sworn by oath to obey Vatican orders even in cases of murder and treason. Mae claimed to have a copy of the oath SMOM members had to sign, with those provisions, but she never produced it when challenged.

Although Calvi is frequently referred to as a "Freemason" in accounts of this case, his known politics have much more in common with SMOM than with Masonry — which has traditionally been radical and anti-clerical. In Catholic countries, Masonry is usually a "revolutionary" force working to introduce such radical 18th Century ideas as democracy and free speech. (These are still very revolutionary ideas indeed in nations where the Church is in control.) Freemasons in England and America have been unanimous in denying that the blatantly fascist P2 was a genuine Masonic lodge. Calvi seems much more typical of SMOM than of Masonry.

Along with Roberto Calvi, a few other prominent members of SMOM in recent times have included:

Franz von Papen, the man who persuaded President von Hindenburg to resign and appoint Hitler the Chancellor of Germany;

General Reinhard Gehlen, Hitler's Intelligence chief, who later became the director of the CIA's Russian "penetration" section;

General Alexander Haig, White House heavyweight in both the Nixon and Reagan administrations, who claimed "diabolical forces" had created some of the evidence against Nixon;

Alexander de Marenches, former chief of French Intelligence;

William F. Buckley Jr., foremost spokesman for the "bombs-and-Jesus" faction of U.S. Catholicism;

Clare Booth Luce, wife of the founder of *Time/Life*, longtime Congressional enemy of the New Deal and later U.S. Ambassador to the Vatican;

Umberto Ortolani, wealthy Italian fascist, P2 member and founder of secret right-wing groups in Latin America. An associate in business of Roberto Calvi — and of Bishop Paul (the Gorilla) Marcinkus, manager of the Vatican Bank, and Michele (the Shark) Sindona, president of the notorious Franklin National Bank;

Otto von Hapsburg, descendent of the former royal family of Austria and a prominent member of the Bilderbergers, a secret society of financiers which meets once a year and will seemingly go to any length to prevent the press from learning their full membership roster or what they are meeting to discuss.

And, of course, another Knight of Malta was *Mad Bill Casey,* the man who was always Absolutely Right.[*]

---

[*] I owe this list of Knights of Malta to *Covert Action Information Bulletin,* No. 25, Winter 1986.

Mom & Olga Achieve Communication With The Other Side

> If one wants to recognize effortlessly the essence of politics, let one reflect upon the fact that it was a Hitler who was able to make the world hold its breath for many years. The fact that Hitler was a political genius unmasks the nature of politics in general as no other fact can.
>
> — Wilhelm Reich, *The Mass Psychology of Fascism*

In 1942 I saw a more war movies than ever, and they all made the war seem like a wonderful crusade of Good against Evil, but I always remembered that my mother and father had a different view.

So did uncle Mick, the Father Coughlin fan. He was convinced that the Wicked Jews, in connivance with the Munitions Makers like du Pont, had created the war to make themselves even richer, and that Roosevelt had gone along with the scheme because nothing else he had tried had cured The Depression.

My brother got classified 4F (he had had polio, too) and the whole family celebrated, in a subdued way. Too many neighbors had sons or husbands in the Army for us to feel comfortable about being spontaneously glad my brother's life was not going to be put in danger. That was the sin of Treason, which was almost as bad as the sin of Pride, because it also meant you were thinking for yourself.

Around then, Errol Flynn got himself in trouble. According to the newspaper, he was standing trial for rape. When I asked what this meant, my parents became very evasive, so I consulted the dictionary when they weren't looking. The dictionary proved equally evasive, at least for a boy with a limited vocabulary. I somehow got the idea that rape consisted of making a woman lie still while you were kissing her. I think I only got the right definition clear in my head after entering high school.

Errol, meanwhile, got acquitted of rape. He was now making war movies instead of pirate movies. I saw him shoot and blow up thousands of Germans and Japanese, and never once wondered why a man in such great athletic condition wasn't really in the Army and really fighting in the war.

Early in 1942, my mother made friends with a new neighbor, who wasn't Irish. She was named Olga Liebertoff and she was a Jew, although not a Wicked one. (But my mother was careful that Olga never met Uncle Mick.) Olga was a big fan of the ouija board, which she soon persuaded my mother to try. They both liked the results so much that they sat, night after night, with the planchette moving between them, while I listened to the radio. A nun at school had warned us that ouija boards were tools of the devil, but when I told my mother that she said "Nuns don't know everything."

I knew that disagreeing with anything the nuns said was the Sin of Pride, but she was my mother, so I didn't dare tell her that.

The first notable success with the ouija board came when Olga lost something — a piece of cheap jewelry, I think. She and my mother asked the board where the lost object was, and the board obligingly gave the correct answer. (Years later I heard the "explanation" that the information was somewhere in Olga's brain and the board just helped bring it out... At the time, however, I was startled.)

One night, while they were sitting at the board, I had an inspiration. I was lying on the floor, doing homework, and I suggested tentatively, "Ask it when the war will end."

They asked, and the planchette moved. Olga spoke out the letters and numbers of the answer as it emerged: AUGUST 14, 1945.

I was shocked again. The answer seemed incredible. Hypnotized by the professional optimists on the newscasts, I had the impression the war would be over much quicker than that. Nonetheless, I copied the answer inside the back cover of my notebook.

AUGUST 14, 1945. There it stood in the notebook for over three years, as the war dragged on and on. When the peace treaty was signed on August 14, 1945, I was discombobulated. It seemed to me that either the ouija board really was a tool of the devil, as the nuns claimed, or something had happened that I just could not understand.

I spent a lot of time wondering about that.

FILMS OPEN DOORS FOR ME

And So Does Probability Theory

When it came time for high school, I convinced my parents I wanted to be an engineer. That persuaded them to send me to Brooklyn Technical High School, and I didn't have to listen to the nuns drone on about God and Satan and Hell and all that horror movie stuff anymore. That was my real goal — getting out of the Catholic nexus. I didn't want to become an engineer at all. I wanted to become a writer, but whenever I mentioned that to my parents they told me writers all starved to death and I could never make a living at it.

All through the war, the union had steadily renegotiated better and better contracts for the workers at the Navy Yard. We moved to Bay Ridge, so I'd be closer to Brooklyn Tech, and, in general, we were living so well, compared to The Depression, that I imagined we were lace-curtain Irish at last.

The Catholic Church had never given me anything New Agers would call a "spiritual" life; it had merely filled me with superstitions and anxieties. Nonetheless, I had a kind of "spiritual" life in the general sense, based on movies. I had found that certain films put me in a high, spaced-out state, which I have been calling Virtual Reality, and these films I would see several times, enjoying deeper and deeper mind expansion with each viewing, and slowly learning to understand *just a little* about what I only later learned to call The Art of Film.

The movies that put me deepest into psychedelic space were *The Devil and Daniel Webster* (directed by William Deterle), *The Picture of Dorian Gray* (directed by Albert Lewin), *Meet John Doe* (directed by Frank Capra), *I Walked With A Zombie* (directed by Jacques Tourneur), *I Married A Witch* and *It Happened Tomorrow* (both directed by René Clair) and *all* the films of Orson Welles, especially *The Lady from Shanghai* with its totally psychedelic climax of the drugged hero lost in a Fun House and then caught in the crossfire of a shoot-out in a Hall of Mirrors.

I didn't know that the camera angles favored by these directors paralleled analytical cubism, surrealism, expressionism and various other developments in modern art, but I knew these films had more visual excitement and "lyricism" than ordinary, run-of-the-mill movies. (I was only dimly becoming aware of painting, then.) All of my favorite film directors created that sense of being outside space-time that I always got from the closing scene of Cooper's *King Kong:* "It was beauty that killed the beast..."

Meanwhile, Brooklyn Tech certainly succeeded in getting me out of the Catholic reality-tunnel. I found myself associating with Protestants and even with Jews, who were not really Wicked at all, contrary to uncle Mick and the Catholic Catechism.

I found that I liked the Jews better than the Protestants, in general. Mostly, the Protestants really wanted to become engineers and had parents who were Republicans. Many of the Jews wanted to become physicists or research scientists, shared my inchoate philosophical questioning, and had parents who were Democrats, just like us Irish Catholics.

Brooklyn Tech taught me a lot. I learned that the Earth wasn't hollow, after all, so there wasn't any Hell inside it. I encountered science teachers who encouraged us to think, instead of discouraging that activity as the nuns had. I even had one teacher, for calculus, who liked to drag philosophical problems into his exposition of math, and especially delighted in ending a class with a logical problem that none of us could figure out.

One day I went to this teacher, Mr. White, and told him the story of my mother and Olga and the ouija board. I wanted him to explain it. Naturally, being the man he was, he made *me* explain it.

"How many ouija boards do you think there are in the world?" he asked me.

I said I couldn't guess, but it must be millions.

"Hundreds of thousands, at least," he said. "How many people do you suppose ever asked their ouija board when the war would end?"

I decided that everybody with a ouija board eventually thought of asking that question.

"Let's assume only half of them asked," he said. "That's still a lot of people. By sheer chance, how many answers would they get?"

"Uh," I calculated, "if there's say four hundred thousand and half of them asked, that would be two hundred thousand, and uh by sheer chance alone they'd get two hundred thousand answers."

"But there haven't been that many days between the beginning and the end of the war," Mr. White said. "How many days have there been?"

I had to multiply 365 by 3 for the years 1942-1943-1944, which gave me 995, add on 24 days in 1941 and 225 for 1945, and arrived at 1244.

"So," Mr. White said, "how many would get the right answer by sheer chance?"

I came up with 152.

"So," Mr. White said, "That gives us 152 families telling the same story as you, and 199, 848 who can only report that they got the wrong answer. Do you think the second group talks *a great deal* about asking a ouija board and getting the wrong answer?"

"No," I said.

"So where do we get our stories about people who got the right answer from ouija boards?"

"From the people who got the right answer, by sheer chance."

"I knew you could figure it out," he said.

WILSON BECOMES A LIBERAL

... At Just The Wrong Time

Meanwhile, my civics teachers were successfully undermining the half-fascist half-radical working class attitudes I had picked up from my relatives. For a while, they almost (not quite) turned me into another middle-class liberal like themselves. They certainly persuaded me of *most* of the liberal doctrines of the time — which was not hard considering my father's belief that the corporations always screwed the workers if the workers didn't have a strong Union to protect them. But the liberals who taught civics (I think Brooklyn Tech had a rule that no conservative could teach that subject) never persuaded me of the innocence of the Hon. F.D. Roosevelt at Pearl Harbor. Uncle Mick's anti-semitism now seemed embarrassing to me (I wished he wasn't a relative) but his angry cynicism about official government propaganda and the horrors he saw in World War I had left a mark on my mind. I furtively read the loathed and forbidden "revisionist" historians — especially Charles Beard, James J. Martin and Harry Elmer Barnes — and decided that liberals were right about most things but not about how capitalist wars get started.

Around then I started reading Orson Welles' column in *The New York Post.* Orson was in semi-exile from Hollywood — because the Hearst family had never forgiven him for *Citizen Kane,* one of my civics teachers told me — and, while working on a new Broadway play, he unburdened himself of some thoughts about the Cold War which were much like what I was spontaneously thinking at the time.

For more than five years the government and almost all the media had been insisting that the Germans were all Nazis and all equally evil, but the Russians were our friends, even if they were Communists. Now the government and almost all the media reversed themselves like the Ministry of Truth in *1984.* The Nazis had all been hanged by the neck at Nuremberg (we weren't told about the numerous Nazis, like General Gehlen and Klaus

Barbie, who were now working for the CIA). The remaining
Germans were now our friends and all good guys, but the
Russians had turned totally evil, again, and were planning to
blow us all up any day if we didn't keep them off balance by
building more and more atom bombs.

This total reversal of the Official reality-tunnel concerning
Russians and Germans occurred while I was between 13 and 14
and I never quite believed it. It seemed to me that the government thought we were all dumber than toy poodles and didn't
even have enough neurons to remember from one day to the next
who we were supposed to hate.

Orson also regarded the Cold War as a crock, and said so in his
columns with wit and vigor.

He also did a great stage production which I saw — *Around
the World in 80 Days.* It was a musical comedy with 20 scenes in
the first act and 14 in the second. It included a Chinese circus, a
train wreck, and a scene in which movies were used, with the
actors on stage interacting with the actors on film. Orson played
a dozen characters, including a Chinese magician and a Western
gunslinger. It was utterly unlike any of his films, but it was lots
of fun and made musical comedy on stage almost as spectacular
as Hollywood could do it.

His political columns had added to his list of enemies. Pretty
soon there was no work for him in this country and I didn't see
another Welles film for many years — and then it came from
Europe.

He was only the first of many domestic victims of the Cold
War. Everybody who tried to preserve New Deal Liberalism into
the late '40s and early '50s eventually got blacklisted, deprived
of a livelihood, roundly smeared in the Hearst and Luce publications. (*Life,* which had praised Welles' stage *Macbeth* extrava-
gantly in 1938 now did a viciously snide review of his film
version, under the headline, "Orson Welles Doth Foully Murder
Shakespeare.") Henry Wallace, former Secretary of Agriculture,
was smeared as a "Communist" and belted with tomatoes when
he ran for President. Professional informers earned full-time
salaries accusing people of being or having been Communists,
making the accusations before Congressional Committees for

maximum media coverage. To defend any Liberal cause virtually guaranteed you would get on their hit list.

A fellow named Harvey Matusow made his living for a few years identifying people as Communists he had known while in the Party. Then he suddenly confessed that he had never been in the Communist Party, at all, and had been making everything up out of his rich Slavic fantasy life. Everybody was furious at him — both the Left and the Right — and eventually he went to jail for perjury.

When he got out of prison, Harvey made a documentary film about his adventures, which I saw. A lot of it involved his testimony about the Stringless Yo-Yo Company, which he had claimed was run by the Communist Party. None of the Congressmen who heard this testimony asked him what the hell a stringless yo-yo was.

The film may still be available. It's called *The Stringless Yo-Yo* and I heartily recommend it to anyone who wants to understand how politics works.

The carefully created hysteria and witch-hunt Matusow had exploited and then satirized reminded me of all the anti-Nazi movies I had seen, but now it was happening in my own country.

Meanwhile, my scientific education, having delivered me from anxiety about the demon who might drop ground glass in my eyes at night, gave me new terrors. My social science teachers all thought the atomic bomb might destroy humanity and that neither our government nor any other was willing to give the UN enough power to prevent wars from happening. To make sure we understood the horrors of nuclear war, they scared hell out of us. Like almost all my generation, I spent my adolescent years and early adulthood seriously unsure if I would be alive the next day or the crazy bastards in Washington and Moscow would start throwing nukes around and blow up the planet.

I was meanwhile reading every novel that I had any reason to think "important." There are so many writers around today who don't seem to have ever read *anything* that my attitude toward the Art of Literature now seems archaic, but I believed, in my youth and ignorance, that in order to write well one must know what good writing is, by studying it. Starting at 14, I dived into James T. Farrell — because he wrote about Irish Catholics and

Depressions, subjects I could understand — and then moved on to Sinclair Lewis, who introduced to me how people talked and thought in mainstream Protestant Republican America. I proceeded through Fitzgerald and Faulkner and Steinbeck and many who now seem totally "unimportant" and finally discovered James Joyce, who seemed to me so earth-shaking that I have by now devoted 41 years to the study of his works. (I began my study of writing with my contemporaries or near-contemporaries, because I thought I could judge their accuracy and relevance better than I could judge that of people writing about other and earlier ages.)

Orson Welles' last American film, the one *Life* trashed so totally, was a violent and barbaric version of *Macbeth* — without Black actors this time, but with all the murky and clammy atmosphere of one of James Whale's horror movies. I loved it and it managed to turn me on to Shakespeare. (I spent a whole summer reading and relishing his plays, in chronological order.) Then I dived into the other English-language poets and soon was awash in Keats and Shelley and Blake and Whitman and, eventually, Yeats and Eliot and Pound.

This pleased my English teachers.

Then I discovered science-fiction and went completely bonkers over Heinlein and Sturgeon and Olaf Stapledon, among others.

This did not please my English teachers at all.

I think Pound influenced me almost as much as Joyce. Together, they convinced me that our century was going through so many radical changes simultaneously that the techniques of literature, like the other arts, had to become "experimental" in order to capture the orders and magnitudes of the breakdowns and breakthroughs we were experiencing — *breakdowns* of old reality-tunnels, *breakthroughs* to new ways of orchestrating our perceptions.

What Joyce did to prose and Pound did to poetry, in my opinion, made those arts contemporary with both quantum physics and the films I liked. They had broken linear order into luminous fragments — quanta — which they reassembled into synergetic wholes, like a Bucky Fuller design. To read them involved stepping outside subject-predicate order into the modes of thought

you find in differential calculus or in the montages of directors
like Welles, Eisenstein, Kurasawa.

To quote the opening of Pound's *Canto 74:*

> The enormous tragedy of the dream in
> the peasant's bent shoulders
> Manes! Manes was tanned and stuffed

Here we have the age-old cyclical tragedy of the Patriarchal
Sun-King Age, the peasant's bent shoulders, the lost dream, and
set against it one unique individual horror — the execution of
Manes, who taught that Christ and Mithra were the same god
under two names, and was crucified, tanned, stuffed and hung up
like a scarecrow on the wall of Rome — which could be the fate
of any intellectual or visionary. This juxtaposition of concrete
particulars, like a film's montage or a Japanese *haiku,* moves us
out of the Aristotelian linear mode of thought into modes of synergy only found in the Orient until modern science rediscovered
them.

And nobody else but Ezra has ever written lines as lovely as
"The water-bug's mittens show on the bright rock below him" or
lines that leap off the page like

> there
> are
> no
> righteous
> wars

Of course, I had very ambiguous feelings about Pound. His
poetry seemed more beautiful than anything in English since
Shakespeare, to me, and his humor was appealing, but his political attitudes seemed as bad as Uncle Mick's. (The beautiful
passage about the peasant's dream and Manes is followed by a
lament for the death of Mussolini.)

But by then I discovered painting, fell in love with Picasso and
soon realized his politics were as batty as Pound's, in the opposite direction. I stopped being ashamed of the politics of my
artistic heroes and decided that people who judged an artist by
his or her politics were imbeciles. I still hold to that view, today.

My next passion was "social commentary" and/or "philosophy" (I didn't make much distinction between them.) I read and had my brain reorganized by Spinoza and Hume and Marx and Veblen and Henry George and Sir James Frazer and H.L. Mencken and all sorts of folks like that, who had reality-tunnels very different from Irish Catholicism.

I had moved in Virtual Space from the one square mile of Gerrison Beach and its Irish Catholic grid to several square miles of Brooklyn/Manhattan and the world of modern thought and modern art generally.

Finally, I went to my father one day and told him I didn't see why I should have to go to Mass anymore, since he never did. He was quite calm about it. He said he didn't believe in the Church anymore and regarded it as racket devised to make money, but he thought some of what the nuns taught was true, and children needed it. This was not a profound philosophical discussion by any standard, and it occurred about 44 years ago, so I can't guarantee I understood perfectly what Dad's view was, but I think he believed that, while the Church was full of superstition and commercialism, children raised without any religion can become frightfully selfish and amoral adults.

A lot of people still believe that and send their children to Sunday Schools that teach a great deal of bizarre nonsense, just because they know these institutions also teach a few ideas that prevent the whole human race from acting as dishonestly and murderously as the blood-thirsty pirates and gay banditos who govern us.

My mother's view was simpler. She believed in God and Heaven and Miracles, because that made her happy, but she didn't see why that compelled her to believe all and everything the Church proclaimed, especially if it didn't make her happy and didn't even make sense.

Once I no longer had to go to Mass on Sundays, the Catholic reality-tunnel began to retreat into the past. It wasn't until a decade had passed and I was in my mid-20s that I realized you don't get rid of early conditioning that easily: I still had some Catholic anxieties and repressions. It required psychotherapy to begin to get rid of them.

Since my parents only had two children in all their years of marriage, I have deduced that neither of them believed the Church's weird notions about contraception.

COSMIC ECONOMICS

"A Great Saving Of Stuff"

In Ludlow Park, in the middle of Hamilton, Ohio, stands a monument to the town's most colorful native, Captain John Cleves Symmes, a hero of the War of 1812 (in which he distinguished himself at the Battle of Lundy's Lane).* The monument, however, does not commemorate Captain Symmes's military prowess. It says in lean, unlovely English:

Captain John Cleves Symmes was a philosopher, and the originator of "Symmes' Theory of Concentric Spheres and Polar Voids." He contended that the Earth is hollow and habitable within.

Even earlier a local poet had written:

> Yes! History's pen may yet inscribe the name
> Of SYMMES to grace her future roll of fame.

Captain Symmes believed, and thought he had "proven scientifically," that the Earth is shaped more or less like a fat doughnut. Although his books and pamphlets appear turgid and somewhat opaque, he was an indefatigable orator and toured the nation, arousing great enthusiasm for his new theory, which he defended chiefly on the grounds of cosmic parsimony, arguing that a hollow Earth represents "a great saving of stuff" as compared to a solid Earth. This had gut appeal for shrewd Yankees in those days, who were accustomed to the thought that Nature's God,‡ like a good shop-keeper, seeks always the most economic solution to every problem.

---

* Curiously, Arlen grew up near there and was educated by Canadian teachers who claimed the American troops were guilty of "atrocities." Could that be? I thought only the armies of other, and hence lesser, countries commit atrocities...

‡ An entity created by the philosophers of the previous century and invoked in our Declaration of Independence. Nature's God is impartial, progressive, obsessed with mechanical economy and, unlike the

A young lawyer named Jeremiah Reynolds persuaded 50 members of the Pennsylvania State Legislature to petition the President of the U.S. to send an expedition to the South Pole to find the hole that Symmes claimed was there. When the President, John Quincy Adams, provided only enough money for three small ships, Reynolds optimistically led the expedition himself. Alas, he knew more about law than sailing and the ships, beset with malnutrition and mutiny, had to turn back before they were south of Chile.

Reynolds consoled himself by writing a melodramatic and popular book about the cruise, including all the good sea-yarns he had heard along the way. Herman Melville read it and one chapter — about a giant white whale that had almost incredible cunning and good luck in escaping whalers again and again — inspired *Moby-Dick.* The whale, of course, symbolized all sorts of ghastly and mysterious aspects of the world, but mostly, I think, he symbolized the "colorless allcolor" of the materialist reality-tunnel which Melville hated, because it made art meaningless, and feared, because it might be true.

Captain Symmes continued arguing for his hollow Earth theory until he died in 1829.

Christian God, will not perform miracles and has no interest in being flattered.

KONG — & THE WHITE VIRGIN

One day in 1948, when I was a junior at Brooklyn Tech, I stumbled upon a book called *An Essay on Morals* by Philip Wylie in the public library. Opening it and skimming, I found a long paragraph made up of rhetorical questions, all pointing to a basic unity in all the myths of humanity. E.g. why have so many other demi-gods and heroes died and risen from the grave, like Christ? Why is it the seemingly weakest of the three brothers, in most fairly tales,* who slays the dragon? Etc. The last question, as well as I can remember it after all these years, was "What is the meaning of this thousand-times-told story of Beauty and the Beast?"

I went tingly all over — or, as Stephen Dedalus would say, my soul swooned softly — as the last scene of *King Kong* and all my other Virtual Reality experiences flashed through me.

"No, it wasn't the airplanes — it was Beauty that killed the Beast..."

I checked the book out and read it that night. Despite the title, it was more about psychology than about ethics, and it was about Jungian psychology in particular. With a viewpoint closer to an old fashioned "village atheist" than Jung's own (as I later came to see) Wylie explained the Jungian theory of the archetypes — genetic programs from the "collective unconscious" that appear as numinous Symbols when they enter normal consciousness. Wylie also offered his own version of Jung's theory about why such Symbols can trigger a total upheaval in the personality leading to either psychoses or to integration on a higher level of self-insight.

I suddenly had a Theory to account for the powerful, irrational and somewhat "mystic" sensations that some kinds of art could provoke in me. Such Virtual Realities simply placed me in juxtaposition to an Archetype. I also had a better explanation of the data in Frazer's anthropological classic, *The Golden Bough,* than

---

* And in one of the most popular movies ever made, *Jaws.*

Frazer himself had provided. Myths of all ages and races told the same stories, not because these stories were allegories on the cycle of the crops, as Frazer claimed, but because these stories expressed the genetic programs that unconsciously govern us.

I began to read Jung voraciously, which led me to Freud, Jung's original teacher, and then to the post-Freudian and post-Jungian psychologists who were then beginning to appear. This is dangerous stuff for a teen-ager. It soon became clear to me that I was neurotic, that everybody I knew was neurotic, that the world as a whole was mildly paranoid, and that none of the theories of any of the psychologists offered any real hope of curing the madness of our species. They were all good at diagnosis, but either vague or unconvincing about how they hoped their theories might be used to cure the aberrations and obsessions of our tormented species.

Most of my own neuroses, Freud convinced me, resulted from sexual frustration, but, no matter how much I read and re-read him, I found no clues as to how to end this frustration. (I knew by now that brothels existed, but I also knew that you could catch awful diseases there, and my still-somewhat-Catholic imagination harped on those diseases unwholesomely.) I followed the advice of James Joyce to penurious bachelors: "Masturbation — the wonderful availability of it!" This never quite ended the frustration satisfactorily, but at least added some hours of pagan hedonism to my over-intellectual life.

As a result of my extracurricular reading, my school marks were dropping dangerously. Having graduated elementary school at the top of my class, I now found myself near the bottom — even in English, because I was reading the books that interested me instead of the books they wanted me to read. (I still haven't read *Ivanhoe.* The year they wanted me to read that and *The Mill on the Floss,* I was reading *Studs Lonigan, The Sun Also Rises, Darkness at Noon, Ulysses, The Great Gatsby, Elmer Gantry* and other books that helped me understand the 20th Century world I lived in.)

I was in an engineering school but was really more interested in literature. I had landed in another double-bind: literature was my passion, but nobody I knew believed I could make a living from that, so I had to go on trying to become an engineer, since I was good at math and might make a passable engineer if I could find the time to study it in between devouring Melville, Chaucer, Dante and Cervantes.

Meanwhile, Jung had convinced me there were four types of humans — the Rational, the Sensational, the Emotional and the Intuitive. I was obviously the Rational type ("left brain," people say nowadays) and I determined to end this imbalance by developing my sensory, emotional and intuitive faculties.

I didn't have a clue about how to accomplish that.

TROTSKY, AYN RAND &
THE SEARCH FOR A GURU

At seventeen I became a Trotskyist. That was hot stuff in New York in the late 1940s. We Trots were more Red and Radical than anybody, or we thought we were. (The Stalinists had "betrayed the Revolution," but we were carrying it on.) Of course, I was lying to myself, or had voluntarily entered self-hypnosis again. Who the hell knows enough, *at seventeen,* to make an intelligent or informed choice among competing political ideologies? (I'm not sure I know enough at nearly 60.) I had picked Trotskyism because one part of my mind was still Catholic and needed a hierarchy; the Central Committee made a good "secular" substitute for the Vatican. It allowed me to feel modern, scientific, "altruistic," brave, rebellious etc. and it did all my thinking for me.

Besides, the Trots agreed with me about how capitalist wars get started, but they weren't anti-semitic nuts like Uncle Mick and Ezra Pound. They had the same analysis, in many ways, as my favorite historian, Harry Elmer Barnes — capitalist nations make endless wars to protect themselves from economic competition by other capitalist nations, and they have brainwashed the masses to believe each war is a holy crusade for "peace."

Uncle Mick was right and wrong at the same time. As Marx said, "Anti-semitism is the socialism of fools." It is a Mickey Mouse model, picking a scapegoat group to blame, instead of analyzing the structural factors within the Capitalist system and the Nation State itself that perpetuate poverty and war.

Every war results from the struggle for markets and "spheres of influence" and every war is "sold" to the public, by professional liars and totally sincere religious maniacs, as a Holy Crusade to save God and Goodness from Satan and Evil.

Barnes caricatured the rhetoric of the warmongers with the ironic slogan, **Perpetual War For Perpetual Peace.** As the decades have passed, and our government has invaded some new country every few years — always for reasons declared "noble" and "idealistic" — Barnes's arguments seem more and more cogent to me.

At eighteen I quit The Party just before they could expel me. The ironic thing is that at that date my major difference with the Central Committee concerned art, not politics. (But then art and politics are not distinguished as separate in the Marxist BS.) I liked all the "wrong" writers, and I would not accept party dogma about who were the "right" writers. (Besides, my continuing interest in Jungian psychology was regarded as heretical.) More and more often, the party dogmatists accused me of having "bourgeois tendencies" — which I thought was really quite amusing, since I was the only one in our cell who did *not* come from a middle-class background. I was the only son of the proletariat in the group, and these middle-class Ideologists hadn't the foggiest idea what a real worker was like. (They would all hate to admit how many workers share my uncle Mick's anti-semitism, for instance.)

Once out of the Marxist reality-tunnel, I pledged allegiance to the principles of individualism, free thought and agnosticism. From now on, I said, I will not by hypnotized by groups: I will think for myself. Naturally, I then spent over 20 years following various intellectual and political fads, always convinced I had at last escaped group conditioning and finally started "really" thinking for myself. I went from Agnosticism back to dogmatic atheism, and then to Buddhism; I bounced from Existentialism to New Left Activism to New Age Mysticism and back to Agnosticism. The carousel turned around and around but I never found a way to stop it and get off until I was middle-aged and had done so much Acid the only choices left were to really think for myself or to go crazy.

The first new dogmatism I embraced after rejecting the Marxist BS (belief system) was Ayn Rand's philosophy (not yet called Objectivism in those days.) *The Fountainhead* had exactly the appeal for me that it has retained, decade after decade, with alienated adolescents of all ages. (The average youthful reader of *Thus Spake Zarathustra* decides he is the Superman, and the average youthful Randroid decides she is an Alienated Genius.) Like most Randroids, I went around for a few years mindlessly parroting all the Rand dogma and imagining I was an "individualist."

Some years later, after becoming a published writer, I actually was invited to meet Ayn Rand once. (I was "summoned to the Presence," Arlen said.) I confessed my doubts about certain of the Rand dogmas and was Cast Out Into the Darkness forever to wail and gnash my teeth in the Realm of Thud. It was weird. I thought the Trots and Catholic priests were dogmatic, but Ayn Rand made both groups look like models of tolerance by comparison.

I thought she was a clinical paranoid. It was nearly 30 years later that I found out Rand was merely on Speed all the time, which creates an effect so much like paranoia that even trained clinicians cannot always tell the difference, and some even claim there is no difference.

Without Trotsky or Ayn Rand as Guru, I started making up a philosophy of my own. Of course, I borrowed most of it, unconsciously, from Bertrand Russell, H. L. Mencken and Nietzsche...

All this, mind you, occurred within the network of language — *the Virtual Reality created by the strange symbol-making capacity of the upper quarter inch of our front brain.* Language created God and Satan and Hell, in my childhood, and it created Liberty and Equality and Justice and Natural Law and other fictions that obsessed me at other stages of my "development." *Language creates spooks that get into our heads and hypnotize us.*

It is obvious, once one considers the subject at all, that our eyes cannot see the whole universe. They can't even see the whole room in which we happen to be sitting (they only see what is in front of us, or a bit of the right and left, and not all of that; they never see what is behind us...) Similarly, our stomachs cannot swallow the whole universe, and our brains cannot "know" the whole universe (they only know the signals they have received up to this second, and do not remember all of them consciously...)

Nonetheless, language programs us to try to speak as if we possessed the kind of infallibility claimed by the Pope, the Central Committee of a Marxist party, or Ayn Rand. That is, language allows us to say things like "The rose is red" — which looks very innocent, doesn't it? Yet in the mild hypnosis of this

Virtual Reality we then promptly forget that the rose "is" *more and other than red* — that it is fragrant, for example, and that it is temporary and will wither soon, and that it is made of electrons, and other wave-forms — *and that it "is" only red to creatures with eyes like ours, etc.*

Every over-simplification becomes a lie quickly (if we are not very cynical about language); ergo, language always lies, just because it over-simplifies. From "The rose is red" to "The National Debt forces us to raise taxes again" to "ARKANSAS MOM RAPED BY MIDGETS FROM MARS" to "Pornography is murder" (Andrea Dworkin) we proceed from one fiction to another, every time we open our mouths to speak.

As Wendell Johnson wrote,

> A rose by any other name
> Would never, never smell the same
> And cunning is the nose that knows
> An onion that's been called a rose

FURTHER SECRETS OF
THE KNIGHTS OF MALTA

But Who Has The Maltese Falcon?

In addition to von Papen and Buckley and Gehlen and Mad Bill *et al.* two other important Knights of Malta in recent history were the aforementioned *Michele ("The Shark") Sindona* and *Licio Gelli* — two names hardly known in America, but the subject of endless conspiratorial theorizing in Europe, since both were associated with Roberto Calvi's weird banking empire. The real beginning of the Calvi-Sindona-Gelli story, however, goes back to the 1940s and the (temporary) collapse of fascism.

In Spring 1945, when Nazi Germany was in ruins, General Reinhard Gehlen, Chief of Intelligence under Hitler — and another Knight of Malta, remember? — loaded a truck with Top Secret documents and drove to the nearest American Army division he could find, to negotiate a separate peace. General Gehlen was evidently a very, very good negotiator. (Of course, he had that truck full of God-knows-what Secrets...)

Gehlen soon had an American General's uniform and was flown to Washington, where he negotiated further. According to papers secured by Prof. Carl Oglesby* under the Freedom of Information Act, by the time Gehlen was through negotiating, not only was he the head of what became the CIA's Soviet penetration section, but a number of other top Nazis soon had CIA jobs as well. Oglesby regards this as the beginning of the "Nazification" of the American intelligence community.

The O.S.S. (parent organization of the CIA) already had a working relationship with the Mafia in both America and Italy by then. This had been masterminded by the convicted pimp, Charles ("Lucky") Luciano, who in return for an early parole from prison, arranged that the Sicilian Mafiosi would help the invading American Army. This accelerated the American con-

---

* Personal communication to R.A.W.

quest of Italy but it also married the American intelligence community to the Mob for many decades — up to the present, in fact. One might say that if General Gehlen began the Nazification of the CIA (and thus of America), Luciano presided over the Mafiazation of our government.

Of course, in the symbiosis between the Mob and the Spooks, the Mob thinks it is using the Spooks, and the Spooks think they are using the Mob, and at least one of them is badly deceived...

At this point Licio Gelli entered the picture — long before he became involved with Calvi and the Vatican Bank. Gelli had honed his skills in the Spy Game by working, during World War II, as a double agent for the Gestapo and the Communist underground, and had managed to convince both that he was faithfully serving them and betraying the other guys. In post-war Rome, Gelli began a new business — creating false I.D. for Nazi war criminals fleeing prosecution, and finding them jobs in Latin America. Many eventually ended up working for the CIA or the Latin American Death Squads — which, as everybody knows, have absolutely no connection with the CIA except for being recruited, trained, armed, financed and "advised" by them.

While recruiting Nazis for the CIA, Gelli formed strong links with ODESSA, the secret society of former SS officers, who seem to be devoted chiefly to (a) evading capture by Israeli intelligence and (b) creating a Fourth Reich in Latin America, the part of the world that seems most ripe for a fascist take-over. Gelli assisted many fascist regimes down there, including buying guns for the Argentines before the Falklands war and helping restore Peron to power, for which Peron once knelt before him and kissed his hand.

Gelli had been on the CIA's payroll since the mid-1950s. He had originally been hired by them to strengthen the right wing in the Italian labor movement and weaken the left wing. Gelli had done this, most efficiently, by bribing those union officials who could be bribed and arranging to have the Mafia assassinate those who couldn't be bribed. You must admit that this technique was neat but not gaudy.

Signor Gelli also, sometime in there, got himself on the payroll of the KGB. Thus, in addition to the billions he and his P2 gang were soon earning on their financial fun and games, Gelli was being paid by both Washington and Moscow. Both sides of the Cold War seemingly believed he was betraying the other side. Why not? A man who could convince both the Nazis and the Red Underground that he was on their side in World War II could play the same game in the Cold War years.

By the 1970s, Gelli and his fellow Knight of Malta, Mike the Shark Sindona, had fairly well taken control of Vatican finances, with the connivance of Bishop Paul "the Gorilla" Marcinkus (so dubbed because of his Gargantuan anatomy: he had served as bodyguard for two Popes.)

Paul the Gorilla was soon manager of the Vatican Bank and had set up in the Bahamas another bank, called Cisalpine, which he co-owned with the late Roberto Calvi, who at one point owned more banks than anybody in the world — except that most of the banks later turned out to have no existence in the sensory space-time world.

These supernatural entities have been called "ghost banks" by Italian magistrates who cannot find them outside Calvi's phantasmal ledgers.

THE GREAT ONE WHO MAKES
THE GRASS GREEN

> The Austrians always claim Beethoven was Austrian,
> even though he was born in Germany, and that Hitler
> was German, even though he was born in Austria.
> — Swiss joke

Between Munich and Berlin the train passed through the
D.D.R. — the *Deutsche Demokratikische Republik,* usually
called just East Germany where I came from. It was the first time
I had been in an overtly totalitarian nation, and as soon as we
crossed the border and entered Marxworld I was as wary as a
rabbit in fox territory. It was 1987, and I was 55, snowy white on
top but tan and (vanity told me) youngish-looking otherwise.

Back in Munich I had taught a quantum psychology seminar,
and Tom, a TV producer had taken me out to see one of the
castles of Ludwig II — the "mad" king of Bavaria, who (some
Conspiracy Nuts claim) was not "mad" at all but merely a pacifist who opposed the 1872 war against France and was therefore
murdered by a conspiracy of the nobles.* Ludwig, a great patron
of the arts in general and of Wagner's mythic operas in particular, also appears, mysteriously, as one of 114 "saints" of Gnosti-
cism in the Gnostic Catholic Mass celebrated by initiates of the
Ordo Templi Orientis. I've always meant to find out more about
Ludwig the Mad.

The castle was "much as I expected" (as Oscar Wilde said of
Niagara Falls) — opulent, gorgeous, a bit silly, about as subtle as
a charging rhinoceros, weirdly beautiful: a true High Camp
Classic. Whether Ludwig was over the hill with the fairies or not,
he was obviously not a man to be afraid of the phrase "too much
of a good thing."

---

* Historians still disagree as to whether Ludwig's death by drowning
was suicide, accident or assassination.

139

Now, Tom and I were headed for Berlin where he had another gig lined up for me, and we were, as usual when we get together, more than a little bit stoned. Then the train entered the D.D.R. and I jumped up quickly and closed the window. It didn't help.

"What the ring-tailed ramgling *hell* is that smell?" I asked.

"The D.D.R.," Tom said, with a Berliner shrug, as if to say: Isn't it obvious?

"Yeah, yeah, I know it's the D.D.R." I said. "But why does it smell like that?"

Tom explained, patiently: when the Communists took over, Stalin wanted to industrialize fast (he had a Paranoid Suspicion that the American ruling elite was plotting against him), and the only fuel for factories was the cheapest grade of coal. Once the factories were built, it was too expensive to convert them to something else, so now, over 40 years later, the same rotten coal is still burning and the whole D.D.R. smells worse than a drainage ditch in August.

Pig-headed Marxists can pollute an environment even more horribly than Capitalist corporations.

The smell seeped through the locked window. It was almost acid in its corrosiveness and, even after Tom's explanation it was hard not to suspect deliberate malice in it, as if somebody had set off a tear gas canister and a stink-bomb at once. We never escaped it until we reached Berlin.

We talked for a while, and then Tom said, with a sixth sense developed by many trips through the D.D.R. "Here they come."

In a minute or so, the Border Guard or Secret Police or whoever they hell they were pushed open the door of our compartment and barked and growled in German. As Hotspur said, I would rather hear Lady my brach howl in Irish. I couldn't catch a single word and looked enquiringly at Tom.

"Our passports," he said.

I got out my passport and handed it to one of Them. There were two and they both looked exactly like the actors who play Nazis in American movies. There are many types of German faces, but the type that looks as if it never stops relishing some exquisite new form of prolonged sadism is the type I mean. This was combined with eyes full of suspicion and insinuation. I have never seen such brutality combined with that kind of paranoia in a human expression, and I thought, *Orwell was right: real totalitarianism looks exactly like a parody of itself.*

The Two Paranoids with Guns both looked at my passport. They muttered and at least I caught one word: *"Amerikanishe."* I suddenly had a distinct vision of dark tiny room, a bright light, one of those machines for pouring electricity into your penis and myself saying over and over, "No, no, no — I've never worked for the CIA."

They handed Tom's passport back. They addressed me in words too fast and Bavarian for my comprehension, took my passport and left.

"What are they doing?" I asked Tom.

"It's a standard routine," Tom said. "Don't worry."

"But they took my passport. My fucking passport."

"Don't worry. Over here the cops are all, how you say, retarded. They went to look up the regulations."

Five minutes passed, like a herd of turtles.

The Two came back and gave me my passport, together with a piece of paper. One of them barked and snarled again, they both looked at me as if they thought I'd pull a dagger any minute, and they left.

"That's your Travel Permit," Tom said. "You're supposed to give it back to them when we get to East Berlin. I bet they'll forget."

We had another joint, after that, and talked until Tom dozed off in his chair. I was still too full of adrenaline to sleep. I started reading the signs as we passed through one depressed little town after another. *Leninstrasse... Marxstrasse... Luexembourg-strasse... Ludwigstrasse.... Ueber-Hamburgerstrasse... Grosse-Schlangestrasse.*

Suddenly I saw *Heiligefliegendekindersheissestrasse* and realized that, even though I was full of cannabis and adrenaline, sleep had still crept up on me and I was dreaming with my eyes open.

Tom was right. The Two never did come back to collect my Travel Permit. I still have it, as a memento of my journey to the end of night.

THE SQUARE ROOT OF MINUS ONE
& OTHER MYSTERIES

As my mathematical education at Brooklyn Tech proceeded, I began to encounter what New Agers nowadays think can only be found in Oriental mysticism — concepts too ethereal to be reduced to sense data.

For instance, 2 is the square root of 4, because if you multiply 2 x 2 you get 4. In mathematical notation, 2 x 2 = 4, or $2^2 = 4$. Three is the square root of nine, by the same logic. ($3^2 = 9$). But minus one (-1) also has a square root, even though we can't write it as a number. We arbitrarily (or conventionally) write it as the letter i (or j if we are electrical engineers, because they already have an i, which indicates a dimension of electricity the French originally discovered and named *intensite* — plain old "current" in English.[*])

We also have multiples of i, such as $2i$, $3i$, $4i$ etc. These are called "imaginary numbers" because, when they were invented, nobody could see any use for them. To practical artisans in those days, and to some of the mathematicians as well, it seemed that i and all of its multiples were just some kind of fantasy that mathematics had blundered into, like the little man in the famous poem:

> I saw a man upon the stair
> A little man who wasn't there.
> He wasn't there again today —
> Gee, I wish he'd go away!

The square root of minus one and its phantasmal multiples did not go away. These imaginary numbers gave birth to complex

---

[*] The difference between current and voltage can be pictured in a metaphor. Imagine an airplane accidentally dropping a hundred thousand watermelons on a city. Each street would have a different number of watermelons, just as each branch of an electric circuit has a different current. But all the watermelons would fall at the same speed, just as each branch of a circuit has the same voltage. Got it?

numbers, which are written in such forms as 3 + 2*i*, 4 + 7*i*, x + 5*i*, y + 12*i*, etc. You can't mark a place on a line and say this is where such a complex number lives, as you can with an ordinary ("real") number. To indicate where a complex number belongs you need, not a line, but a plane.

For instance, if you draw a line of any length on an ordinary page and divide it with a mark at every inch, 3 would indicate the location of the mark for the third inch. 3 + 2*i* would be two units "above" that, floating in space, as it were (but in the same plane with the line.)

So far, these complex numbers with their imaginary numbers as parts of them seem like some "head game" or the mathematical equivalent of Abstract painting. The amazing thing is that, over the past 300 years, scientists have found dozens and dozens of systems in the physical world that can only be described with this occult symbolism. For instance, you can describe direct current electrical circuits (DC) without them, but you need them to describe alternating current circuits (AC). You also need them in Relativity, quantum mechanics, television and computer design — and in dozens of other areas of our technology.

It's as if we can't describe and predict the world of matter and energy without including in our description a factor just as inscrutable as the Cabalist's Head That Is Not A Head or Zen's Sound of One Hand Clapping.

As this gradually dawned on me, I asked my teachers a lot of questions about the meaning of it all. The usual answer was, "Well, it *works*, so why worry about something a little weird in the math?" The only other answer was, "Well, you can get into that in college, if you decide to major in Pure Math."

(Pure Math deals with all the mathematical systems humans can invent. Applied Math deals only with the mathematical systems that have some scientific or mercantile use. Another joke here is that anything in Pure Math can become Applied Math as soon as somebody finds a use for it. For instance, Reimanian geometry was Pure Math until Einstein used it in his theory of gravity, whereupon it became Applied Math. Since 95% of Pure Math is not known even to most mathematicians — nobody has the time to read and understand all the published theorems — we don't know how much Pure Math may be lying around in dusty

books containing the scientific models that can explain phenomena that are now considered inexplicable. I can't imagine why
parapsychologists and UFOlogists haven't looked into this.)

Even stranger to me was the concept that we are living in a
colorless world. For instance, from where I sit at my computer
writing this, I can see a *black-and-white* chess board, a *brown*
book case, a *beige/yellow* dresser, a *red-and-yellow* tapestry
(done by an Indian artist in Panama) and a *green* overstuffed
chair. All of this is hallucination, according to physics. What is
actually out there consists of clusters of colorless atoms and
photons, and all the "colors" are my brain's way of reacting to
various wave-lengths of light carried by the photons bouncing
off the atoms.

Melville understood, and felt profoundly disturbed by this aspect of modern science. The phrase from *Moby-Dick* that I mentioned earlier, "the colorless allcolor of atheism," summarizes
the horror that most artists feel at this bleached-out, emotionally
empty view of a monochromatic world — which also terrorized
Blake and Dostoevsky and absolutely nauseated Whitman. (See
his "When I Heard The Learn'd Astronomer.") This colorless,
seemingly "abstract" world reappears in the pale dead white
decor of some of the gloomier films of Bergman and Woody
Allen. It has the inhuman and emotionless flavor of Theravada
Buddhist meditation, without the hope of Enlightenment.

If "reality" is this Buddhist/scientific White Light, or Imaginary Math, or No-Thing as the Nihilists and Chinese Buddhists
say, why did we develop brains that persistently invent a hallucinatory "solid" world full of colors and sweat and music and
purposes and fun and suffering and even such haunting presences
as Justice and Injustice? Why do our brains go on hallucinating
that technicolor fantasy even after we have learned the scientific-
mathematical truth?

Temperature turns out to be even stranger than color. It registers on instruments — e.g., the thermometer — as well as on our
eye/brain system, but it only exists on certain levels.
Specifically, it exists at the molecular level and above, since
what we call temperature is actually the rate of movement of
molecules. Thus, if a desk top is 100 degrees Fahrenheit on a hot
day, it makes no sense to say that the atoms in the desk top are

also 100 degrees Fahrenheit. *Atoms have no more temperature than they have color.* Only the clusters of atoms called molecules have temperature, and only in relation to their movements.

The more my technical education progressed, the more I realized that what's real is not what we see, and that what we see isn't real at all. What is "real," evidently, is colorless, temperatureless, abstract and only expressible in terms of surrealist mathematics like the square root of minus one. I found this increasingly hard to believe, yet (as I keep insisting) experimental and experiential evidence supports it.

But calculus presented me with even worse problems. The form of a simple calculus function looks like this, as usually written:

$$dx/dt$$

This means the rate of change of some variable (x) — which might be gallons of water pouring out of a leaky tub, or miles traveled by a jet airliner, etc. — as a function of the rate of change, or duration, of time (t). The trouble is that this is an abbreviation. It was derived, by Newton and Leibniz, including an additional term, known as the infinitesimal. The infinitesimal is always omitted (after the original theorem is understood) because "it is so small we can ignore it."

If we don't ignore it, if we are impertinent enough to ask questions about it, we find ourselves in a fine metaphysical mess. The infinitesimal is smaller than any number you can write. Thus, you know that 1/100 is smaller than 1/10, and 1/1000 is even smaller than 1/100, etc. Well, if you keep adding zeroes to the denominator (the bottom of the fraction), you get a smaller and smaller number...but you never get to the infinitesimal. The infinitesimal is not only smaller than 1/1,000,000,000, but smaller than:

1/1,000,000,000,000,000,000,000,000,000,000...

and if I filled the rest of this book with a denominator made up of as many zeroes as you could fit in this many pages, the infinitesimal is still smaller...

In other words, no matter how small a number you can write or think about, the infinitesimal is still smaller than that. It seems like "the ghost of a departed quantity," to quote Bishop Berkeley.

Now, you obviously can't find such a spook in the existential or sensory space-time continuum, anymore than you can find the square root of minus one, the Jabberwock or the Holy Ghost there. Where can you find the infinitesimal (and the imaginary numbers, for that matter)? In the realm of the pure laws of physics which — although invisible, colorless, weightless, massless, temperatureless and impalpable — "controls" or "determines" or at least "underlies" the sensory space-time continuum (i.e., the world we see and smell and feel and taste).

Thus, scientific "reality" is not something we can see or otherwise experience. It is something we deduce from mathematical systems that look, to me, as spooky as anything in Platonic metaphysics — or Cabala. Yet most scientists, who use this *mathemagic* every day, remain blind to its implications and espouse a philosophy of "materialism" that seems to say that the sensory-sensual world is real, after all.

By the time I realized this, it became obvious to me that the majority of scientists, just like Catholics or Trotskyists, can ignore anything they don't want to think about, even if it is staring them in the face or even biting them on the arse. The scientists who do not ignore these issues are generally treated as suspicious characters; if they publish their thoughts, the usual response of their colleagues is something like, "Interesting book of philosophy you wrote there, but when are you going to do some science again?"

This gets even more mind-boggling when you enter the realm of Relativity. Two of Einstein's basic equations, in simplified form, look like this:

$$x_1 = x_2 + bt$$
$$t_1 = t_2 + bx$$

b represents a complicated function which, if I wrote it in full, would require several pages of explanation; it contains the velocity of light and the velocities of both the observers and the observed. We do not need to explore all that here. What matters is that these equations represent the different readings of space and time that will be obtained by people (or instruments) in different "inertial systems."

For convenience, we will regard our inertial systems as space ships. That makes for nice, easy illustrations — and, incidentally, shows you how far pure math and inborn genius can carry a person. Einstein was creating a system that describes space ships (among other things) the year before the Wright Brothers got their first monoplane off the ground for a few seconds.

Okay: I am in space ship *Goddard,* and you are in space ship *Ley* and we both measure the length of a river on the planet we are passing. If we are both traveling at the same velocity, no problem arises: we get the same measurement. But if we are traveling at different velocities, then we get different measurements. *Length is not an "essence" in the thing being measured — the river — but a relationship between the inertial system of the thing and the inertial system of the observer.*

The first equation above tells you what that relationship will be, where the x-terms represent our different measurements and the **b** represents that Einsteinian function including our velocities and the velocity of light.

Now suppose we decide to measure the time interval between two events — Mr. A starting for work and Mr. A arriving at the office. The second equation tells us what will happen if we are not moving at the same velocity — if we are moving at different velocities. You will measure, maybe, one hour and I will measure perhaps an hour and a half. *Time, like space, is not an "essence" in the thing being measured but a relationship between the inertial system of the thing and the inertial system of the observer.*

Now, the Relativity of space and time seems startling enough, but the Einstein theory contains a second, more amazing aspect, which one might call its abstract expressionist Absolutism. That is, your measurement and mine remain relative to our velocities (and the velocity of light) but the *mathematical formula describing the differences between our measurements does not share this relativity; it remains Absolute.* In other words, however much our instruments may differ, the Einstein equations — pure mathematical abstractions — will still tell what your reading will be, if we know mine, or will tell what my reading will be, if we know yours.

My measurement only exists for me as a function of my instrument and my inertial system; your measurement only exists for you as a function of your instrument and your inertial system; but the abstract mathematical relationship between our two tunnel-realities remains constant, or Absolute.

Sense date thus seems less "real" than the mathematical relationship between my sense data and your sense data.

If math is a human invention — if it doesn't descend upon us from some "Divine source" — this seems hard to explain. If, on the other hand, math does have a Divine origin, the whole philosophy of scientific materialism collapses, as hinted in Sir Arthur Edington's observation that "the universe now seems more like a great thought than a great machine." It seems, more precisely, like a great mathematical theorem.

(But poets would prefer to consider it a great poem, musicians a great symphony...)

At this point, if one has the temperament that philosophers call "naive realism," one may decide that science is just some intellectual game like the Thomist theology I told you about earlier, in which something that looks and tastes like bread really has an invisible "essence" which is the flesh and blood of a dead man. But the truth is even weirder than that: the Einstein equations, for instance, have been checked with atomic clocks in rocket ships circling the Earth, and space and time are indeed as relative as Albert thought. Strange as it seems, the abstract and spooky Virtual Reality of mathematical science does allow us to make accurate predictions about the sensory-sensual world of our ordinary "reality."

The direct experience of this "fit" between math and sense data can come as a tremendous emotional experience, as Alfred North Whitehead has noted. Indeed, the experience is not unlike that produced by great art (a fact unknown to the artists who find science "cold" and "inhuman.") I felt the shock of this "fit" between math and sense data as almost a "mystic experience" in one very trivial experiment I had to conduct in electrical engineering lab.

This experiment involved the use of an oscilloscope to measure the amplitude and direction of voltage in an alternating current system. In accord with instructions, I placed tracing paper over the screen of the oscilloscope and traced the wave form that appeared. Then I sat down and drew the wave that the equations predicted — equations involving that damned mysterious square root of minus one. Then I put the two pieces of tracing paper on top of each other.

The two waves were exactly the same.

Hundreds, thousands, of students do this experiment every day in high school labs and most of them are perfectly happy to get the "right" result, turn in their papers and get an *A* on the experiment. A few of them, here and there, stop to think, as I did, and feel an emotional-intuitive sensation so damned strange that it is not at all extravagant to call it a "mystic" shock to the system.

Somehow, the seemingly unreal world of math (which science treats as real) does connect with the seemingly real world of our senses (which science treats as largely hallucinatory.) But the further you read into the "philosophy of science" the more obvious it becomes that the connection has never been explained and looks even more mysterious today than it did 100 years ago.

Let me try to make this more clear. The invisible spooks of pure mathematical physics, including the infinitesimal and the square root of minus one, have a haunting resemblance to the invisible spooks of traditional theology, such as the Son Who is Himself His Own Father or the "invisible grace" behind the "visible symbol" of a sacrament. The difference between scientific spooks (or models) and religious spooks (or models) lies only in the fact that *you can actually use the scientific models to predict precise results in the sensory-sensual continuum* — precise as my neat fit of a physically-measured wave with a mathematically projected wave — and those predictions must work (within reasonable limits) or that model gets thrown out of science.

But why do our mathematical systems fit the "hallucinatory" world projected by our mammalian sense organs so exquisitely (as they do in the best cases)? Does the universe actually consist of mathematical abstractions? That's a rather weird thought, even if a few mathematicians, ancient and modern, have been logical enough or nutty enough to accept it. But try to imagine a continuum made up only of mathematical entities, some of them as simple and honest as 1, 2, 3, and some of them bizarre as the infinitesimal, and then try to explain how the seemingly "solid" and multi-colored world we perceive somehow emerges from that abstract and colorless "real world." Go ahead. Really try to imagine and feel it.

Then, coming back to common sense, try to figure out how humans invented mathematics, over a period of thousands and thousands of years, and in what sense this human invention — this symbolic group art work — can be more real than the bacon and eggs and coffee you can buy in a restaurant for breakfast. Can you really believe the world of our most abstract symbols is more real than the world where we drink our orange juice and flirt with the waitress?

If, on the other hand, mathematics is "less real" than the smell of the coffee, why does math have the tremendous accuracy and predictability it has shown over millenniums? Certainly, human perception can be demonstrated, in any close examination, to be much more fallible than a valid mathematical theorem.

This gets more mysterious, not less, as one looks deeper into it. The great mathematician Eric Temple Bell concluded, after a lifetime of pondering this, that *nobody has ever explained satisfactorily why mathematics has any connection at all with the world we perceive and seem to live in.*

For instance, there are four theories of how the root concepts of math can be validated: 1. the logical theory; 2. the formalist theory; 3. the intuitionist theory; and 4. the set theory.

The logical theory, pioneered by Bertrand Russell, holds that math derives from logic. Hardly anybody believes this anymore because (a) others have equally good arguments that logic derives from math and that Russell got the relationship backward, and (b) there are several competing types of logic and several competing types of math, so if we have somehow arrived at truth by any of these it was a remarkably lucky accident.

The formalist theory, pioneered by David Hilbert, still has defenders, but it amounts to treating math as a game, like playing chess in your head. This theory seems the strongest of the four, insofar as it does appear to explain how math was generated and does not lead to contradictions or Strange Loops (as the Russell theory does), but it leaves us more in the dark than ever about why math coincides so exquisitely with experiment (when it does).

The intuitionist theory of Brouwer and his associates is far more recondite and obscure than its name suggests and every single part of it is still subject to endless and violent debate. I have never been able to perfectly convince myself that I understand it, so I dare not try to explain it to others. It does not just say we obtain math by intuition and let it go at that. It develops the theory in a way that leads to such remarkable conclusions as A can be B and not-B at the same time and that you can take the Earth apart in a way that allows you to put it back together as a sphere the size of a basketball, without throwing away a single part of it.

The set theory of "Nicholas Bourbaki" (actually a group of French mathematicians, writing under one pen-name) seems very strong at present. It argues that all other parts of math derive from the root concepts of set and class, just as our computers do (i.e., from propositions like "If Joan is red-headed, she belongs to the set of red-headed people" and on to "The set of all-red headed people is smaller than the set of all people" and onward yet to abstruse technicalities about operations that define or constrain sets) — but this still leaves us unclear where and how the concepts of set and class were ever invented or validated.

Worse yet: Mathematical sets, being abstract, can yield absolutely true statements, but the sets of things in the sensory world, being concrete and quirky, never quite mesh with mathematical sets and yield only relatively true statements. Many statements are "true" or at least valid about all circles, because circles only exist in mathematical theory — any "circle" in the sensory world is only an approximation: a ring, in fact, not a pure mathematical circle. But no statements about sensory sets, like all red-headed people, can be true in that sense, since every red-head is different even in degree of redness...

However you look at it, whether we derived math from logic or from game-rules or from "intuition" or from the concept of class or set, both the actual *history* of math and the debates about "the foundations of mathematics" that have raged for over one hundred years now lead to the same conclusion: humans *somehow invented* math, just as mysteriously as they *somehow invented* language. *We don't understand how we did it, but it allows us to understand our hallucinations better.*

In short — as Einstein once said — the most incomprehensible thing about the universe is that it is comprehensible.

Taking The Name
Of The Lord In Pain

"God, God, God," I moaned.

Dr. X — not his real initial — went on manipulating my chest armor. "You're still holding back," he said, and increased the pressure.

"GOD," I howled, feeling real pain.

"That won't do," he said calmly. "Let out a scream. A real scream."

I tried to scream.

"You won't get punished," he said patiently. "Stop holding back."

I tried again. He applied new pressure at a new point. Suddenly I was screaming like a wounded animal. The sound frightened me. It seemed pre-human, like the Killer Ape in Robert Ardrey's *African Genesis*. It was the shriek of the murderer, the cannibal, the "war hero."

"That's it," he said, applying more pressure. "Let it out...let it all out..."

I screamed a Holocaust and a My Lai and then began to weep as I had never wept in my whole life. He relaxed the pressure and watched me.

I was in Reichian therapy because my previous shrink had given me lots of wonderful insights but my anxieties had never quite really gone away. Then I had read about Dr. Reich, when the Food and Drug Administration invaded his laboratory, smashed his equipment with axes, burned all his books and threw him in jail.

I didn't believe that was the proper way to settle scientific disputes, so I got interested in Dr. Reich. Eventually, I decided to try Reichian therapy.

"Breathe the way I showed you," Dr. X said.

I tried. He pushed, gently, on my stomach. "From here," he said.

I began to breathe deeply, still sobbing a bit.

153

"No more tears now," he said. "You're learning to feel your pain, but you also have to learn to feel your joy. Just relax and breathe."

I let the tears taper off slowly and went with the breathing. He pressed again on my chest and gut, gently. I went deeper into relaxation and felt the familiar warm pulsations start — just as if I were on pot. But I wasn't on pot. I was doing it by just relaxing — after my muscles were loosened up and my rage and fear had been expressed.

The pulsations got better, sexier. I was floating in the kind of bliss that Freud prudishly called "polymorphous perversity."

In a moment, Dr. X asked, "Why do you call on God when you feel your muscles start to untense?"

"I don't know. I don't believe in God."

"When did you believe in God?"

"When I was a child."

"Were you afraid of God?"

"Of course. I was raised Catholic."

"Do you think God will punish you if you express your anger?"

"My eyes..." I said.

"What?"

"I think he'll take out my eyes."

Dr. X brought an instrument over to the couch. I recognized it: an orgone shooter. "Is that an orgone shooter?" I asked.

He looked evasive for a moment, then answered. "Yes. Do you want me in jail? Go tell the A.M.A. about this." He applied the shooter to my nose-eyes-forehead area. I felt tingling and prickling for about five minutes. He asked me about my eyes and I told him about the demon with ground glass.

"Is that when the sinus attacks started?" he asked.

"Yes," I said. "But I never saw the connection before."

From about the time I heard of that ground glass demon until my mid-20s I had had periodic bouts of violent sinus headache. I have never had another sinus headache since Dr. X treated me.

Until orgone research is legal in this country again, I will never know if that symptom went away because of the muscle manipulations (which are now accepted, in one form or another, in many schools of therapy) or because of the Damned and Heretical orgone shooter. Or both working synergetically, as Dr. Reich claimed.

Those who do "know" for certain that orgone devices are unscientific remain determined that such research never will be legal.

It all reminds me of the Sister Kenny story. I seem to go around getting cured of various things by methods that aren't officially supposed to cure anything.

Maybe I am "suggestible." Or — maybe, just maybe — the A.M.A. is no more infallible than the Pope, or Trotsky, or Ayn Rand...

INFORMATION DOUBLES AGAIN ... EVERYBODY GETS A CAR

By 1900, when my father was eight years old, information had doubled again. The process had only taken 150 years this time.

That year Max Planck published his first paper on quantum mechanics, beginning the process by which science in this century would gradually abandon Aristotelian logic and evolve in a non-Aristotelian, almost Buddhist direction. We were learning that the "one" "objective" Aristotelian "real world" previously posited by all Western thought existed only as a concept in our linguistic structures: that the only worlds we knew were plural and created by our senses and scientific instruments, all of them uncertain to some degree and all of them given structure by the inbuilt hardware and software of our senses and instruments.

The Boer war was raging in South Africa, as the English and Dutch fought over which of them should govern and exploit the native Black population. In China, the Boxer Rebellion represented another of the countless efforts by Third World peoples to throw off the domination of any and all white conquerors, British, Dutch or whoever.

In 1900 also the king of Italy was assassinated by idealists who thought the liberation of the workers could be achieved by murdering the Masters one by one. In Russia, Lenin returned from three-years exile in Siberia, and went on plotting to liberate the workers by organized world revolution. The International Ladies Garment Workers Union was formed in New York by those who thought the workers could be liberated by forming coalitions and bargaining collectively with the Masters.

All this followed, inevitably, from the general increase in living standards throughout the Industrial world. In the new Second Wave civilizations, the ruling class was living maybe 100 times better than the ruling class of ancient Rome; the middle classes were living better than ever before; and the idea that even the lower order had the right to a decent life, formulated by the most radical thinkers of the 18th Century, continued to reassert itself, in dozens of forms now forgotten in addition to the two forms we all know:

(1) the Democratic Socialism which, by learning to co-exist with free enterprise, has permanently improved life in Europe, Canada and most of the industrial world, outside the U.S.; and (2) the Totalitarian Socialism of Marx, which has recently collapsed after making a mess of all its Utopian dreams.

Also in 1900... Major Walter Reed discovered that yellow fever was not contagious by persuading volunteers to sleep with blankets taken from fever victims who had died, and then he correctly deduced and later proved that the fever was spread by a mosquito. Mendel's great essay on genetics, ignored for 35 years, was suddenly rediscovered by the scientific community. Freud published *The Interpretation of Dreams.*

Human life span in the U.S. had quantum-jumped to 47 years. *For the first time in history, a newborn human had a good chance of living longer than 30 years.*

Also in 1900... The U.S. Navy bought its first submarine, and the Kodak company sold its first camera.

Only one U.S. home in seven had a bathtub. As Sinclair Lewis records, the Reagan-Bush mentalities of the period often said, "Why give bathtubs to the poor? They'll only put coal in them."

Brooks Adams had already published *The Law of Civilization and Decay,* in which the Westward movement of Capital throughout history was documented for the first time. Adams did not realize that this trajectory was, more fundamentally, a movement of information — capital being the fruit of technology, i.e., of *information that is totally accurate* — but he did see that, if the trend continued, the English Empire would collapse by about 1950 and be replaced by an American Empire.

AN INTERVIEW WITH
ROBERT ANTON WILSON

From ROC Magazine

ROC: Who are your favorite writers?

WILSON: You'd learn more about me if you asked who are my favorite film directors. However, my favorite writers are Joyce, Chandler, Faulkner, Mark Twain and H.P. Lovecraft. Joyce taught me multiple vision — looking at the same scene from several angles. Chandler taught me to dread sloppy sentences and pay attention to every word, every rhythm. Faulkner and Mark Twain showed me how to employ my "unique" (or eccentric) talents, which are essentially humorous and satirical, in a way that can include "serious," even tragic, subjects. Lovecraft gave me my basic technique of mixing real facts with fantasy in such a way that the reader is genuinely disoriented and unsure about where one leaves off and the other begins. H.P.L. used that kind of literary "counterfeiting" only to make his horrors more horrible, which I've copied, but I also use it to make my jokes into real intellectual time-bombs, like Zen riddles.

ROC: Why did you say we should have asked about your favorite film directors?

WILSON: I suspect movies have shaped my mind more than books have. Orson Welles' late films are a much stronger influence on my novels than any books have been — or any theories about deconstructionism and postmodernism either. The way a Welles film turns around in your mind, reversing its meanings and melting into endless ambiguities, is the way my novels function. The montages of Eisenstein and the cross-cutting between parallel suspense themes in Griffith and Hitchcock also shaped a lot of my nonlinear narrative structures. And I have a great affinity with the Monty Python group; I always try to build up to the kind of controlled, logically consistent lunacy that's their specialty. To me, the world — especially the world of politics —

seems more like a Monty Python routine than it seems like a mainstream "realistic" novel.

ROC: Why do you live in Los Angeles?

WILSON: Well, you know what Willie Sutton said when a psychologist asked him why he robbed banks: "That's where the money is." Los Angeles is where the money is. I've had several of my novels optioned, but none have gone all the way to production. I want to live to see at least one of them actually produced as a film. My only regret is that Orson Welles isn't alive to direct it.

ROC: Your books all seem to combine horror, humor, sex and philosophy. How did you select that formula?

WILSON: Those topics just overwhelmed me when I started looking at the world and trying to understand it; I didn't choose them. Horror is the natural reaction to the last 5000 years of history, from the first Bronze Age armies setting out to enslave their neighbors right up to having an old CIA hand like George Bush sitting in the Oval Office, plotting wars and invasions and lecturing us about his "pro-life" morality. Humor is the only mental health technique I know that allows us to go on living in such a mad, mendacious, clandestine world. I survive with relative sanity, for instance, because when I was growing up in Brooklyn, *bush* meant pubic hair and *quayle* meant vagina. Amid the madness of our times, I can read the headlines without totally wigging out because I remember it's just Pubic Hair and Vagina making pretentious speeches, and it all seems like a surrealist novel. Like something I might have written myself, in fact.

ROC: That covers the horror and humor. How about the sex and philosophy?

WILSON: My novels are all about fear, and how people cope with it. Sex is the hidden core of every anxiety, except for those pure survival terrors that result directly from bad politics and bad economics. As for philosophy, we're all philosophers to some degree. We're all trying to figure out how to cope with this predicament called history, or how to get out of it. That's philosophy, if you're doing it for yourself. If you need help, it's psychotherapy or a Twelve Step program.

ROC: Your next three novels are all fantasy. Why did you switch over from science-fiction?

WILSON: I didn't switch. "Science-fiction" and "fantasy" are just merchandising labels. I would call my books "gonzo ontology" or maybe "postmodernist slapstick," but they don't have a shelf for that in the bookstores. I'm writing about the same theme in all of my novels — "the nightmare of history" — and the books are all parts of one continuous saga, tracing the ups-and-downs of five or six families over the time span 1750-2000 AD. Some of the later parts of the story got published before some of the early parts, but it's all one continuous yarn — the transformation of human society from the agricultural/religious/Sun King/slave-and-serf era to the industrial/secular/democratic/capitalist-vs.-socialist stage and onward into the Green/computer/psychedelics/space age.

ROC: When you put it that way, it sounds as if you have some kind of mainstream realistic saga buried underneath all your fantasy and *grotesquerie*. Would you agree?

WILSON: In a sense. But I don't like what's generally considered "realistic" fiction (I regard Joyce as a premature postmodernist.) I think borderline literature, such as sci-fi and fantasy, is closer to human experience than the conventional "realistic" novel. For instance, Victorian "realists" were very evasive, or downright dishonest, about sex. Modern "realists" are equally afraid of the macabre — the element of the inexplicable and anomalistic or the so-called "paranormal" that enters everybody's life some time or other. What is called "reality" is always a set of conventions based on what people have agreed not to mention in public. To breech those conventions creates anxiety, and that's why there's always hostility toward those crossing the border into the antipodes of the psyche. Those of us who do cross the border are regarded as the literary equivalent of crack dealers.

ROC: If your novels are about social evolution, as you seem to imply, why do you put every part of the story in the form of a conflict between secret societies or rival conspiracies?

WILSON: For several reasons. I'm trying to cross borders, as I said — to break all the taboos that constrict our thinking. One of the major taboos when I was in college was "Thou shalt not think about conspiracies." Only a certain limited class of conspiracies could be discussed, and only by officers of the courts, within the parameters of the criminal conspiracy statutes. To think beyond that was allegedly paranoia, or at least "extremism." I started to challenge that after the Kennedy assassination, and the first thing I discovered was that if you keep an open mind and examine alternative conspiracy theories impartially and critically, you will immediately get denounced by two groups — those who still have the taboo against thinking about this subject at all, and those who believe they are such clever fellows that they have uncovered the One Real Worldwide Conspiracy which controls everything. The first group calls you paranoid and the second group claims you're a CIA agent assigned to confuse people and muddle the search for truth. I found this amusing once I saw how mechanical it was: all the real paranoids think I'm a government agent and all the people without a sense of humor think I'm a paranoid.

ROC: In all your research, have you ever come close to believing in the One Big Conspiracy that controls everything?

WILSON: Never. There are three basic attitudes toward the universe: atheism, polytheism and monotheism. Metaphorically, you can apply these views to history also. Atheist history says it all happened by accident, polytheism says it happened as the clash of rival forces, and monotheism says it happened because of one dominant intelligence. I don't believe everything happens by accident, so atheism is out for me. On the other hand, I agree with H.L. Mencken, who said he wasn't a monotheist because the world looked to him like it was designed by a committee. The world would make some kind of sense if there was one group of "insiders" who really run everything. Since the world obviously doesn't make any sense, there is no such group. There are just rival coalitions trying to become the group that runs the world, which is probably just as hopeless as trying to become God and "run" the universe. These Apes of God all get defeated in the end by what I call the Snafu Principle.

ROC: What's that?

WILSON: In the power game, the more successful you become, the more motive people have for lying to you. They lie to flatter you, to avoid contradicting your prejudices, to keep their jobs, to tell you what you want to hear, etc. Have you ever told the truth, the whole truth, to anybody from the government?

It's the same in any authoritarian organization, be it an army, a corporation or a patriarchal family. People say what those in power above them want to hear. In the big power struggles, the most successful conspiracy of the decade becomes the stupidest conspiracy of the next decade, because it never hears what might offend its self-image. *Communication is only possible between equals.* The power game creates total communication jam and everybody near the top drifts slowly but inexorably into a kind of schizoid fantasy. Then they get replaced by younger, hungrier predators who are not successful enough yet to frighten everybody into lying to them, and hence have at least a partial knowledge of what the hell is really going on.

ROC: You said you had several reasons for writing about rival conspiracies. What are your other reasons?

WILSON: Well, in addition to the above sociological analysis, or parody of a sociological analysis, I have literary and artistic preferences. One big conspiracy is mere melodrama, but dozens of rival conspiracies are black comedy. I tend to see the universe more as black comedy than as melodrama. Also, in a book, dozens of conspiracies create that irony and ambiguity that seem to me the basic features of human life, since men and women are creatures who always try to find a pattern or meaning in what's happening to them, and most of what happens to us is so god-awful and senseless that every possible pattern or meaning eventually becomes dubious; your favorite model or map of history may be *part* of the truth, but something bigger and weirder is obviously going on. In modern physics, the researchers realize they need more than one model to cover the data. My view of history and politics is that we need more than one model there, too. Whenever people are certain they understand our peculiar situation here on this planet, it is because they have accepted a religious Faith or a secular Ideology (Ideologies are the modern form of Faiths) and just stopped thinking. If you don't stop thinking, you will finally face the Chaos that every one of my heroes and heroines eventually confronts.

ROC: You seem to push all your characters into situations, not just of physical danger, but of psychological emergency. They all seem to reach a point where they're about to snap. Why is that?

WILSON: Well, you can't really convey true physical fear on the printed page; you can only approximate it. Only Grand Opera and films, hitting all nervous centers at once, can really knock the audience over emotionally with straight melodrama. Indiana Jones hanging off a cliff in a film hits you in a way that printed words never hit you. Books can't compete on that level. But books can create an eerie ambiance, a psychological *malaise,* that you can't get onto a stage or a film screen. For instance, if your hero is not just in prison, awaiting execution, but then is visited by an official who offers him a deal, which may be a complicated double-cross...and if your character worries that this official may be a hallucination because anybody left in isolation long enough will hallucinate, and if you can hint the visitor may actually be a demon or an extraterrestrial zoo-keeper, then the reader really does share your character's doubt and anxiety. Especially if you have built up to it by presenting some good arguments that every mind, *including the reader's,* can snap and start hallucinating under sufficient stress, and that the case for demons and extraterrestrials is stronger than we generally realize... You see? The deepest fear is the fear that you can't trust your own mind — that your sanity may be lost, or at least your ideas may be inadequate to explain what's happening around you. The whole human race has been experiencing that to some extent ever since 1750, when the industrial revolution started to break up the dogmas and traditions that have governed us since the Bronze Age.

ROC: Conspiracy, then, functions largely as metaphor for you? A way of communicating the uncertainty and ambiguity of the modern world?

WILSON: To a great extent, yes. A world of clandestine groups engaged in covert operations is a world of uncertainty. To try to grasp it, you have to start thinking like a quantum physicist — in terms of indeterminacy and probability, not in terms of religious or ideological dogmas. The period I have chosen to record, 1750-2000 AD, is the age in which certitude died and more and more of us had to confront what Nietzsche called the Abyss. But I also write about conspiracies because conspiracies exist. The KGB once set up a bank in San Jose, California, to monitor computer corporations and see who might be in financial hot water and willing to sell U.S. military technology for a suitable bribe. They even had profiles of financial irregularities to identify which executives had expensive mistresses, which had cocaine habits, and so on. That's true, it really happened, but it sounds like one of my plots, doesn't it? And it's typical, rather than unique. Half the citizens of California are conspiring to get enough marijuana for next Saturday's party, and the U.S. government is conspiring to prevent them from doing that. The arts-and-literature world is a constant warfare between rival conspiracies, which call themselves "schools of art" or "schools of literature" or "affinity groups" — but each "school" or "affinity group" looks like a damned self-serving conspiracy to those outside it. Corporations continually get caught buying Congress-entities (I am trying to avoid the human chauvinism of saying "Congresspersons") or fixing prices or lying to the public about safety issues or even paying for CIA covert operations. The Vatican conspires to make the Western world Catholic again, or at least make us obey Catholic laws, and the Freemasons plot to keep us Protestant. The Arabs, whenever they stop conspiring against each other, get together and conspire to take some of the power away from the Western "imperialists." Washington, the lethal crown of world power, is such a hotbed of rival conspiracies that Henry Kissinger once said, "Anybody here who isn't paranoid must be crazy." In a world like this, the liberal dogma that no conspiracies ever effect history is on all fours with the Flat Earth theory or trying to cure cancer with the hair of the seventh son of a seventh son.

ROC: If conspiracy is more than a convenient literary metaphor to you, how many conspiracies do you think really exist?

WILSON: At minimum, two. Whenever any coalition gets enough power to seem to be "in control" of any hunk of land, another gang starts plotting to unseat them. Conspiracy, as Prof. Carl Oglesby once said, is "the normal continuation of normal politics by normal means." The maximum number of conspiracies is something I wouldn't try to guess, but it seems to have been steadily increasing in the last 200 years, just as population and information and technology have increased.

ROC: You seem serious about this, and yet in all of your books, you carry this multiple conspiracy theme to the point where it becomes absurd. Why?

WILSON: In my own way, I am some sort of realist. I only carry this theme, or any theme, to the degree of absurdity that precisely corresponds to the madness of the world that I read about in the newspapers.

ROC: But you *are* satirizing conspiracy buffs part of the time.

WILSON: I am satirizing everybody part of the time. I am also satirizing myself, and the techniques I use to obliterate the line between "reality" and "fantasy." Every kind of novel is a species of magic trick and a close relative of the con-game. As somebody said, art is lies that look like truth. A so-called "realistic" Leonardo-style painting, or pre-modernist painting, is *a two-dimensional object that almost convinces you it's three dimensional.* It was only after modern art appeared that we could see how magical and weird that kind of "realism" is. Every affinity group looks like a conspiracy from outside. Every conspiracy thinks of itself as an affinity group, and only becomes a true conspiracy in the legal sense when it creates "lies that look like truth" — when it becomes magic, or a con-game, or a cognate of the art tricks that look like "realism." Where does fraud leave off and art or entertainment begin? If you could tell worthless bonds at sight, nobody would ever buy them. In certain meditative states well-known in the Orient and among pot-heads, the difference between a "real" dollar and a counterfeit becomes obliterated; they're both just pretty designs on paper. A counterfeit dollar could even become worth more than a "real" dollar, if a popular artist put a frame around it and exhibited it in a gallery. I was in a TV documentary called "Borders" recently — which was about the vanishing of borders in our world — and when I saw the final cut, it included an artist who declared an air conditioner at the Museum of Modern Art to be a work of modern art itself and wanted credit for discovering it; I can only congratulate him for crossing more borders than I have. If I said "game" instead of "conspiracy" throughout this interview, many sociologists would say I'm just popularizing their analysis of how society works. My novels look like melodramas part of the time and then switch over and look like black comedies, but isn't that true of politics also? If you believe somebody's war propaganda, the world is pure melodrama — the good guys versus the bad guys. If you start doubting all propaganda, the world becomes black comedy — "a darkling plain /swept by confused alarms of struggle and flight /where ignorant armies clash by night," i.e., a more violent and ugly version of the Three Stooges. I can't see things from every possible perspective, but I try to see them from enough kinky new angles that my books never degenerate into war propaganda for any of the ignorant armies that go on clashing by night.

THE PROBLEM OF "REALITY"

Another Look At An Old Riddle

> The pure and simple truth is rarely pure and never
> simple.   — Oscar Wilde

One day when I was still in Brooklyn Tech I was browsing in the public library and found a book with the title *Science and Sanity* by somebody called Alfred Korzybski. I sampled a few pages and saw that Korzybski had tackled the Big Questions (or Wig Questions) about how scientific "reality" relates (if at all) to ordinary sensory "reality." I checked the book out and took it home to read.

Later I met many people interested in Korzybski's ideas and none of them ever seemed to believe me when I said I read *Science and Sanity* in one week-end, the first time. Well, I did...and it dazzled me. And then I returned it to the library and went and bought a copy, because I knew I would have to re-read it several times before I could hope to understand it fully.

Even at first reading, I could see that Korzybski had the answer to at least one question that had perplexed me for years — namely, What is "reality?" According to Korzybski, the only correct way to answer the question begins with recognizing that "reality" is — *a word.*

This seems either too obvious or not obvious at all to most people, at first glance anyway. Nonetheless, "reality," like "sex" and "communism" and "breakfast" and "horse-radish" and "Thursday" etc. happens to exist as a word in the English language. All words have multiple meaning<u>s</u> (plural) and therefore the word "reality" has many meaning<u>s.</u>

To explain by analogy: the word "sex" means any or all of the following: the normal method of reproduction among animals more complex than amoebas, violent rape in an alley, Jack tenderly making love to Jill, Jack making love to Joe, Jack masturbating, Jill making love to Jane, male-female cunnilingus, female-female cunnilingus, male-female fellatio, male-male fellatio, two dogs fucking in the street, Jack having a fantasy about making love to Marilyn Monroe, a hard-core porn movie, a soft-core porn movie, a painting of a nude by Renoir, Jill simply hugging Jack when he feels depressed, Jill in childbirth, Jill nursing her baby, a *Playboy* centerfold, a necrophile in a morgue, the Marquis de Sade flogging a whore and paying her to flog him in return, etc. etc.

Millions of events occur in space-time, each one different and in some respects unique, and onto many of them we affix the label, "sex," which *helps us classify things but also lulls us into forgetting their differences.*

Similarly, millions of events occur in our nervous systems, each one different and in some respects unique, and onto many of them we affix the label "reality," which *helps us classify things but also lulls us into forgetting their differences.*

Thus, it does not appear accurate to say the world of our perceptions — the sensory-sensual world — "is real," which implies that everything else "is unreal." More accurately, we should say that we find it convenient to *label that world as "real"* most of the time, and that sometimes we have to revise the label and replace it with "optical illusion" or "hallucination" or "maya" or whatever.

And it does not appear accurate, either, to say that the world of our most abstract concepts — the mathematical-scientific world — "is real," which implies that anything else, including the sensory world of ordinary perception (or of Art, or of marijuana) "are all unreal." More accurately, we should say that *we find it convenient to use specific mathematical models to solve specific problems,* and that sometimes we have to throw out one model and create a completely new model.

The world *is not* the colorful model created by our senses or the abstract and colorless mathematical models created by our frontal cortex. These merely represent various ways of making maps of the world. The conflict between Art and Science turns out to be a conflict between different maps, and no one map shows "everything." A political map is not inaccurate because it shows a different reality-tunnel from a weather map. A geological map is not wrong because it shows a third reality-tunnel. Etc.

Up to this point, Korzybski has just found an unusually precise way to repeat what several scientific philosophers c. 1870-1930 had already begun to realize. But then came his truly original thought — one that still seems to stagger people over half a century after he wrote:

> *Any proposition containing the word "is" creates a linguistic structural confusion which will eventually give birth to serious fallacies.*

In other words, to begin to make sense of any proposition presented to us we have to reformulate it without any form of the verb "is" or its cognates ("be," "being," etc.) This runs directly against our earliest and deepest conditioning, and trying to apply it creates a sense of stress similar to some yogic or Gurdjieffian exercises. (David Bourland, a commentator on Korzybski, has noted that Korzybski himself relapsed into using some form of "is" in 37% of the sentences in *Science and Sanity*.)

However, if we can succeed in abolishing "isness" from our concepts we find ourselves forced into writing (*and thinking*) in the manner that physicists call Operationalism and modern philosophers call Existentialism.

For instance, if we try to rewrite "Men are more visually oriented than women" without the is-of-identity we soon find out if our observation belongs in the Operational-scientific area or in the Existentialist-subjective area. In the former case we re-write it (and scientifically limit it) as something like "In our study of 67 white males, 33 nonwhite males, 70 white females and 31 nonwhite females, all of them reared within American culture, we found 85 percent of the males and only 67 percent of the females showed rapid eye response to visual material." Note that, as we operationalize and limit our statement, we leave open the possibility that further research on people raised in Europe, Asia or Africa might modify or even nullify our generalization. We also force ourselves to note and remember that any generalization about a class or set, *Outside Pure Mathematics,* refers to some-but-not-all members of that set.

(I have coined the word "sombunall" to make this clearer. See my book, *The New Inquisition,* New Falcon Publications, 1987.)

Even more crucial, if, after removing the "is" we find that all we write consists of, "I think I've observed that men notice

visual material quicker than women," we have limited our statement even more and, in doing so, have learned a lesson that may
prevent us from one of the more common types of uncritical
over-generalizations. In the rewriting we "discovered" no hard
evidence but only anecdotal subjective impressions.

Or consider: "This is a second-rate book." Rewriting without
the "is," there seems no possible operational content to this statement, because we lack instruments or techniques to establish
first-rateness and second-rateness in literature. We therefore
must assign this to the existential realm and state precisely, "This
seems like a second-rate book to me."

Language without "isness" seems so important to me that I
have written one book entirely without "is" — my *Quantum
Psychology* (New Falcon Publications, 1990.) Mostly, however, I
prefer to frame the word with dubious quotation marks, indicating irony — "is" instead of is — and rewriting without "is" only
in passages demanding maximum clarity.

Before moving on, I would like to explain the Korzybski
critique of language a bit further, in terms of a metaphor that
Korzybski considered very useful.

*The map is not the territory.** In using this proverb-like statement — which he repeats many times — Korzybski intends to
convey many things:

Our words are *not* the sense impressions they denote (the word
"water" will not make you wet.)

Our sense impressions are *not* the events in space-time which
trigger these impressions. (When a rock hurts you, the hurt is not
"in" the rock but in the interaction of the rock with your senses.)

Our scientific or philosophical or religious models (orches-
trations of words and other symbols) are *not* the non-verbal
universe they seek to describe or explain;

The menu does *not* taste like the meal or have the same nutri-
ents or additives as the meal; etc.

---

* Bourland would rewrite this as "We should not confuse the map with
the territory," to avoid any use of "is." I, however, agree with Korzybski that the denial of identification (as in "is not") has opposite neurolinguistic effects on the brain from the assertion of identity (as in "is")
and therefore I see no harm in "is not."

In short, our mental filing cabinet may serve us well — or serve us very poorly — in classifying and comprehending the world, but even in the best case, where it serves us very well (for a while...) we should never confuse it with the world.

The map does not show all the territory. A map of Los Angeles that showed "all" of Los Angeles would have to occupy the same space as Los Angeles and hence would not serve as a map at all. Also, to show "all" about Los Angeles, the map would have to include *time* and evolve as L.A. has over a period of aeons, from an uninhabited desert, to a temporary camp of Native Americans, to a small Spanish mission, etc. up to the present and on into the future indefinitely.

Note that the "lowest" forms of bigotry — e.g., statements about "all Jews," "all Blacks," "all men," "all women" etc. — implicitly assume that a "map" (model) does show all the territory. *Since no map or model can do this, training in Korzybski's semantics might cure racism, sexism and similar dangerous follies quicker than any other educational technique.* But note also that even the more sophisticated and educated bigotries — e.g., the scientists convinced that they have the only correct theory and all scientists with rival theories "are" "incompetent" "dolts" — rest upon a similar delusion about having a map that can show *all* the territory.

Once we have a map, we can make a map of the map, and a map of the map of the map, etc.

On the simplest level, this means that once humans have sense impressions they can (unlike any other known animals) make "maps" and models to classify and organize these impressions.

Once I learn the word "chair," I can classify everything in the house into "chairs" and "not-chairs."

Later, I can make a map of this map of a map and classify chairs into the larger category of "furniture," and so on, until I come to concepts like "the Gross National Product" and find myself developing an economic model of the world, or until I come to concepts like "energy" and "mass" and start developing a mathematical-physical model, or until I come to 92 "elements" and start developing a chemical model, etc.

There seems no reason to believe this process of mapping our mapping of mapping etc. ("abstracting to ever-higher levels") has any termination. Already we have sciences like physical chemistry, mathematical biology, sociobiology, neurogenetics, neurolinguistics, psychoneuroimmunology etc. etc.

Once we grow accustomed to thinking of maps in conjunction with maps of maps, and maps of maps of maps etc., it becomes easy to work our way out of the confusions about "reality" which have perplexed many others besides myself.

Our first-order map — "raw" sense data — has one kind of "reality," in the sense that it reveals something about what sort of world we live in and how our brains classify their impressions.

Our second-order maps, i.e., maps of maps — simple folk-wisdom or "brute empiricism" like the traditional "red sky at morning, sailor take warning" or the momentous discovery that women do not give birth if they haven't had sexual intercourse with a male — have "reality" if they work and also have some fallacy, as we discover when some of them don't work. (I don't know about that "red sky at morning," personally...)

Third order maps — maps of maps of maps — like astrology and reading omens etc. often contain a lot of "reality" mixed with fantasy.

Fourth order maps, like primitive algebra and early physics, have another degree of "reality," etc.

Fifth order maps — like the abstract mathematical models of a colorless and decentered world I have discussed earlier — have another degree of "reality."

From this perspective, the naive scientists who claim these high order maps "are" "reality" seem as semantically ignorant as the artists who recoil from this kind of map because they think *if this "is reality" than all ordinary life and perception, including artistic perception, "is not reality."*

Since the ultimate map of all maps which includes *all* the territory of existence does not exist, and we cannot even imagine how to produce it, the best we can say of any reality-tunnel — sensory or mathematically abstract, philosophical or "superstitious," created by our tribe or by a different (and therefore "inferior") tribe, "scientific" or "political" or "artistic" — can only consist of, "This map here seems to work pretty well for my purposes, in most cases, so far." (Or, in more academic language, "The data does not yet justify revising the theory.")

Every "reality" remains relative to the instrument used in detecting or measuring it. In most cases, for most humans, in ordinary life, the instrument that determines our "realities" — or reality-tunnels, more accurately — remains our nervous system in general and our brain in particular.

All of this does not derive directly from what Korzybski wrote in *Science and Sanity* in 1933, or what I read in that book when I discovered it circa 1949. It derives also from the many other scientists and philosophers whose works Korzybski cited and I then read (especially Wittgenstein, Bohr, Bridgman, Whitehead and Poincaré) and from others who wrote on language and communication after Korzybski (especially Shannon, Whorf, McLuhan and Bateson.) I have merely found the Korzybski model the most general and useful "bag" into which the insights of other linguistic analysts could all blend into a coherent whole system.

I perhaps have seen Korzybski in a different light than many other commentators because I re-read him several times while on marijuana. On grass, it seems quite easy to understand that allegedly "raw" perception contains as much inference and orga-nization-or-orchestration as our more obviously brain-generated mathematical formalisms or religious dogmas.

If I have managed to make Korzybski clear the reader should now understand that the redness of roses belongs to the realm of our sensory experience, while the no-color of atoms belongs to the realm of our most abstract brain software. You should also see why social scientists have largely given up the word "reality" entirely and speak of glosses or grids or models or (the term from Tim Leary I find clearest of all) reality-tunnels.

To attribute "reality" to any one level of abstraction, from the most sensory to the most theoretical, implicitly damns other levels to "non-reality" even though they, too, represent normal human experience.

I found all this very helpful in understanding Einstein — every instrument, like every brain, creates a different reality-tunnel, and our highest brain functions creates mathematical models to translate the different reality-tunnels into *abstractions that serve science even though they contradict sensory or Existential experience.*

Around about the time I digested all this and finally accepted the colorless mathematical abstractions of pure physics as "*a* reality" but not "*the* reality," and sense-data as another "reality" but not "*the* reality," I went through my annual re-reading of Joyce's *Ulysses.* To my astonishment, it now appeared that Joyce had not only written a great Freudian-Jungian "psychological novel," but had also written the first novel based entirely on Relativity. In *Ulysses* every narrator (or "narrative voice") acts like an instrument recording a different reality-tunnel, and the reader, like a mathematician, gradually intuits an abstract structure that seems to "contain" all of these, or at least allows them to co-exist as Existential Reports from various psychological "inertial systems."

For instance, just as four space-ships can measure four lengths of the same river, in Einstein Physical Relativity, four narrators can see the same dog four ways, in Joycean Existential Relativity.

Garry Owen, the dog in question, represents one of the nearly-a-hundred "real, live" Dubliners who got incorporated into Joyce's "fiction." A pedigreed Irish Setter, Garry (born, 1888, therefore 16 years old when the events of *Ulysses* occur on 16 June 1904) belonged to one J.J. Giltrap and first appears in the Good Book as seen by a drunk with gonorrhea and a bad opinion of everybody, who describes Garry as a mangy, dirty and unfriendly beast. The next "instrument" Joyce uses, the voice of an Animal Lover with a penchant for Theosophy, insists that Garry has imbibed so much "humane culture" that he actually recites poetry in classic Gaelic. (The one sample of Garry's verse provided to us scans well and vehemently curses a Dublin publican for not placing a water pale on the floor for thirsty dogs.) A third voice, that of a sentimental young girl, sees Garry as a "lovely dog, so human he almost talked." The last voice, that of Bloom in the cabman's shelter, describes Garry as a savage and terrifying hound. The reader recognizes the Relativity of these "instruments" and registers only the abstract Cosmological Constant: all readings agree in classifying the animal as a member of the canine species.

The Absolute canineness or dogginess of Garry Owen, however, has the same abstraction as the mathematics of colorless infinitesimals. We have arrived at it by abstracting — by discarding or forgetting the individual habits, physiognomy, temperament etc. of the concrete Garry Owen in sensory-sensual space-time. To put those sensory-sensual or "colorful" characteristics back into our picture of Garry, we must leave the arena of scientific "truth" and return to the Existential level, where every instrument (or brain) reports a slightly different hound.

If the reader thinks of *Citizen Kane* and *Roshomon* now, she or he might realize why, after reading Korzybski, I have always felt a deep similarity between modern science and modern art, and have wondered why the two always seem to misunderstand each other.

ATTACK OF THE
DOG-FACED DEMONS

In a farm in Mendocino, 1972, I was preparing for the Mass of the Phoenix, a ritual designed by Aleister Crowley in which the magician attempts to activate his "True Will." I had taken 250 micrograms of Acid, played some Beethoven, and, when I felt ready, I went to my makeshift Altar and began the Invocation.

> East of the Altar see me stand
> With Light and Musick in mine hand!

I lifted the Cakes of Light and chanted the next lines:

> This Bread I eat. This Oath I swear
> As I enflame myself with prayer:
> "There is no grace: there is no guilt:
> This is the Law: DO WHAT THOU WILT!"

Suddenly, the room was invaded by dog-faced demons who formed a ring around me. They were black and quite sinister, and they slavered or frothed a bit at the mouth, and they looked quite as solid as the bed and writing table behind them.

Oh, *damn*, I thought. Crowley always warned us this sort of thing could happen, but I never took that seriously. I thought it was another of his jokes. Now what do I do?

On one level I was seriously frightened; but on another level, I felt confident of my hard-learned ability to navigate in the Infernal regions of psychedelic space — or in the qliphotic astral realm, or whatever you want to call this particularly unlovely reality-tunnel.

I recalled something from H.P. Lovecraft: "Do not call up any that you cannot put down." That was not helpful. But then I remembered from some book on shamanism: "If you feed Them, they will become Allies instead of Foes."

I concentrated on party food and the Altar was suddenly full of shrimp cocktails with hot red sauce. I hadn't planned that, and it surprised and amused me. I had unconsciously invoked one of my favorite snacks.

I began distributing the shrimp cocktails to the demons. They accepted them and then turned into all the nuns I remembered from my grammar school days. They also shrunk into rather comic dwarfs. In school they had been bigger than me, but now I was bigger than them. The had lost all ability to terrify me.

I started to laugh, and realized the ritual was, in one sense, ruined. (In another sense, it had been a great success...) I broke the circle and "grounded" the energy as the nuns faded away.

Then I sprawled on the bed and laughed like a blithering idiot for a half hour. That was one of the many, many times I felt totally convinced that all the "entities" invoked in Magick are parts of our own minds.

Then the room started to shake. The bed was jumping like a scene from *The Exorcist* and the whole house seemed to shift on its moorings.

Just another California earthquake. Coincidence. Only a minor trembler, actually. It would be best to not even think of it as synchronicity. I banished all "superstitious" thoughts from my mind, firmly.

It was about two months later that I began to think I was receiving telepathic communications from Sirius.

INFANTICIDE ... & RUMORS
OF BLACK MAGICK

After two years in Ireland, it still seemed wonderful to me, but no longer quite so mystical and mysterious. Arlen and I were living in Howth, a little fishing village and art colony north of Dublin mentioned in the first sentence of *Finnegans Wake:*

 ...back to Howth Castle and Environs.

After over 30 years study of the Good Book, I had finally crossed from the unmarked state to the marked state (in the terminology of G. Spencer Brown's *Laws of Form*) and found myself living in its first sentence.

Then the Kerry Baby Case broke and the whole country proceeded to provide me with a classic anthropological demonstration that you can never fully understand a culture in which you weren't raised.

It began on 14 April 1984, when the body of a newborn infant boy was found on the beach at Cahiriciveen, in southwest County Kerry, dead of 28 stab wounds.

If you try to imagine yourself stabbing a baby once, you will feel revulsion and disgust, but trying to imagine the kind of person who could stab an infant 28 times, trying to really understand the mind that could do this, is to experience vertigo and raw horror. Naturally, rumors of Satanism and human sacrifice were soon circulating among the farm people (Kerry is almost entirely rural); but that was only the overture to the malign fiesta that followed.

After the Cahiriciveen baby was found, the Irish police (popularly called the Guards, although the correct Irish word is *gardai*) did not spend much time looking under beds for Satanists. They very intelligently went looking for a an unmarried woman who had been visibly pregnant and was no longer pregnant.

In a Catholic country where abortion is illegal, that makes sense. I had discovered this when researching an article on "the abortion situation in Ireland." I had interviewed a woman from the Well Woman Center in Dublin, which arranges English abortions for Irishwomen. She had told me, "In places like Kerry, they never heard of centers like this. Infanticide is their form of abortion."

On 1 May 1984 the Guards found one Joanne Hayes, 25, of Abbeydorney, about 70 miles from Cahiriciveen. The Guards also learned that local gossip said Joanne had been having an affair with a married man, Jeremiah Locke; that she had appeared pregnant to some neighbors; and that she had been treated for the aftereffects of a miscarriage on 15 April — one day after the Cahiriciveen baby was found. The whole Hayes family was brought in for questioning — Joanne, two brothers, a sister, the mother and a senile aunt, Bridie. Within eight hours all had confessed that the Cahiriciveen baby was Joanne's, that she had stabbed it to death, and that the two brothers had driven the tiny corpse 70 miles to dump it on the beach.

I'm sure the Guards felt well satisfied with themselves. Six confessions in eight hours. Quick, efficient work. Case closed. Nobody inquired into the savagery of Joanne's alleged crime — the psychotic fury of the 28 separate stab wounds.

Five members of the family were released on bail. Joanne, who had appeared normal before arrest, was removed to a mental hospital in Limerick in a catatonic state, mute, semi-paralyzed.

THE INWARD-TURNING SPIRAL

"Time Is An Illusion"

We were living in San Miguel de Allende, which is in the hills northwest of Mexico City. It was 1971, and my earnings from my new career as free-lance writer had been meager for several months; worse, my savings from the years at *Playboy* were running out. When a royalty check arrived in the mail, it seemed so large to me that, after depositing it in the bank, I insisted on taking Arlen and the kids out to lunch. Afterwards, the kids wandered off to see some friends and I took Arlen to a silver shop to buy her some jewelry.

She said that I had to buy something for myself, too, so I looked around the shop and finally picked out a silver ring, with an inward-turning spiral design. I have worn it ever since.

A picture of me, in which that ring appears rather conspicuous, appeared on the jacket of one or two of my books. From then on, whenever I went out on the lecture circuit, people would ask me what the ring "symbolized." (Many people appear to believe I am a deep and mysterious fellow and that everything I do or say has hidden mystical and symbolic meanings.) I started thinking about the ring myself.

An inward-turning spiral, I decided, is the shape of our galaxy. Oddly, it is also the shape of the DNA molecule, the code of life, *seen from above*. The ring thus suggests the old Hermetic notion of the macrocosm in the microcosm, "That which is above is contained in that which is below."

Hmmm... That certainly wasn't on my mind, consciously, when I bought the ring.

Later I realized that if one can look at the DNA from above, one can also look at the Hindu kundalini serpent that way, too. Seen from above, the kundalini also looks like an inward-turning spiral. According to the Hindus, this kundalini energy underlies all manifestations of life, "however small," which would seem to include the DNA.

The controversial neo-Freudian, Wilhelm Reich, also believed there was a life-energy underlying all biological systems. He called it "orgone" and claimed it had a spiral shape.

The same spiral appears over and over in the late paintings of Van Gogh, work done when he was either going crazy from paresis, or from too much absinthe, or from both.

In the mid '70s, when Arlen and I were living in San Francisco, I got involved in the pagan revival. By then, I was a gourmet of religions — sampling all, believing none, much like Adolphus in Bernard Shaw's *Major Barbara*. Neo-paganism was definitely a growing force in America, and I wanted to know about it from inside. I learned a lot, which I will write about sometime, but the most interesting detail right now is that Celtic pagan rituals take the form of a dance made up of an inward-turning spiral followed by an outward-turning spiral.

Some say these rituals have come down to us from the Stone Age, through underground cults and sects which survived even during the Inquisition. Others say that is a Romantic Lie and modern paganism was created out of anthropology books and Aleister Crowley's poetry by an English eccentric named Gerald Gardner, in the early 1930s.

(Curiously, Gardner, who certainly popularized neo-paganism even if he didn't also invent it, lived on the Isle of Man, where an ancestor of mine was once king...)

Reading a book on Celtic myth around 1980 I found that ancient Irish burial grounds were laid out to form a double spiral when seen from above — an inward spiral and an outward spiral. This was alleged to represent death and rebirth.

I wasn't sure all this meant anything, but at least it gave me a bright line of chatter to reel off when people asked me what the spiral ring symbolized.

THE RETURN OF THE HEAVY SQUAD

And The Doctrine Of Super-Fecundation

The day after the Hayes family confessed and Joanne Hayes was hauled off to the nut-house, the Guards were not feeling well at all, at all. The five family members repudiated their confessions and Kathleen, Joanne's sister, led the press to the Hayes farm and produced another dead baby, which she said was Joanne's.

Holy Ireland, mother of Saints and Sages, reeled — and reeled again when Pure Science went to work on the Forensic evidence. Science said the evidence established that this infant (another boy, by the way) "had not attained separate life," or in ordinary language "was born dead." It had no marks of violence.

Forensic evidence also showed that this child — the Abbeydorney baby, it came to be called, after the town where the Hayes farm was located — had Type O blood, as did Joanne and her lover, a married farmer named Jeremiah Locke. The Cahiriciveen baby, the one that had been stabbed 28 times, was Type A and could not be the child of Joanne and Jeremiah.

When news of this reached the mental hospital, Joanne Hayes spoke for the first time since her psychotic breakdown. "Thank God," she said to a nurse. "Now they know I didn't kill my baby." She recovered thereafter and was released in 11 days.

It was a Celtic Mystery indeed. All six members of the family had confessed that Joanne not only stabbed but strangled and beat her baby on the head with a brush.

The Abbeydorney baby, which could be hers and Jeremiah's, was born dead and showed no signs of such violence.

The Cahiriciveen baby *could not be hers and Jeremiah's* and there was nothing to link it to Joanne Hayes.

The newspapers, and especially Feminist writers, began asking how the Guards had obtained six false confessions in eight hours, and driven Joanne into a mental breakdown in the process. The Hayes family did little to clarify that mystery. One brother claimed the Guards beat him, but he had no bruises to substantiate this. The others said they couldn't remember everything that happened while in custody, but that a lot of conversation concerned the Catholic doctrine of Eternal Damnation and the Guards were all of the opinion that the one sure way to escape Hell was to confess and ask God's forgiveness. Confession, indeed, was the only path to Salvation in the theology of the Guards.

Newspaper criticism grew vehement. The Guards had been accused of brutality in the past, when the I.R.A. was still active in the Republic, and some asked if those days had returned.

In the bad old days, the Guards had a branch to deal with the I.R.A. and everybody soon called it "the Heavy Squad." Charges of brutality and torture made the Heavy Squad infamous, and eventually it was dissolved. The I.R.A., meanwhile, had moved its activities north of the border, to Northern Ireland.

Now many in the media, and even in the government, were asking if the Heavy Squad was back again.

The Guards rallied, with Hibernian imagination. One of them invented the Doctrine of Superfecundation. This could only happen in a Catholic country where people are indoctrinated from childhood in such multisyllabic mystifications as the Dogma of Transubstantiation or the Immaculate Conception. The Superfecundation, for all I know, may someday take its place beside these and be made official by the Vatican. It holds that Joanne Hayes had two babies on the same night, *fathered by two separate lovers.* The Abbeydorney baby (Type O) was fathered by Jeremiah Locke and was born dead, as the forensic evidence indicated. The Cahiriciveen baby (Type A) was also Joanne's, by an unknown Second Lover, and had been killed by her after all.

Presto! The confessions were not false (except that they hadn't mentioned *two* babies...) and the Guards were vindicated, sort of.

It is not at all clear if anybody ever believed in the Superfecundation, but it is not certain either if many Catholics really believe in the Immaculate Conception. There is "Sunday truth," which you hear in Church, and there is the other kind of truth, which you deal with when buying or selling potatoes, and adult Catholics, like other religious groups, have a marvelous faculty for mentally segregating the two. (Only children believe religious doctrines literally.)

What did appear was that in a country where people can discuss the Immaculate Conception with straight faces, Superfecundation is not going to seem too bizarre for legal contemplation. When the Minister of Justice appointed a Tribunal to inquire if the Guards had used dirty tricks in securing six false confessions, the judge, Kevin Lynch, ruled that Superfecundation was a legitimate defense.

INFORMATION DOUBLES AGAIN

By 1950 information had doubled again. The acceleration factor was becoming more and more obvious to more and more observers.

It had taken Life more than three billion years to arrive at the first tool. It had taken more than three million years to achieve the information density of the Roman Empire in 1 AD. 1500 years for information to double again. 250 years for the next doubling in 1750. 150 years for the next doubling in 1900. Now information had doubled in only 50 years, within the lifetime of some human beings. The fully educated person of 1950 could, at least in potential, learn two facts for every one fact known to his father in 1900, four facts for every one known in 1750, eight for every fact known in 1500, 16 for every fact known at the time of Christ.

During this doubling, Fascism had risen to power and then fallen, or at least the survivors learned to hide themselves behind more plausible masks. Communism was continuing to rise and now controlled more than one-fourth of the Earth.

Back in the 1920s, as these trajectories were becoming clear to a few, Prof. H. J. Mackinder in England was formulating a new philosophy of Global Thinking. Mackinder saw a New World Order rising eventually out of the chaos of competing Empires and tried to teach people how to think and plan globally.

Karl Haushofer came from Germany to study with Mackinder. He returned and passed his version of the New World Order on to a charismatic and messianic young man named Hitler, and we all know what that cost the world before the carnage was over.

Haushofer and Hitler had taken Mackinder's ideas and added the assumption that the only way the New World Order could emerge out of chaos was if one nation were strong enough and cunning enough to outwit all its rivals.

In the U.S., R. Buckminster Fuller also read Mackinder and developed the Global idea in a different direction. He began to visualize and plan very concretely a "synergetic" system for the planet which would "advantage all without disadvantaging any."

With warfare becoming increasingly omni-lethal Fuller predicted that humanity would be forced to choose peace and synergetic cooperation before the end of the 20th Century.

The discovery of the 92nd and last natural chemical element and the splitting of the atom the year I was born, 1932, had created the explosions of Hiroshima and Nagasaki and a knowledge explosion in all the hard sciences as one new fact quickly led to five or six more. By 1950, Bucky Fuller was becoming more and more recognized as an architect-mathematician of genius but his City Planning and Global Planning ideas still seemed too far out for ruling elites to consider seriously.

On April 19, 1942, chemist Albert Hoffman of Sandoz Laboratories in Basel, Switzerland, mixed up a compound he hoped would be a new and better cure for headaches. Not knowing he had inhaled a great deal of the fumes, Hoffman got on his bicycle and started to peddle home for lunch. He began to notice strange sensations.

A 10-dimensional universe cracked into a 6-dimensional universe and a 4-dimensional universe. There were gold ornaments and silk curtains and heavy incense: it hurt like a bastard. Wild technicolor Maui trees and shrubs everywhere as Mother Superior raised the steel yardstick again — Uncle Mick understood with the same mathematical certainty that those 60,000 body-bags would be filled. An egg within an egg gave birth to a quantum jump, huge lumbering reptiles. These Sun-Kings walking across the Brooklyn Bridge, hiding behind a bush going *cluck-cluck-cluck* — the inertial system changes — he could see every black-head, every wart, every bead of sweat. Art works considered "pagan" bowed to Rev. Yoshikami and came down the stairs to New York 1959... "He wears thick goggles and a kind of scuba-diving suit"...they help us to understand our hallucinations better.

Dr. Hoffman got off the bicycle, a wild surmise dawning upon him.

The first Xerox machine and the first Japanese tape recorder came on the market in 1950. There were already over 100 television stations in 38 of our states, and the great era of radio drama on which I had been raised was dying as the new medium brought "movies" into the living room.

The population of the world had reached two and a half billion.

Average life expectancy for all classes in the Industrial world had reached 60. For the first time in history the majority of people were living *twice as long* as the majority of people in all history before the French Revolution.

The center of information-and-power — ideas that work — had again migrated Westward. As Brooks Adams had foreseen, the British Empire had collapsed during the doubling of knowledge 1900-1950, and an American Empire was rising to replace it.

The only serious rival to the New Empire seemed to be the Union of Marxist states of the East. Public hysteria against Russians was whipped up to a fever pitch and you could not be "normal" or "ordinary" in America in 1950 if you did not have a violent hatred of our recent allies and a near-hysterical fear that their spies were everywhere in your community, perhaps even hiding under your bed.

Alger Hiss was found guilty of perjury (for denying Communist involvement) on January 25, 1950, thereby proving, at least in the public mind, that "their agents were everywhere," even in the highest ranks of our government. In England, Dr. Klaus Fuchs was convicted of espionage, and the witch-hunt for further traitors in the scientific community spread back across the Atlantic growing more irresponsible and frenzied every week. Senator Joe McCarthy gave his name to the Era by "finding" more Communist Traitors than anybody, although his admirers did not note that he never found enough evidence to convict a single person of the hundreds and hundreds he accused. Black lists decimated the arts and entertainment, and a fading actor named Ronald Reagan leaped back into the spotlight by leading the Hollywood witch-hunt.

As the Industrial Age rushed to its apotheosis, death and total transformation, the Old Bronze Age System still survived in much of the Third World, and before 1950 was over the Pope announced the dogma that the Blessed Virgin Mary rose not "as a spirit" but *in her body* directly to "heaven," apparently at an angle of 90 degrees perpendicular to the Earth like one of the rockets being tested that year in New Mexico.

We continued to fire rockets but none of them went high enough to reach "heaven" or knock the Blessed Virgin off her throne.

And I was working in the Corrosion Engineering Department of a large consulting engineering firm.

CORROSION ... ALL THINGS ARE IMPERMANENT

The fool says, "These are my sons, this is my land, this is my money." In reality, the fool does not own himself, much less sons, land or money.   — Gotama Buddha

After I graduated from Brooklyn Tech, I had obtained a job as an engineering aide at the engineering firm mentioned above. I then enrolled in Brooklyn Polytechnic Institute, where I attended night school and majored in electrical engineering (because I still thought I could eventually make a living as an engineer) and minored in mathematics (because that really interested me.)

I worked in the Corrosion Department. That consisted of about a dozen engineers who traveled around the country finding out why pipelines or power plants had corrosion problems and what was the most economical cure. I did the graphs and charts for their reports, and all the incidental shit-work they didn't want to bother themselves with. I learned a lot about corrosion, which is inevitable because all structures outside of Pure Math are, as the Buddhists say, impermanent. In fact, the Buddhist metaphor of the world as fire seems to fit the realm of corrosion engineering very neatly, since fire and rust are both based on oxidation. The best we can do is slow down the process of decay and metamorphosis.

The corrosion of metals is frequently accelerated by anaerobic bacteria in the soil and may be treated in some cases with corrosion-resistant paints but in more cases requires a "cathodic protection" system — a bunch of anodes buried nearby and electrically linked to the system being protected. Quite in accord with the theory of electricity, the anodes would corrode before the cathode (the object being protected.) Again, as in my lab courses, I saw over and over that even the weirdest Wonders of the Invisible World of pure math have practical applications in our sensory world.

The work I was doing involved the electrical theory I had learned in school plus a lot of chemistry I had to pick up as I went along. Every bit of it depended on current geology which insisted the Earth was not hollow, contrary to Captain Symmes. That cheered me. There were no devils living down there and they couldn't come up and drop ground glass in my eyes.

Working eight hours a day and attending engineering college two hours a night four nights a week, with all the homework engineering courses pile on you, cannot be called an easy schedule. I made it harder on myself by writing dozens of short stories, all of which got rejected by the magazines I submitted them to.

Most of the stories were bad imitations of H. P. Lovecraft, a writer I recognized as minor but who nonetheless fascinated me. I never considered his works "horror fiction," since they never scared me; I regarded them as a special kind of prose-poetry that lifts the reader into a perspective far, far beyond human prejudice, a perspective in which Earth and its denizens are very unimportant, virtually accidental parts of the cosmic drama. (Later I came to think of H.P.L. as "the poet of materialism" — the man who could really make his readers feel Melville's "colorless allcolor of atheism.")

I was also writing a lot of poetry, which consisted of bad imitations of the dramatic monologues of Browning and the early Ezra Pound:

Bridge britten beneath us and dingsail ripped ragged
Bull-seal bellowed in the Norden night. Waves whipped us.

That's from "Lucky Lief," a monologue "spoken" by Lief Erikson and typical of the rubbish I wrote in those days. The alliterations attempt to imitate Pound's imitations of Olde English poems like "The Seafarer" and "The Wanderer." Fortunately for the reader, I cannot remember any more of this abortion, which I lost years ago.

Of course, I had to have some social life, too, but I was in headlong flight from my whole Roman Catholic tribe and quite shy about making new friends. (My father had retired by then and he and my mother moved to Miami to live on his small pension and Social Security.)

Eventually, my interest in jazz led me to the clubs in Manhattan where Be-Bop was then thriving. It would make a good story if I told you I heard Charlie Parker play and recognized his genius at once. The truth is that he already had a narcotics conviction and was barred from employment in New York nightclubs — including Birdland, which had been named after him. It was like locking Michelangelo out of the Metropolitan Museum of Art but law isn't supposed to make sense. It's just supposed to make us frightened of the government.

I did hear John Lewis and Miles Davis and Thelonius Monk and recognized their genius.

Naturally, in this environment, I began to have Black friends. I don't know if that is still possible for a young white intellectual today, but back the '50s the jazz world was still amused but basically tolerant of its white fans. Martin Luther King hadn't been assassinated, Malcolm X hadn't been assassinated, the high hopes of the '60s (still ahead of us) hadn't been crushed by the Republican Counter-Revolution, and we all sort of shared the lovely dream that Racism could be abolished in our generation by people of good will. Now, when Racism seems as entrenched in our society as ever, and in some respects even more virulent than in past days, Blacks usually feel rather suspicious of whites who want to be their friends. I can't say I blame them.

I also had an affair with a Black woman, which was even more educational than worrying about the foundations of mathematics. Previously, I had learned to despise Racism, but only in an intellectual way; now I began to feel the emotional horror of what Racism does to all its victims.

At the age of 24, after my lady friend and I parted, I had a kind of slow-motion emotional "breakdown." I quit night school for six months — although I continued my job — and began seeing a psychiatrist. Since the company I worked for paid for the therapy, I got to see the forms that went from my doctor to me, to the company, to the insurance people. Under "diagnosis," he had written, "Severe anxiety, compulsive rumination." In lay language, I was afraid of something but didn't know what it was and spent a lot of time philosophizing about everything in the universe, trying to find clues to what terrified me. By now I was sure it wasn't a demon waiting to drop ground glass in my eyes as soon as I tried to sleep, but I didn't know what else it might be.

Partially, I was afraid of nuclear war; like most Liberal Intellectuals of the Eisenhower decade I considered American foreign policy a species of suicidal mania and expected Apocalypse "next Tuesday after lunch." To some extent, of course, I had anxiety *because I had anxiety.* That is, the emotions or neurological reflexes of a Catholic education linger years and years after the ideas of the Church have been rejected by the objective intellect. James Joyce was terrified of thunder all his life.

Around that time, Dr. Albert Ellis wrote a book listing over 100 types of psychotherapy available in the U.S.; more recently, I saw a similar list of over 300. In this psycho-smorgasbord, I lucked out. The doctor I found had no special dogma and used an open-ended eclectic approach. Within six months, he had helped me to see that most of my emotional jim-jams arose from the fact that my life profoundly bored me, and that it bored me because I was doing what other people wanted me to do instead of what I wanted to do.

The implications of what I had learned were perfectly clear to me. My parents always wanted me to work in an office — *indoors,* not out in the weather like Dad and other longshore-men — and I was afraid to challenge that Life Script. I had other, even more "ambitious" goals but nobody in my environment regarded those dreams as attainable. I therefore thought about what I had learned in therapy for two years afterward but did nothing about changing my circumstances. I continued my job, returned to night school and avoided the obvious step of becoming a bum and writing full time.

CHOOSE YOUR HALLUCINATIONS

Meanwhile, something else happened. A jazz musician — not a famous one — turned me on to marijuana. The first experience was typical of the novice pot-head: I saw colors brighter, heard music better, and spent a lot of time giggling over nothing in particular. I also felt "melting" sensations of warm energy running through my body, especially in my arms, legs and penis.

Most pot-smokers, evidently, simply enjoy this sort of thing and never think about why a simple herb changes so many of the parameters of the nervous system. Since I had already been diagnosed as a compulsive ruminator, you will not be surprised that I found that question almost as interesting as the marijuana experience itself.

The world consists of colorless atoms, I had been taught, and our brain imposes colors on the large-scale lattices of atoms that we call "objects." *Why, then, do the colors change when we get stoned?* The colors represent our brain's "interpretation" of wave functions, which themselves have the structure of equations including that damned square root of minus one. The wave forms (equations) cannot possible change when we let the cannabis molecule into our neuro-chemical broth (can they?), so our brain "software" must do the changing.

Brain software in this case seems to include the management of the "traffic" — which chemical signals are routed to which synapses. Our brain undergoes a kind of organizational quantum jump.

Thus, in scientific terms, the cannabis experience obliterates one hallucination (our usual way of seeing colors that aren't there) to open us to multiple hallucinations (countless new ways of seeing colors that aren't there.) But that Strict Materialist explanation did not seem satisfactory to me, for reasons having to do with my experiences of Art and other Virtual Realities.

Whether one is transported out of one's habitual Realty Tunnel to the multiple-choice labyrinth of Virtual Reality by marijuana or by Charlie Parker or by sexual orgasm or by meditation or by Picasso or by King Kong or by the Wicked Witch of the West, the experience has a quality of timelessness and liberation about it. One *feels less mechanical* and seems on the edge of grasping what the mystics mean by "Awakening"; sometimes, especially with Beethoven, one almost feels that one will never forget the "absurd good news" (as Chesterton called it) of that Awakened state.

Reichian therapy (which I would soon experience) and some Oriental varieties of chiropractic can also put one in that timeless state seemingly suspended between parallel universes or neurological reality-tunnels — all equally "real" as possible experiences — and all equally "unreal" scientifically as mere *mnemonic icons* created by our brains out of colorless atoms and the void and then used by us to file and index our hallucinations. That is, between pot and Korzybski, I could see all possible reality-tunnels as human products and lost all tendency to turn any one of them into an Idol or Dogma. (After Reichian therapy, my body began to awaken from the rigidity imposed by Catholic education.)

What I experience "is" *not* "reality." What I experience registers my brain's way of filing and indexing its impression. The bright colors and lovely music of the marijuana state "are" not more "real" or less "real" than the colors and music of other neurological states. Whatever we are talking about, as Roger Jones says in *Physics as Metaphor,* our brains cannot be separated from it.

(Most of my books attempt to help people see our "mnemonic icons" — perceptions and conceptions — as models or maps, instead of treating them as Idols or Dogmas. You'd be surprised how much hate mail I get from Fundamentalists of all persuasions; the Fundamentalist Materialists seem even more violently emotional than the Protestant Fundamentalists, as Jung's analysis of the Rationalist Complex predicts. One recently accused me of being a "psychological terrorist.")

Meanwhile the pot experience was changing me in a way that I could understand in Jungian terms. I had already analyzed myself as a compulsive Rationalist and wanted to learn how to develop my sensory, emotional and intuitive capacities, but I didn't know any "schools" that taught those subjects. Now I found that marijuana definitely enriches the sensory-sensual manifold. I not only saw more colors, and more beauty generally, but I also found that I heard music better, including the more complex forms of progressive jazz and the more intricate baroque composers such as Scarlatti.

The first time I made love while stoned, I discovered that even orgasm was better with the Devil Weed.

(I am not the only one to have made this discovery. In a 1968 study — "The Marijuana Problem: An Overview" by McGlothin and West, *American Journal of Psychiatry* — 73 percent of all pot-smokers said the main reason they liked the Weed was that it improved sexual enjoyment.)

So I was graduating from pure Rationalist-Esthete to Rationalist-Sensualist-Esthete, due to my cavalier disregard for the laws of the land — i.e., because I regard Congress as a bunch of crooks and dunderheads who had no right to interfere with my private life.

The next question for me was: How do I find a similar formula to increase my emotional freedom and my intuition, the way pot had increased my sensory awareness? I knew that, as an ex-Catholic I was still emotionally armored and repressed, and that, as a compulsive rationalizer, I was "afraid" of nonlinear thinking.

But, again, I didn't know where to look for the tools to deal with the problem. I had to wait a few years... Then — as noted earlier — the U.S. government burned the books of Dr. Wilhelm Reich, smashed his scientific equipment with axes and threw him in jail. I got interested — a scientist who arouses that much fury must have something important to say — and ended up by embarking on a course of Reichian therapy.

I learned to scream and weep again, as I had as a child. Then I learned to relax and play, like a child. I was becoming Rational-Sensual-Emotional, or three-fourths of a human being.

I still didn't know what to do to develop Jung's fourth faculty... Intuition.

That had to wait until I discovered Acid and Aleister Crowley.

ANOTHER BLOOMSDAY ...
THE POOKAH RETURNS

On June 16, 1985, I went to the office of the *Dublin Evening Herald* to turn in my review of the new "corrected" edition of *Ulysses*. I had found four gross errors in it and suspected that there were more. (Since then, one Joyce scholar has claimed over 1000 errors. The most Relativistic novel ever written has become even more Indeterminate as pedants quarrel over virtually every line of Joyce's crabbed eccentric handwriting and whether or not the galleys he approved, when his eyesight was failing, really said what he hoped they said...)

As I crossed the lobby of the Herald building, Arlen asked the time and I looked at my watch.

12:31.

I suddenly remembered two things.

The Herald building had been the office of the *Freeman's Journal* in 1904, and in *Ulysses* on Bloomsday at about 12:31 Stephen Dedalus and Leopold Bloom cross the same lobby I was in, without meeting. It is the first of two near-meetings before Stephen and Bloom finally do really meet at 11 p.m. in a maternity hospital.

I was handing in a review of a book containing 1000 synchronicities and I seemed to be part of a larger synchronicity containing both me and the book.

I mentioned this to Arlen and we chatted about it a bit. I handed in my review and we walked back to the Quays and headed for the Ormonde where we planned to have a bite of lunch. Walking along the Quays, looking at the lovely river Anna Liffey, I thought of Joyce's pun linking her to Huck Finn's river: "Missus Liffey."

We ate pub grub in the Ormonde...and listened, entranced, as a man at the bar read aloud from the Sirens chapter of *Ulysses*, to two friends.

A man reading Joyce aloud on Bloomsday is not a synchronicity, or even a coincidence. In Dublin, it is an inevitability.

We listened, and ate, and I reflected on the Sirens chapter, set in the hotel we were in. That's the chapter where Bloom, in the restaurant, starts to write, "Dear Martha," and "coincidentally" hears Simon Dedalus, in the bar, start to sing "Martha," the song. Bloom becomes Stephen Dedalus's "spiritual father" later because Simon, a hopeless alcoholic, has abandoned all parental responsibility. In the Ormonde, Simon and Bloom are linked by spiritual and biological paternity and by the name "Martha," sister of Lazarus — and also the name of a young lady with whom Joyce had a brief affair while writing this chapter.

After lunch, Arlen and I headed down Grafton Street — still "gay with awnings" as it was when Bloom looked at it on June 16, 1904 — and headed for Stephen's Green.

Arlen asked the time again. I looked at my watch and realized it had stopped.

In *Ulysses,* Bloom realized that his watch had stopped right after he left the Ormonde.

I was still in Joyce's synchro-net.

"The unconscious Joyce represents is not merely an area within the brains of his creatures. It is a network of connections through time and space that extends beyond any awareness but the most absolute." — Sheldon Brivic, Crane Bag, *VI, 1.*

The Ormonde is named after the Earls of Ormonde, one of whom persuaded King Charles II to "give" Phoenix Park to the people of Dublin. (The king had originally planned to give it to one of his mistresses.) I had visited the home of the Ormondes, Kilkenny Castle, on a tour, and I had sat in a chair given to the family by Charles II — the chair in which he had been crowned king.

All I could remember about Charles II, while I was sitting in that chair, were his epigrams. Hearing the popular joke about himself, "He never said a foolish thing and never did a wise one," Charles replied, "That is because my words are my own, but my acts are those of my ministers." During the Titus Oates affair, when Oates was stirring up anti-Catholic paranoia, Charles refused to intervene on either side, saying, "The more you stir a turd, the more it stinks." His next-to-last words were, "I am an unconscionably long time dying." His very last words were, "Let not poor Nellie starve," referring to his favorite mistress, Nell Gwynn.

Nell, when attacked by a mob who mistook her for Barbara Villiers, the king's Catholic mistress, had cried, "Gentlemen! Gentlemen! I am the king's Protestant *whore."*

The Irish Catholics had suffered abominably during the Puritan Era — the atrocities of Cromwell and his troops are still bitterly remembered. Charles let Ormonde persuade him to give Dublin the beautiful Phoenix Park because he wanted the Irish to believe they would fare better with a religiously indifferent king than they had with a Puritan "democracy."

I came back to Consensus Reality and we found a shop where I got a new battery for my watch.

That evening, at the Joyce Tower, I met James Joyce's grandnephew. He told me his hobby was collecting photos of his famous relative and I asked him if he ever saw a photo of Joyce with a brown mackintosh. He said no, he hadn't.

If he had said yes, I would have a new solution to another of the Bloomsday puzzles that Joyce scholars love to mull: Who was the "lanky galoot" in the brown mackintosh who appears at Paddy Dingam's funeral at 10 a.m., ducks across the street just before the Royal Procession at 3 p.m., reappears at Burke's pub at 11 p.m., and leaves the whorehouse just as Bloom is entering at midnight?

I still think he's Joyce, but I can't prove it yet.

THE ELUSIVE TOM FLYNN

Er Ist Nicht Hier, Er Ist Nicht Da...

When the Tribunal on the Kerry Baby Mystery and possible misconduct of the Guards began, the lawyers for the Guards immediately went to work on demolishing Joanne Hayes, endeavoring to prove that she was so shockingly *immoral* and *depraved* that she might have had two lovers at the same time. They did this by cross-examining her about her whole sexual history for five full days in January 1985. (By comparison, a full sexual history for the Kinsey Institute takes only a few hours.)

Mr. Justice Lynch also permitted Radio Telefis hEirann, the Irish radio-TV network, to carry the trial live on the airwaves. Everybody in Ireland, where X-rated movies are illegal, had the chance to listen to endless discussions and debates about the size of Joanne's vagina when examined at the hospital 15 April, where and when she had her first orgasm, how many times she had made love in motels and how many times in cars, and in general all the gynecological details for which *Ulysses* was once banned.

The lawyers were merciless; that was their job. ("All's fair in love, war and cross-examination," one of them explained to the press.) Judge Lynch lived up to his name and was equally merciless. It was the most prolonged gang-rape of a woman's psyche in history. Joanne Hayes broke down repeatedly and had hysteric attacks so acute that some reporters thought she was on her way back to the mental hospital.

It was the best possible defense for the Guards. In Ireland, a woman with two lovers would be considered capable of any other enormity, including murder and piracy on the high seas.

Her lawyer begged for recesses several times, so she could recover; Judge Lynch ruled that she was well enough to continue. By the fifth and last day, she was so heavily sedated by her doctor that she appeared catatonic again.

No evidence of the elusive Second Lover emerged from all this. Joanne, weeping and hysterical, insisted through every kind of badgering and bullying that she had only had one lover, Jeremiah Locke. It began to look as if Superfecundation, like Transubstantiation, would have to be taken on faith.

Feminists in thousands — huge masses for a small country like Ireland — began picketing the Tribunal. Judge Lynch denounced them from the bench. The word "witch-hunt" appeared in print so often I thought I was back in the Joe McCarthy era; in fact, the only Inquisitorial detail missing was that Judge Lynch did not allow the lawyers to shave Joanne's pubic hair to see if the devil was hiding there.

I can't explain how they forgot that.

Somebody in the Guards helped their defense along by leaking to the press the name of the still-elusive Second Lover. It was Tom Flynn, we were told, and his name was written on Joanne's mattress.

But by then the Plain People of Ireland, as Myles na gCopaleen called them, were getting fed up. Sweaters saying "I'm Tom Flynn" appeared and hundreds of men wore them, marching around the courthouse with the Feminists, taunting the Guards, who were allegedly working 16-hour shifts like 19th Century coal miners trying to find the phantom fornicator.

And do you know what I'm going to tell you, faith? Tom Flynn *was* finally found, in the United States, where he had emigrated in 1969. He said he had been a mattress salesman in Kerry in the '60s and wrote his name on every mattress he sold. If he were the father of the Cahiriciveen baby, everybody calculated quickly, he must have seduced Joanne when she was 10 and she must have gestated for 15 years. That was too much to swallow, even in the context of Superfecundation.

The Second Lover remained elusive. No other candidates for that role were ever found, although I'm sure some of the Guards, in desperation, thought of invoking the Holy Ghost again. If people could believe that yarn when it was invented 2000 years ago, they might have believed it again.

At least in Ireland.

THE INWARD-TURNING SPIRAL

"And here," said the tour guide, "is the site of the Battle of the Boyne. It was right at this part of the river that the troops of James I met the army of William of Orange in 1692."

We got out of the bus and walked around. Nobody had bothered to put up a plaque to "authenticate" the guide's claim. Since this was Ireland, the Battle of the Boyne might have occurred here, or ten miles away. (Irish Facts, as Hugh Kenner has noted, have the plasticity of rubber inches.) All we could see were trees, each of them spectacularly flashing those gorgeous greens that make Ireland "the Emerald Isle."

This special green is the result of high copper concentration in the soil. Ireland had copper mines at least 3000 years ago, when Phoenicians and others from the Mediterranean first began sailing there to get this valuable metal,* and it still has the largest copper mines in Europe today.

"Some tourists ask me what the Battle of the Boyne was all about," the tour guide said. "Well, now, I'll tell you, ladies and gents. It was a donnybrook between a Scotchman and his Dutch son-in-law, fighting on Irish soil over which of them should be king of England."

I've never seen a history book explain it better.

(Well, if you want to know a little more, when Charles II died — the bloke who gave Dublin its Phoenix Park, remember? — his brother James II succeeded to the throne, almost. Parliament threw him out and imported William of Orange. William of Orange was Protestant — which is why the Northern Protestants in Ireland still call themselves "Orangemen" — and had the support of the Bank of England and James II was a Catholic and had no claim to the throne except that legally he was next in line for succession after Charles II died. For insisting on this nitpicky legal point and going to war over it James became disparagingly known as the Old Pretender, but only after William won the war.)

---

* Valuable because, together with tin, it makes bronze. Remember?

I thought of Yeats' claim that "Ireland was part of Asia until the Battle of the Boyne." I think he meant that when the Protestants won, everything non-linear, "mystic" and intuitive about Irish culture got buried alive.

We got back in the bus and drove toward the Hill of Tara. It was a warm, Van Gogh sort of day, and Arlen and I were on the Boyne Valley tour to wallow a bit in our common Celtic heritage.

At Tara, where the High Kings of pagan Ireland had ruled, we climbed to the top of the hill and enjoyed a splendid view of the whole Boyne valley, which is as Irish and mystical as you can get, because it is full of mysterious monoliths that archaeologists do not attempt to explain. The builders of these Kubrick *koans* are identified only as "pre-Celtic," which is about as helpful as knowing something is "not cheese."

I walked over and touched the *Lia Fial* — "the Stone of Destiny" — which looks so penile that I think the concept of "phallic symbol" would have come to the mind of anybody looking at it even if Freud had never lived. Alas, the Stone did not cry out "in a voice of thunder" when I touched it, which it is supposed to do when a True King arrives to liberate Ireland. But then, even according to the Irish, who are great yarn-spinners, the Stone hasn't done that since Brian Boru was crowned there in 988 AD.

I went back to the summit and looked over the Boyne Valley megaliths again. They had been built before Stonehenge, according to carbon dating. They were literally older than the pyramids. Myles na gCopaleen once claimed they were built by Corka-dorky Man, the first denizen of County Kerry, just to baffle future archaeologists. I'm sure von Danikan or one of his clan or ilk claims the real builders were extraterrestrials.

Before taking the tour, I had read a book called *The Boyne Valley Vision* by Martin Brennan. He claimed to have found a system by which all the Boyne megaliths, together with the Stone of Destiny atop Tara and the huge egg of Newgrange, across the valley from the Stone, formed a giant astronomical-astrological calendar, based on a symbolism both sexual and mathematical, like the hexagrams of *I Ching*.

I had found, or thought I had found, a similar system, both sexual and mathematical, underlying *Finnegans Wake,* so I tried to get in touch with Mr. Brennan. Alas, inquiries around Dublin intellectual circles revealed that he had been thrown out of Ireland for possession of LSD. He had his supporters, though, and they claimed the archaeologists from Trinity College had framed him. But it is a firm axiom in *some* Dublin circles that those Protestants at Trinity are always up to dirty tricks of some sort.

(A few years later, I heard of Brennan again. He and John Michele, an Irish friend of mine in London, had formed the Concordance of High Monarchists in Ireland. They wanted to end the Catholic/Protestant struggle in Ireland by reviving paganism, appointing a pagan king to serve as spiritual leader of the united Republic, and allowing each county to make its own laws, like a Swiss canton. I never found out if there was a third member of the Concordance of High Monarchists in Ireland.)

We got back in the bus and drove to Newgrange. This is the most important symbol in *Finnegans Wake,* the egg from which all Creation emerges (sometimes personified as Humpty Dumpty, and sometimes calendarized into 28 flowergirls representing the 28 day cycle of the human ovum). Like the other Boyne Valley monuments, this is pre-Celtic, older than the pyramids and we know nothing about who built it or why. It is the biggest of the Boyne Valley structures, and the most eldritch. Archaeologists recently discovered that at dawn on Midwinter morning every year, the sun, coming over the Hill of Tara, sends a beam down the vaginal tunnel from the entrance of Newgrange to its central chamber, which is then suddenly and shockingly illuminated like a dark theatre when the houselights come back on.

Arlen and I joined the group that agreed to follow the guide into the central chamber of Newgrange. We had to crouch, and almost crawl, going down the tunnel. The Irish are generally small people, but whoever built Newgrange was even smaller.

When we got to the central chamber — which, like the whole of Newgrange, is egg-shaped: an egg within an egg — somebody in the crowd said to me, "Oh, look, it's just like your ring."

I had noticed that myself. The walls of the whole central chamber of Newgrange are covered with the inward-turning spiral design of the ring which I picked up in a Mexican silver shop 13 years before.

That design — as I had found over the years, trying to answer the question, "What does your ring mean?" — suggests the galaxy, the DNA, the Hindu kundalini and Reich's orgone. It was also the shape of a witch's dance.

I suddenly had a "leap of intuition." I could see the builders of Newgrange, back in the Stone Age, gathering in the central chamber for Initiation Rituals on Midwinter Eve. They ate their magic mushrooms and explored Virtual Reality in the womb-like dark all through the long winter night and then — at dawn — Illumination flooded the chamber as Father Sun shot his seed over the phallic Stone of Tara into the egg-within-the-egg of the Earth Mother's womb at Newgrange. A "symbolism both sexual and mathematical," from which Freemasonry had emerged...

Since my intuition is no more infallible than any of my other faculties, I know not whether this be truth or Romantic Fiction; but then most of the things that go on in this world have elements of both in them, don't they?

Back outside in the Van Gogh sun, surrounded by Cézanne trees, we rested. Somebody asked the tour guide what he did in the winter, when the tourist season ended.

"Sure, I'm a government artist," he said. He waited for that to register, and then delivered the punch line with a straight face. "I draw the dole."

HARLEM NIGHTS

A few months after I began smoking pot, I quit my job as an engineering aide and took a much lower-paying one as medical orderly. I also enrolled at New York University in the English Education program. It was my new Life Script or myth that I would become an English teacher, spend a few hours each day sharing my love of fine literature with appreciative students (I didn't visualize what a real high school class is like in modern America) and have the rest of my time free to write either the Great American Novel or an Epic Poem on Evolution or maybe both.

I went on smoking pot while taking courses on Education Theory (which bored me) and on every branch of English literature (which I loved.)

Meanwhile my nights were spent in the vicinity of East Harlem. Part of my duties as medical orderly consisted of riding the ambulance and helping the driver decide if the suffering victims could be taken to the hospital at once or if moving them was so dangerous that we needed a duly ordained M.D. to come and pronounced a verdict on that legal-medical problem. (If a wrong decision were made, the hospital could be sued for malpractice.)

I remember a case of a Black woman who had a concussion because the toilet-tank (mounted above the toilet in that style of bathroom architecture) had fallen on her head. Her husband was careful to get the names of the ambulance driver and myself and let us know he planned to sue the landlord "for everything but his truss, hee-hee-hee!"

I remember a case of a young Hispanic guy who was shot in the gut. A cop rode in the ambulance with me and kept trying to get this fellow to tell who shot him.

"I'll take care of eet myself," the victim answered.

"We should know, in case you don't pull through," the cop said.

"Then my *brothers* will take care of eet," the guy said, logically. He didn't want the police involved in his life in any way, not even to apprehend the galoot who shot him.

I remember countless obstetric cases, in which the deficiencies of the sex education provided by the Catholic Church and Brooklyn Tech were rapidly corrected by pure Existential Reality.

Obstetric cases, incidentally, usually make everybody feel good — the ambulance staff, the mother, even the cops. There seems something very deep in all our psyches that makes us feel proud of ourselves if we help during childbirth, even in a minor way. I think the cops enjoyed it especially because so much of the time they have to be tough, mean and suspicious; it is a real relief for them to be in a situation where nobody fears them, hates them or plans to shoot them when they're off guard — a situation where they can safely express the kindness and tenderness that all humans have buried somewhere under their armor.

I remember the time we took a Black woman into Harlem Hospital (the legal rule was: take the sufferer to the hospital nearest to them, even if your hospital "caught the squeal" — got the call.) All the way, her husband was complaining: "I don't want her in that place, *you hear*? That place ain't no proper *hospital* — it's a Slaughterhouse!" Like the guards as Buchenwald, we followed orders, and took the poor woman to Harlem Hospital where the emergency room staff "received her" — did the paper work — while we gently placed her in a wheelchair. The wheelchair was so old it suddenly collapsed and the woman landed on the floor, where she didn't utter a sound of pain and seemed in a state of nervous shock — or total terror. She obviously had acquired more bumps, bruises and assorted medical problems than she had the moment before entering the door of the hospital.

I never before or again saw the old proverb "Go to the hospital, and they'll make you worse" come true that fast.

And I remember a Black woman who had attempted to hang herself in a closet. Her mother called Emergency, and the cops were there when we arrived. (All psychos, in those days, had to be accompanied by a cop on the way to The Bin — Bellevue Hospital Psychiatric — and is axiomatic in our culture that we have achieved such a perfect system of Equal Justice For All that anybody who tries to take a quick exit to Nirvana Terminal must be psycho.) While we were busy with the usual bureaucratic paperwork, the would-be suicide casually said she wanted a smoke, and opened her purse as if reaching for cigarettes.

A cop dived across the room and grabbed her hand as it came out of the purse with a wickedly long knife in it.

The woman tried to ram the knife into her gut, but the cop held on to her hand, and they both were breathing hard, and then he gradually forced her to drop it, and all the time I was standing there like a damned fool with my mouth open. The other cops had spread around the room, hands on their guns, but no guns were drawn.

The woman did not get angry or seem frustrated. She returned to the expression of total despair she had worn since we arrived.

Off she went The Bin. I would like to be able to believe they helped her.

I have thought a lot, over the years, about that cop. He had a high degree of a kind of intelligence that I only possess in much smaller, almost microscopic amounts and very intermittently. In the jargon of Dr. Timothy Leary, this is called Emotional-Territorial Intelligence.

Leary distinguishes eight types of intelligence. *Bio-Survival Intelligence* seems mostly genetic and tells an animal or human how to find the nourishing and "supportive" and how to avoid the predatory or toxic. *Emotional-Territorial Intelligence,* as shown by the cop I am remembering, seems partly genetic and partly "learned" — it tells an animal how to read the body-language of another animal and know what the other animal is *feeling* (and, hence, what it will probably do next.) The cop read the woman's body-language correctly and knew she was not reaching for cigarettes.

Semantic Intelligence is based on genetic potential and early imprints but mostly is learned slowly, over years, from peers and instructors. It allows us to understand one or two symbol systems (or even several if we are clever) and perhaps to create a symbol-system of our own, sometimes. *Socio-Sexual Intelligence allows us to manage our social and sexual relations in ways that* keep us reasonably happy or at least out of jail.

Leary's other four types of intelligence, which are rare in our society, are: *Neurosomatic Intelligence* — the "wisdom of the body" holistic physicians talk about; *Neurogenetic Intelligence* — access to the "collective unconscious" or "species mind" where archetypes like the inward-turning spiral or King Kong are stored and, when activated, trigger leaps of intuition; *Metaprogramming Intelligence* — the capacity to turn on and tune in to each type of intelligence as needed; and *Non-Local Intelligence* — which enables one to endure "mystical" experiences without coming out of them as a raving loony.

Our schools only teach Semantic Intelligence (and only a primitive Aristotelian variety of that, unless you go on to major in physics). Most people acquire any of the other seven kinds of intelligence only by lucky accident — a remarkable set of genes, a model close by in childhood whom we imitated, or stumbling into Virtual Reality via Art or Dope and remaining sane enough to learn from the experience.

I didn't understand all this for many years, but that cop taught me that there were types of intelligence I lacked — types that most "intellectuals" do not even know exist.

I learned other things outside my reality-tunnel, too. One night I had to pick up a Black man from a police station because he had been injured "resisting arrest." As an ex-Trotskyist, I knew that could be a euphemism for Police Brutality; as a refugee in headlong flight from all dogmatism, I tried not to jump to conclusions.

The cop who rode the ambulance with us was an old veteran of New York's street wars and, seeing how young I was, decided to put on a show for my benefit.

"What were you arrested for?" he asked the suspect.

"Nothing. It was a mistake," the man said wearily.

"It's *always* a mistake," the cop said. "What were you wrongfully accused of?"

"It's a mistake," the man repeated, more wearily.

"Oh," the cop said. "The boys at the station house said you raped your daughter."

"That's what *she* says," the man cried with a great show of outraged innocence that seemed totally unreal and unconvincing to me.

Nowadays incest is recognized as a major problem, but back in the 1950s the very possibility was quite shocking to me. I guess I had believed Freud's verdict that girls who claim their fathers have sexually molested them are all hysterics.

Every day, at NYU, I would be living in the world of Shakespeare, Swift, the Brontes, Chaucer, Melville, T.S. Eliot and Education Theory; every night, on the ambulance, I entered the world where Black Harlem and Spanish Harlem intersect. Perhaps each half of my education in those years helped balance the other half.

Many years later, in the East Bay Bus Terminal in San Francisco, I saw a Black man, alone on an island between bus lanes, talking very loudly to an invisible companion. He was quite incoherent but his body language had the urgent eloquence of total terror. Two Black people, near me, stopped and looked at this poor lunatic. "I wonder how he got that bad," the woman said.

"He just couldn't *handle it* anymore," the man said.

I think that's the best explanation of "mental illness" I have ever seen. If you can still *handle it,* society will tolerate you and only your Ideological foes will call you crazy; when you can no longer *handle it,* our society would like to put you in the Bin — and only the gallant Libertarianism of Thomas Szasz, M.D. and the tight-assed economics of Ronald Reagan has dumped these cases, who can't *handle it,* back on the streets where they wander like the tormented ghosts of mad refugees from the Third World.

Working on the ambulance, I learned not to fear "psychos." Every "squeal" — phone call — came to us from Emergency as a pink slip with an address and an abbreviation on it. "Obs" meant obstetric — a woman in labor. "AIS" meant accident in the street — a car had hit a pedestrian or another car. "Psycho" meant what it always means. "D&D" meant drunk and disorderly. I soon learned that the psychos were much easier to handle than the drunks.

The typical psycho we picked up was nothing like Norman Bates or any conventional Hollywood image. They were frightened, withdrawn, depressed and usually not very talkative. They did what they were asked, sat quietly looking gloomy when not asked to do anything, and seemed not quite clear about what was happening to them. The drunks, on the other hand, all wanted to fight with me. That was strange, in a way, because they had required medical attention in the first place because the cops had been called to stop them from wrecking a bar. Maybe, having failed to wreck the bar completely, they wanted to wreck the ambulance instead.

They were the toughest cases I had to handle. I would rather have a psycho in the ambulance with me than a drunk.

ONCE AGAIN WE RETURN TO
PAUL THE GORILLA
& MIKE THE SHARK

Unlike most of the Calvi-Bishop Marcinkus "ghost banks," the Cisalpine Bank of the Bahamas really existed, and soon came to the attention of the D.A.'s office in Dade County, Florida. The D.A.'s investigators had uncovered Cisalpine's links with what they called "the biggest cocaine laundromat" in the world. This was an outfit resonantly named the World Finance Corporation and was run by a "former" (or allegedly former) CIA agent, Hernandez Cataya.

The World Finance Corporation was reported to the Dade County cops by garbage men who said they often found marijuana stalks in the bank's rubbish. That sort of thing attracts attention by Florida law enforcement people. Further inquiry revealed that the CIA was using the bank for payments to "deep cover" agents in Latin America and that most of the cocaine money from Latin America was being laundered through the WFC and then sent on to the Cisalpine in the Bahamas, where Paul the Gorilla and Roberto Calvi ran it through the Vatican Bank and Banco Ambrosiano and a merry-go-round of Shark Sindona's banks in a system so tricky that not even God Himself knows where most of the money finally landed — although students of this caper generally believe a large chunk of it might be found in those Swiss accounts with which Liccio Gelli was later to be obsessed to the point of foolhardiness.

The Dade County D.A. convicted a few WFC officials but claims the CIA prevented him from getting the evidence he needed to convict eight others, all of whom seemed to have links to the Agency.

Also in the 1970s Paul the Gorilla and Mike the Shark set up a deal in which the American Mafia — specifically, the Johnny Roselli family, acting through New York's Rizzo family — printed a cool billion dollars (yes, that's $1,000,000,000) in counterfeit stock which was deposited in the Vatican Bank and then disappeared almost totally from the sight of profane investigators. Only one hundred million has ever been tracked down: the other nine hundred million is probably still circulating.

The Vatican Bank is the financial equivalent of a Black Hole. Anything that goes into that extra-mundane realm is forever lost to observation from outside. The Vatican Bank is not subject to bank examiners coming around and probing into the records, because the Vatican is not part of Italy. It is a sovereign nation, like the Sovereign Military Order of Malta which serves it.

You might wonder why so much counterfeit stock was printed — a whole *billion* dollars?

Businessmen in tight spots often buy counterfeit stock, deposit it in a bank long enough to establish a hefty "line of credit" and then sell it to someone equally desperate before the fraud is discovered. Counterfeit stocks sell at 10% of the face value, but if you successfully deposit them without being caught, your line of credit equals the face value: thus, for ten million investment, you can be worth one hundred million on paper.

If the counterfeits are bought and sold fast enough, most of the operators of these scams escape detection. Once printed, counterfeit stocks may circulate through thousands of banks, opening lines of credit for the needy and greedy, before anybody looks at them closely enough to spot the fraud. They are thus much more ubiquitous than stolen stocks, which are listed on a "hot sheet" shared by all banks and seldom escape relatively quick detection. Only the truly desperate knowingly deal in stolen stocks and they sell them as quickly as possible.

Johnny Roselli, who arranged the printing of the counterfeits for Paul the Gorilla and his associates in the Vatican, also had a long track record with the CIA, having collaborated with them in several assassination attempts on Fidel Castro. Many investigators — e.g., columnist Jack Anderson and English journalist Anthony Summers — have claimed there is good evidence that Roselli was involved somehow in the Kennedy assassination. Roselli disappeared while under subpoena by the House Select Committee on Assassinations and was later found dead.

Roselli's close associate, Sam Giancana — who had at least once discussed a plan to assassinate Kennedy, according to one witness before the House Select Committee — was also taken suddenly dead while under subpoena. Sam was shot through the mouth — the *sasso in bocca,* traditional Mafia punishment for suspected informers.

Back in Italy, from which Calvi had been a fugitive at the time of his death, investigating magistrates have learned a great deal more and understood a great deal less. Calvi had fled Italy while under indictment for fraudulent bankruptcy, stock and currency fraud, embezzlement and hiding things from bank examiners, but new charges were soon raised against him and against many of his associates.

Mehmet Ali Agca, the dingbat who tried to assassinate the Pope on May 31, 1981, announced that Calvi's Banco Ambrosiano and the Vatican Bank had both been engaged in laundering heroin money for the Grey Wolves (an Islamic fascist group to which Agca had belonged) — but then Mehmet Ali Agca was simultaneously announcing that he was the Second Coming of Christ. Agca had also claimed, at his first trial, that he had acted alone in his assassination attempt — and then, at his second trial, he swore he had been trained and paid by the Bulgarian secret police.

Nonetheless, for all the owls in his attic, Agca seemed to know something about the heroin laundering business in Rome. Magistrates soon added dope dealing to their (now posthumous) charges against Roberto Calvi.

An even worse can of cobras had opened when the police attempted to arrest Licio Gelli, Calvi's "Master" in the P2 pseudo-Masonic lodge, and another Knight of Malta. (It is entirely possible that P2 was a SMOM operation all along, disguised to look Masonic so that Masons would get the blame if the lid ever blew.)

Gelli skipped Italy before the police could nab him, and investigations about how he had been tipped off revealed that many members of the secret police (devoted to protecting the government) were also members of P2 (devoted to overthrowing the government). This phalanx of double agents included General Musumeci, the Chief of Intelligence, who was subsequently indicted for conspiring, with Calvi, Gelli and others, to take over the government of Italy by a fascist coup.

Musumeci, in fact, was charged with aiding the allegedly left-wing bombers he was supposed to be hunting down. The embattled general died (of natural causes, it seems) before he could stand trial, but meanwhile over 950 other agents of P2 were uncovered in the Italian government, and P2 was being blamed for the Bologna railway bombing of 1980 and assorted other terrorist acts previously attributed to the Red Brigades.

(Gelli had explained this policy of terrorism, which he called "The Strategy of Tension," in a paper written for P2 initiates and found by the police when they raided his home. The strategy of tension was supposed to make Italians welcome a totalitarian coup to save them from Mad Bombers.)

Gelli, after his escape from Italy, was subsequently reported in Uruguay, near the previous home of Klaus Barbie, the Nazi war criminal who had been employed for nearly 40 years by the CIA. It was later revealed that Gelli had helped Barbie get employment with the CIA and that the secret P2 lodges Gelli and Ortolini had formed in Latin America played a key role in supporting Vatican and CIA objectives there.

After his 1982 flight to Uruguay, Signor Gelli later returned covertly to Switzerland, to withdraw funds from a numbered bank account. He was apprehended by Swiss police and placed in a maximum security prison in Basel until he could be extradited to Italy. The "maximum security" prison managed to hold the wily Gelli for only three days — 72 hours — and then, in some manner not yet determined, he escaped and was soon back in Uruguay.

Curiously, Signor Gelli's wife left Rome on a flight that allowed her to meet him as soon as he arrived in Uruguay. Sort of sounds like Gelli's escape was well planned, doesn't it?

Some Swiss wits claim the Basel "maximum security" prison should have a sign showing the famous Three Monkeys ("See no Evil, Hear no Evil, Speak no Evil") and a motto, *"Ficken sie nicht mit P2!"*

Meanwhile, the beleaguered Italian government — falling apart as more and more P2 members were uncovered in its highest offices — was trying to extradite Michele "The Shark" Sindona from the United States, where he was in prison for embezzling $55,000,000 from his own Franklin National Bank and 64 other counts of stock and currency fraud.

The Shark had originally been a lawyer for several Mafia families, but had started a chain of mysteriously interlinking banks in Italy — all of them tied up in strange loops, it has been discovered, with Calvi's Banco Ambrosiano and the Vatican Bank — and had become manager of Vatican financial affairs in the U.S., as Roberto (God's Banker) Calvi had been manager of Vatican finances in Europe.

It was due to Mike the Shark's wheeling-and-dealing that the Vatican now owns substantial shares in the World Trade Center, Proctor and Gamble and Paramount Films. But Mike was loyal to old friends, too — it is thanks to the Shark that the Mafia also owns part of Paramount, and gets royalties every time the anti-Mafia movie, *The Godfather*, is shown on TV again. Once again, one can only say: neat but not gaudy.

Mike the Shark Sindona was a guest at one of Nixon's White House parties. When New York D.A. Frank Hogan tried to extradite Paul the Gorilla Marcinkus to stand trial in connection with the billion dollar counterfeit stock fraud, Nixon intervened to protect Marcinkus.

Licio Gelli, the Puppet Master himself, was a guest at Reagan's January 1981 inauguration: there is even a photo of Gelli and Reagan together and they are both smiling, as if at some private and wonderful jest that the rest of us haven't heard yet.

Bishop Paul the Gorilla Marcinkus advanced to Archbishop.

Everybody was making billions — or hundreds of billions, if you believe some estimates of the profits in the drug traffic.

In the middle of the web were Mad Bill Casey, the man who was always Absolutely Right, and Colonel Oliver North, the man who could never recall what he did when quizzed by Congress.

IN THE HOOSEGOW

Coercion is the central principle of government.
— Lord Armstrong

We arrived at the Greene County Jail and the Yellow Springs Chief of Police turned us over to the County Sheriff, who "received" us. That means they exchanged pieces of paper, after filling in the blank spaces. When you deal with the State, everything goes on those pieces of paper which then are filed somewhere and probably photocopied and sent to the FBI, the CIA, Interpol, the Rhode Island Department of Furniture and Bedding and probably the credit department of every bank in the world.

A sheriff's deputy then began to fingerprint us. While we were lined up for this part of the Ritual — a Rite of Passage, signifying our transfer from the status of Free Citizens to that of State Property — I found that, standing against the wall, I could see into the first large holding cell.

The image of caged creatures was overwhelming. Nobody was getting forcibly sodomized or knifed or anything like that, it was actually all very quiet, but the atmosphere hit me like the first three notes of a death-dirge in Verdi. Virtually all the prisoners were Black and all of them looked as if they had reached a pit of depression and despair I had never known in my saddest hours. A few of them were playing cards at a table but even they looked more dead than alive. The others just stared into space, with no expression. The silence was the silence of a morgue. The only emotion I could sense beyond depression was the boredom of men who had been bored for a very long time and expected to be equally bored forever.

This was not a State Pen, I told myself. It was only a County Jail. Nobody in there was a Lifer. They couldn't possibly be that bored, really. I must be reading too much into their body language. But, still: I have seen zombies in horror movies who had more human hope and feeling in their faces than those men in that cage.

It was my turn to be finger-printed. I stepped forward, losing sight of the caged men, and obediently held out my hand. I remembered all the times I had held out that hand to have it savaged by Mother Superior's steel yardstick. You hold out your hand, in those circumstances, because you know something much worse will happen if you refuse.

All around me I sensed the men with guns. Agents of Law and Order, according to the popular view. Hired Guns on guard to ensure that property remains stolen, according to the anarchists. I looked at them covertly. None of them looked like Nazis or sadists. They were just Good Old Boys who worked for the sheriff because they lacked the education to get a better-paying job. I might even enjoy having a beer with one of them, under other circumstances.

They had the authority to use "reasonable force" if I resisted them in any way. One of them could shoot me, non-fatally, and the others would dutifully testify that I was dangerous and "out of control." They could even shoot me fatally and if they got their stories right on the witness chair the jury would exonerate them.

Two years earlier, at the School of Living library, I had read most of the classics of anarchist theory. The State was created by conquerors, these books said, to police the peoples they had enslaved. The revolutions of the 18th Century failed because, instead of abolishing the State and organizing society into voluntary communes and syndicates, we had stupidly continued the State apparatus, thinking we could "control" it by democratic elections. These elections cannot control the State because the Great Pirates who own the Earth and its resources own the State, too, and know how to buy elections.

"Now the next finger, please..." The officer who was taking my prints seemed pleasant. If he believed in segregation and thought we were "commies" for opposing it, he did not reveal that opinion in his actions.

Wilhelm Reich disagreed with the anarchist analysis. The State did not survive because some Great Pirates needed it to rob us more efficiently, he said: it survived because the masses were neurotically trapped at a childish level. They needed a Daddy Figure above them. That's why "God" survived the attacks of the

Rationalists, Reich said, and why Feminism, after 200 years, had not seriously damaged the Patriarchal structure.

"Please come this way." Another officer led us upstairs. "Please sit down."

We were alone. We could open a window, jump and make a run for it. That did not seem very prudent and we weren't desperate enough to consider it. I doubt that we would have gotten half a block before somebody with a gun said, "Halt in the name of the Law" or whatever they say. Besides, we didn't intend to become fugitives. We intended to go to jail to protest segregation.

We looked at a large camera and a blank white screen. This was where they would take our pictures.

I craned my neck and saw an officer waiting in the hall to take us back downstairs after the photographer was finished with us.

"Well, here we are," somebody said finally.

I suddenly realized we were already falling into the empty silence of the Living Dead in the cages down below.

Trapped.

INTERCEPT & PAVANNE

To plunder, to slaughter, to steal, these they misname
Empire, and where they make a desert, they call it
peace.   — Calgacus

As I write, the United States continues to bombard Baghdad,
hour after hour, day after day. Goddam Insane, who probably
genuinely believes his claim that this bombardment is all a
"Zionist" plot, has just bombed Tel Aviv for the fourth time. The
war in the Gulf is evolving into what an English tommy once
called "a fair bugger."

Egyptian refugees from Iraq, back in Egypt, claim that the
U.S. — contrary to its claims of only bombing military targets —
has bombarded many civilian centers and killed thousands. They
want Egypt to drop out of its alliance with the U.S. (These
claims are receiving remarkably little media attention in the U.S.
I heard them on CNN *once*, and then they were heard and printed
no more.) Jordan is rumbling about all the missiles crossing its
air space — one of which is bound to fall on them by accident,
sooner or later. Goddam Insane is still trying to whomp up a pan-
Islamic Holy War against Zionism and American Imperialism.

All this finally tore me away from the creative "ecstasy" or
*bezonken*state of writing this book and dragged me back down to
Consensus Reality, feeling nasty. I sent a telegram to my
Representative in Congress, the Hon. Mel Levine. He had said he
voted for war in the Gulf in order to protect Israel from Arab
attack — even though it seemed to most of us that such a war
would *inevitably* lead to an Arab attack on Israel.

But, then, Mel's reasoning was not as bizarre as that of others
in Congress, who actually said they voted for war in order to
preserve peace, as if they had been reading Orwell without
recognizing his irony.

Since Mel is my very own Congressman and allegedly represents me, I targeted him for my vexation. I wrote:

WAR IS PEACE
FREEDOM IS SLAVERY
IGNORANCE IS STRENGTH
BEFORE I EVER VOTE FOR YOU AGAIN
I WILL VOTE FOR ZIPPY THE PINHEAD

I have little expectation that the Hon. Mr. Levine will ever see this, but I have some hope that whoever in his office has to read it will find it harder to forget than most telegrams from irate citizens. Meanwhile, Syria has joined Jordan in muttering darkly about switching sides and joining the Iraqis if Israel is so wicked as to defend itself from Goddam Insane's bombardment of its civilians.

At least one group of our citizens is really enjoying this war — the Fundamentalist Protestants. They think this is the beginning of Armageddon and they expect to be lifted up to Heaven in what they call The Rapture.

These Fundamentalists are not quite as wacky as a woman who called a radio talk show I tuned in the other night. She said Islam was a secret branch of the Catholic Church and the Arabs are acting on Vatican orders.

INFORMATION DOUBLES AGAIN

The next doubling of information took *only ten years* and by 1960 "we" collectively knew twice as much about the Universe as we had known in 1950...

Already, the Industrial Age was beginning to transmute into something new, as over 2000 scientific research centers were using computers and finding out what these wonderful new toys could do. Little was left of the tribal partnership societies from which human society had originally evolved, and even the sun-king systems that remained were colonies of the Industrial states, openly or covertly, but now Industriality was mutating into something so radical we didn't even have a name for it yet.

In 1960, I was writing advertising copy — a victory and a defeat; bitter victory, because for the first time, contrary to what my parents and everybody else had told me, I was making a living by writing; moral defeat, because what I was writing was not at all what I wanted to write. Like everybody else in the business, I was drifting into the habit of the two martini lunch, which sometimes became a three martini lunch or a four martini lunch. (In 1962, I saw so many symptoms of alcoholism among the other advertising writers around me that I quit before it could happen to me.)

In 1960, Black sit-in demonstrations against segregation were already occurring throughout the South. The first privately financed nuclear power plant opened at Dresden, Illinois. Grand Juries indicted General Electric, Westinghouse and Allis-Chalmers for conspiracy in restraint of trade — "price fixing" — and the executives responsible got their wrists slapped with fines totaling less than $2 million.

That was just about the last effort of the U.S. government to police the multi-national corporations. Since TV took over, it takes $100 million to run a campaign for the Presidency, $30 million to campaign for the Senate, and $10 million to campaign for the House. (Figures from Buckminster Fuller, *Grunch of Giants.*) Guess where the politicians get that kind of money. Then guess who owns the government.

Also in 1960, the first tranquilizer went on the market —
Librium.

The first U.S. communication satellite went into orbit in
August.

World population reached three billion.

Project Ozma, the first attempt to contact extraterrestrial intelligence, began under the directorship of Frank Drake.

The Information Explosion was beginning to be noticed by
some scientists. Mathematician Stanley Ulam observed that
200,000 new theorems were being published every year and no
single mind could keep up with all this. It was estimated that the
last man to know all mathematics was Alexander Ostrowski,
who died in 1915.

YELLOW ROSES FOR JOANNE

On 20 January 1985 the first yellow rose was delivered to Joanne Hayes, in the courtroom where the size of her vagina had been the subject of such intense investigation — and the search for the Second Lover had yielded no evidence that such a person existed.

The rose had been sent by Bernie McCarthy, a Feminist from nearby Tralee. Word got out, and the next day hundreds of yellow roses were delivered, while Judge Lynch fumed. In the following month, thousands and thousands of yellow roses were delivered to Joanne, mute testimony to what the Plain People of Ireland thought of this Tribunal.

The courtroom began to look like a florist shop. The roses came from men as well as from women, and many came from nuns. One nun even wrote to Joanne, confessing her own affair with a priest and writing, "God is more forgiving than men." (This is quoted in Nell McCafferty's book on the trial, *A Woman To Blame*.)

MENSTRUATION ...
ITS CAUSE & CURE

In 1962, after I quit the advertising business, Arlen and I had taken our four small children and moved to Millbrook, Ohio, where I had been hired as co-editor of *Balanced Living,* the magazine of the School of Living. The first thing I did was change the title of the magazine to *Way Out,* which I hoped would attract a younger, hipper readership. I also persuaded Norman Mailer to write a few poems for the first issue under the new title, which I figured would galvanize the whole intellectual world.

It didn't work out that way. We didn't have the budget for adequate promotion.

The School of Living, founded by Ralph Borsodi around 1928, was based on the idea that, even in 20th Century America, you could attain more independence and live more comfortably if you "returned to the land," grew your own food, and generally imitated the sturdy, mind-your-own-business farmers on whom Jefferson's democratic dream had originally been based. Insofar as Jeffersonian America was dead, or moribund, Borsodi claimed, that was because most Americans worked for wages and *working for wages* turns everybody into conformists and cowards.

Borsodi had retired and the School of Living was now run by a former social worker, Mildred Loomis, who had supplemented Borsodi's ideas with a grab-bag of radical and heretical notions from a variety of off-beat sources. In a nut-shell, she had progressed from Decentralism to Libertarianism and onward to Anarchism, without ever thinking herself either radical or eccentric; she was just looking for a way humans could live more healthy and independent lives.

In her searching Mildred had acquired a lot of knowledge of and respect for such Heresies as Henry George's economics (democracy with free enterprise, except that land speculation was impossible since the government would own all land), Silvio Gesell's rival economics (still basically democratic free enterprise, except that along with government ownership of land *a la* George, there would be a tax of one percent per month on money, and no other taxes, which Gesell claimed would keep government small and Jeffersonian while at the same time preventing usury) and the "sexual revolution" doctrines of Dr. Wilhelm Reich.

I learned a lot about Third Choice systems — social doctrines that were neither Capitalist nor Marxist — at the School of Living, which had a great library of radical and off-beat literature. It was there that I found and read all the issues of *Liberty,* the individualist-anarchist magazine edited by the brilliant Benjamin R. Tucker ("the clearest mind ever, in politics," Joyce called him.) I also read all the issues of *Mother Earth,* the communist-anarchist magazine of Emma Goldman, where I perused with excitement what scholars call "primary sources" — contemporary accounts of the trials of Joe Hill, Big Bill Heywood and other founders of the Industrial Workers of the World.

The most amazing book in the School of Living library, however, was *Menstruation: Its Cause and Cure* by Raymond Bernard, Ph.D. Arlen found that one, and insisted on keeping it on our coffee table, just to see how visitors would react to it. She has a wicked sense of humor.

Dr. Bernard, who — as I later discovered — had a real Ph.D. from New York University, even if he did write like a Clinical Loony, claimed menstruation was caused by "too frequent" sexual intercourse and the unnatural vice of meat-eating. If women had sex only once a year, at the Spring solstice, and didn't eat meat, he proposed, the "curse" would go away.

When I asked Mildred Loomis how she had acquired that book, she was embarrassed and evasive. Her husband, John, insisted on telling the whole story, even though Mildred obviously did not relish hearing it again. She had once loaned Dr. Bernard around $2000 to help him start a Utopian community in Central America. She never got the money back, and John was convinced she had been taken by an expert con-man. He seemed to think that was the sort of thing that happened to gullible women who were not satisfied with Ralph Borsodi's back-to-nature philosophy and insisted on adding all sorts of radical and far-fetched new ideas onto the Borsodi system.

Later, I found another of Dr. Bernard's books in the School library. It was called *The Hollow Earth* and made Captain Symmes doughnut-shaped hollow Earth seem conservative by comparison. According to Bernard, the inside of the Earth is not only "habitable," as Symmes claimed, but already inhabited — by two races of androids designed by the Atlanteans before their continent was destroyed. The good androids, called Teros, were the ones who came out of the hole at the North Pole and flew around in "flying saucers." They would take all the good people inside the Earth to save them in the event of nuclear war. The bad androids, called Deros, were devoted entirely to sadism, and by using fiendish machines which sent invisible rays up to the surface of our planet, these Deros created all seemingly "paranormal" events, especially the more sinister ones, such as Spontaneous Human Combustion.

I recognized most of that, because it had appeared in *Amazing Stories* when I was a teen-ager. The Teros and Deros had been invented, in that sci-fi pulp, by one Richard Shaver, who, like L. Ron Hubbard later, started out writing sado-paranoid science fiction and then went on to invent his own religion.

Just this year, I received a review copy of *Subterranean Worlds*, a history of hollow earth theories by an eminently skeptical writer named Walter Kafton-Minkel. It has a whole chapter about Dr. Bernard and concludes that, even if he did not have the financial rectitude of a Scotch banker, Dr. Bernard was perfectly sincere in his beliefs — especially in the belief that modern women want sex too often.

THE WORLD GAME ...
I BECOME THE MID-EAST

I became all the nations of the Mid-East — the Arab states, the Persians (Iranians), even the Israelis — for a few hours in July 1990.

You see, I had gone to the annual convention of the World Future Society and was playing Bucky Fuller's World Game, under the leadership of Medard Gabel, a longtime co-worker with Bucky.

You play the World Game on a large Dymaxion map of the world. This kind of map, designed by Bucky, is flat but has no distortion of land areas because it uses synergetic geometry. (Mercator maps make Greenland look bigger than Australia, and distort other things less notably, because they use flatland Euclidean geometry for the surface of a sphere.)

I was given the props to represent the Mid-East's share of the world's resources. Eggboxes represented food, light swords represented energy, and balloons represented weapons. I found I had three eggboxes, representing three percent of the world's food. Consulting my information sheets, I found this was adequate, since I represented three percent of the world's population; but I couldn't sell any food without some of my people going hungry.

I also had nine percent of the world's energy which seemed adequate for my population. However, my literacy rate was only 65 percent. I decided to try to raise it to 85 percent in the course of the Game.

Despite having only enough food for my population, I decided to sell some anyway, hoping to buy more later. Alas, the people who needed food couldn't afford to pay for it, and the people who could pay (e.g., the U.S.) didn't need food.

I invested $50,000,000,000 of my capital in buying educational equipment and hiring teachers, which raised my literacy rate to 75 percent in the first round.

I then got another eggbox, since when literacy increases 10 percent, food production increases proportionally. I now owned four percent of the world's food and had only three percent of the world's population to feed. I tried again to sell food, but the hungry had no money and the wealthy weren't hungry.

I decided to give some food away to Africa. This earned me a Good Will Certificate which meant I could collect something from Africa eventually.

I gave away some more food to South America and got another Good Will Certificate. With that much Good Will in two heavily-populated continents, I felt secure in investing another $50 billion in education — and got a bonus light-sword, since energy as well as food production increase when literacy rises.

Quickly, I sold my extra light-sword (representing one percent of world energy) to Southeast Asia and bought more education.

Things were getting exciting. Players were shouting, trying to make deals before time ran out. I gave away some more food, to Southeast Asia, and bought more education. That gave me a bonus in food production, which brought me back to the three percent with which I had started.

When the Game ended, I still had three percent of the world's food to feed three percent of its population, nine percent of its energy, lots of Good Will from Asia, Africa and South America, and had raised literacy beyond the 85 percent I had aimed for to a full 100 percent — higher than the U.S. — meaning that I would have more food and energy in the next round if the Game had continued.

Because of my "generosity" to Asia, Africa and South America, infant mortality declined in those places, meaning that birth-rate would drop in the next round. (Birth-rate always drops when most children who are born survive past their first two years. Most excess birth seems "insurance" against high infant mortality.)

I began to grok the sociological meaning of synergy more fully. If X gives away food instead of letting it rot, X not only collects "good will" but also lowers the planet's birth rate.

Synergy means that there are no isolated systems.

THE MYSTERY DEEPENS AS
THE BVM TAKES A HAND

The Joanne Hayes tribunal, awash in roses, lurched along. On 14 February 1985, a few miles away in Asdee, several children reported that a statue of the Blessed Virgin wept. A few days later, an 80-year-old farmer said the statue made pitiful "imploring gestures."

The tribunal continued, as the pickets outside increased in number and more and more yellow roses arrived. The Guards produced an expert in obstetrical oddities from London. The expert recounted numerous documented cases of Superfecundation among the lower animals.

The Guards smiled.

Judge Lynch smiled.

The defense rose and asked if the expert knew of any documented cases of Superfecundation in *human* females. The expert said there were no such cases, and none among the higher apes either.

The Guards stopped smiling. They had hired the wrong expert; they were beginning to look like Keystone Kops.

And on 14 March at Ballydesmond (in Cork, near Kerry) another statue of the Virgin was seen to make "imploring" or tragic gestures.

On 14 June the Tribunal concluded its hearings. Margarite Egan, a Feminist from Tralee, marched up to the bench and placed a thick envelope before Judge Lynch. He asked what it was. She said it was a petition calling for the abolition of all-male Tribunals in Ireland. Judge Lynch said she might be in contempt of court. They glared at each other, or at least locked eyes, and then Margarite Egan walked away. I don't know if Judge Lynch ever read the petition.

On 15 July in Cashel a few miles away a group of young people between 10 and 14 years of age were crossing a field when they saw a blinding white light, which staggered them. When they could see again, they saw or hallucinated a UFO take off rapidly. An adult male, nearby, saw a "silver disc" ascend from the same field.

On 17 June back in Kerry another "imploring" statue of the Virgin became active in a town with the wonderful name, Ballinspittle. This one not only made piteous gestures but swayed in rhythm and began changing its features so that it looked like Jesus and various saints, especially Padre Pio, patron of the poor, who is very popular in Ireland.

In the next two months there were moving statues of the Virgin reported in 24 towns in Ireland, accompanied by alleged healings. The overwhelming majority were in southwest Ireland, in or around Kerry, and more than half were in Kerry itself. The most active of these hunks of stone turned out to be the one in Ballinspittle, Kerry, which was particularly prone to weep or metamorphize into Padre Pio. It was also in Ballinspittle that the best-documented healing occurred. Mrs. Frances O'Riordan of Cork City, whose deafness had been diagnosed as incurable by an ear specialist at Cork Hospital, went to Ballinspittle, saw the statue move, and regained her hearing.

Journalist Isobel Healy examined this case thoroughly and there is no doubt that Mrs. O'Riordan was deaf before Ballinspittle and is no longer deaf.

On 11 September a Dublin Feminist and free-thinker, June Levine, went down to Ballinspittle to see the phenomenon for herself. In her perception, the statue of the Virgin turned into a "handsome young rabbi." She says she blinked, looked away, rested her eyes — and when she looked back the Virgin was still a rabbi.

Eanna Brophy went down on 15 September, also saw the statue begin to transform (into Jesus) and also blinked, looked away, rested her eyes — and the statue was just a statue again.

You never know who the *pookah* is going to play his tricks upon.

On 13 September a cameraperson from Radio Telefis hEirann reported his own experience at Ballinspittle. The statue remained inert stone, he said, but he saw two strange lights in the sky, performing loop-the-loops and even stranger maneuvers that he found inexplicable. He was quite shaken.

Conner Cruise O'Brien, Ireland's leading agnostic, went down to have a look-see and also saw strange lights. He said they were reflections of automobile headlights on clouds. They did not do loop-the-loops.

On 20 September, parapsychologist Harold Covington of Tralee, published a study. He noted that some of the strange visions had been seen by ex-Catholics, Jews, Protestants, freethinkers, atheists and mildly curious tourists, whereas some pious Catholics had gone to the scene night after night and never seen anything strange. The majority of visions, however, had been seen by believing Catholics.

Nell McCafferty wrote a sociological article claiming the whole statue phenomenon (she ignored the UFOs) was a hysterical response to the explicit sexual details in the Joanne Hayes cross-examination; she also claimed that the Virgin, because she had never had a orgasm (in Catholic doctrine), was the only female in history not feared or hated by Catholic males.

Bishop Thomas McDonell of the (Protestant) Church of Ireland wrote a long letter to the *Irish Times*, learnedly citing scientific texts to prove that some people sometimes see optical illusions.

I myself wrote a piece for Dublin *Hot Press,* demonstrating that Catholics have no monopoly on weirdity; I cited the statue of Mahadeva in India which (according to *Probe India* August 1981) *menstruates* every seven years.

GORBY ACID ... & THE FALL OF THE BERLIN WALL

The big fad in Europe in 1989, while I was on my annual lecture tour there, was Gorby Acid — blotter LSD with Gorbachev's picture on it. Aficionados insisted it was the best acid since the legendary blotter of 1978 that had the Illuminati eye and pyramid on it; some even claimed Gorby was "good as Sandoz." London was celebrating by having huge acid parties which were almost semi-public and verged on overt civil disobedience. Berlin, Heidelberg and Zurich (among other places) all had their own supply of the wonderful Gorby Acid, and rumor insisted the manufacturer was in Amsterdam, which, of course, always has the best acid in Europe.

That year I was doing my European tour with Michael Hutchison, author of *Megabrain*. It was an unusual experience, since I am accustomed to working alone on the lecture platform and also to "taking risks" (using humor that might be offensive to some). Mike and I turned out to work well together and, since we were demonstrating brain machines, we attracted very odd audiences — a blend of physicians, psychiatrists and New Agers that made a very unstable mixture. I'm convinced that half of each audience regarded the other half as so far out the trolleys don't run there, but that was okay. They all gave me new insights into what was happening in Europe in the Year of Gorby Acid.

1989 was always on my mind for the past decade, because in 1981 I read Bucky Fuller's *Critical Path*, in which he stated that by 1989 we would either have nuclear war or a radical change in the whole world order. Fuller had made many correct prophecies before that, so I kept waiting for 1989 to see what would happen; but I never expected Gorby Acid.

In Zurich, where the tour started, I was told that Gorby was the most popular politician of the 20th Century. "Why not?" a lady photographer asked rhetorically. "He's the first statesman to have an original idea since the Congress of Vienna." (That was in 1812, in case you forgot.) Gorby's face was on the acid in

1989 because he appealed to the same sort of people who were *Illuminatus* fans in 1978, when the eye-in-pyramid acid came out.

I will try not to be jealous.

Everybody in Zurich had an idea about when the Berlin Wall would come down. Most said by the mid-1990s; a few optimists said the early 1990s...

I remembered standing at the Wall, in 1986, with an actor named Tobias who said to me, "Look at the birds. They fly back and forth, over the Wall, as if it wasn't there."

I had examined the graffiti that decorate the Western side of the Wall and found them equally hostile to Communism and Capitalism; their attitude was pure anarchism, or nihilism, or perhaps just deep cynicism about all politicians.

"Do you think it will ever come down? In your lifetime?" I asked.

"No," Tobias said bitterly. "Not in my lifetime..."

But that was 1987 and in 1989 everybody in Zurich was asking how soon the Wall would come down. I thought of fractals, those totally unpredictable mathematical functions that are lately being discovered in one science after another.

In June, in Washington, I had heard a mathematician, Theodore J. Gordon, read a paper to the World Future Society, demonstrating that fractal unpredictability increases in any system where information flow increases. Since there is no doubt information flow is increasing exponentially these days, I thought, we should see more and more fractal instability in every social system, and the technical name for that is "chaos."

Mathematical "chaos" in social systems does not mean riot and arson, necessarily. It simply means the totally unexpected.

Such chaos can be symbolized, I think, by the picture of a Russian bureaucrat on the drug that, above all others, symbolizes the Utopian dreams of the 1960s. But then what words better invoke the '60s than *glasnost* (openness) and *peristroika* (restructuring)?

In Heidelberg, I heard about the death of a man who had fascinated me, even though I probably never met him. I had read about his adventures, originally, in a paper given to me after a lecture in Hamburg in summer 1988. The paper was a blurry Xerox of an article by Clifford Stoll of Lawrence Berkeley Laboratory, called "Stalking the Wily Hacker" (*Communications of the Association of Computing Machinery,* Vol. 31, No. 3). The man who gave me the paper said only, "This will amuse you."

Stoll's paper concerned a German hacker who, from his home in Hanover, had penetrated every part of the American defense establishment. He had browsed through the computers of LBL and Lawrence Livermore, where nightmares worse than the hydrogen bomb are being devised, and through the Naval Data Center in Norfolk, and so on through just about every allegedly "secure" system the U.S. has. It took the American intelligence community a year and a half to track him down and then, oddly, the German authorities declined to prosecute him because of "lack of evidence."

Somehow, I had an intuition or a suspicion that the man who handed me that article was the hacker whose exploits it recorded. I will never be sure of this, of course.

Now the Hanover neuromancer was dead. I was shown a newspaper article including his picture — I couldn't decide whether he was the one who had handed me Stoll's article, but I thought he might be. His name was Klaus — I thought ironically of Santa Claus — and he had committed suicide on May 23, 1989. He was 23 years old.

After years of writing about 23-synchronicities, I never expected it would come back on me in so morbid a form.

The article also had a picture of Klaus's computer with a copy of *Illuminatus* on top. The story said it was his favorite book and he often wrote articles for the anarchist press under the pen-name "Hagbard Celine."

Well, I thought, now somebody from the CIA is going to have to read that book and write an analysis of it to be added to their already thick dossier on me. I cannot begin to imagine what a CIA agent will make out of *Illuminatus.* A man from the Committee for Scientific Investigation of Claims of the Paranormal recently complained that when he tells people some things in my books are batshit crazy, they tell him he lacks a sense of humor. I fear somebody in the CIA is also going to have that problem, because the CIA reality-tunnel is as rigid and paranoid as that of

CSICOP. People without humor are always being psychologically terrorized when they try to understand my books.

(One man from CSICOP recently wrote, "Wilson describes himself as a 'guerrilla ontologist,' signifying his intention to *attack* language and knowledge the way terrorists *attack* their targets: to *JUMP OUT FROM THE SHADOWS* for an unprovoked *attack*, then slink back and hide behind a belly-laugh." (Emphasis added, of course.) You can see that this poor man feels under *attack* and probably looks beneath his bed at night to see if I or some other Witch might be lurking there. He also never had a teacher who told him using the same word three times in a short sentence creates a dull mechanical style suggesting a dull mechanical mind.)

In Gottingen, I heard more about Klaus the Cracker. The newspapers mostly called him Hagbard, accepting his *nom de plume,* but had blacked out the case rapidly after the first story. Rumors were now rife that both the CIA and the KGB had tried to recruit him after his escapades became known. Nobody seemed to believe the official verdict that he had committed suicide.

In Cologne, nobody had any new Conspiracy Theories about Klaus Hagbard, but everybody was saying the Wall would come down within two years.

During the brain workshop, I did my standard bit about how information has been accelerating in the past two thousand years, using the same statistics from French economist George Anderla used in this book. Somebody asked me if I thought that process might be a Mandelbrot fractal, as suggested by Terence McKenna. I said frankly that I wasn't sure, but I certainly agree with Terence that there are more wild and unpredictable changes directly ahead of us.

If the rate of increase of information does have the structure of a Mandelbrot set, as McKenna claims, by the year 2012 we should have information doubling *every day* and, later in the year, *every hour* and then *every nanosecond.* I cannot imagine what this means practically in terms of social change, because every doubling of information in the past has resulted in totally unexpected social revolutions, violent or non-violent.

In Berlin, I was taken to dinner by a Punk Rock group called the Klingons and met a young man who had escaped East

Germany a year ago. He said the Wall would come down within a few months — the most optimistic prediction I had heard yet. He also told me a Strange Story.

In Leipzig, where he grew up, there was a "public" library that was not open to the public. (Isn't that a marvelous Marxist oxymoron?) In this library were books which the Communist leaders did not want anybody to read but which, evidently, they didn't want to burn. (Maybe some of them liked to read the Forbidden Heresies themselves?)

My young informant told me he decided to burglarize the library. With patience and observation, he found a way to get in at night and grab a few books now and then. He always returned them, to avoid arousing suspicion, after reading their Heretical Ideas. When he made his escape to the West, he brought only one of those forbidden books with him.

He put it on the table. It was *Illuminatus.* "Would you please autograph it?" he asked.

I was overwhelmed. The thought of my book locked in a sealed library by Communist officials who did not want to burn it outright was dramatic enough, but having the book stolen and offered to me for an autograph was so weird I wondered if anybody would ever believe this story.

I opened the book to sign it and found on the inside front cover the words RAJNEESH INTERNATIONAL LIBRARY.

Is (or was) the Rajneesh International Library in Poona, India, at his original Ashram, or in his later Oregon ashram? How the hell did the book get from either India or Oregon to the hands of a Communist official in East Germany, who decided to preserve it in a sealed library?

I signed the book, thinking Jungians would regard this odyssey of a book back to its author as a synchronicity. I found myself thinking of it, instead, as another wiggle in the fractal process that it is producing more and more unpredictability every year as in-**form**-ation leaps over Walls and jumps borders, and the world moves toward the trans-*form*-ation of all forms that once seemed eternal.

A week after I returned to California, the Berlin Wall came tumbling down. In the next months, more and more Experts began appearing in the media declaring the Cold War over and asking what we would do with our Peace Dividend. Nobody suggested that Huge Berserk Rebel Warthog would use most of it to blow hell out of the Mid-East.

And nobody guessed that Gorby would crush the independence movements in the Baltics with such brutality that he has no more chance of appearing on the next batch of Amsterdam Acid than Huge Berserk Rebel Warthog has.

HELL ON EARTH

There are now 50,000 thermonuclear weapons on Earth.

June 1989: I was back in the World Game seminar, after lunch. We all seemed to agree that playing the Game had taught us very concretely what Bucky Fuller had meant by "synergetic global management" and "advantaging all without disadvantaging any."

Now Medard Gabel proceeded to dramatize the alternative, in which all 50,000 thermo-nukes are used in a global conflict.

Each weapon was represented by a red plastic chip about the size of a dime. On the Dymaxion Map, each "dime" covered the area that would be destroyed totally if a nuke was dropped. Medard carefully spread all 50,000 chips across the map...and slowly *covered every square inch*. No part of Earth was not blown up totally.

I had known for a long time that the world's nukes had reached the level where D.O.E. — Death Of Earth — was possible, but this simple dramatization made me feel it more deeply than ever before.

"This only represents the immediate effects of the blasts," Medard said soberly. "We're not even considering fall-out and nuclear winter and other long-range effects..."

I looked around the room and saw the most sober and saddened faces I had ever encountered. I suppose I looked like that, too.

Later, I chatted with Medard in the hotel lounge. He told me that, to get health care for our children equal to that of Costa Rican children, the U.S. would only have to spend a sum equal to eight days of our yearly military budget.

Imagine that, I thought. Even without trying to get health care equal to Ireland or any European country — a Herculean task after a decade of Voodoo Economics — we could at least achieve parity with one moderately advanced Third World country if we gave up eight days of bomb building.

Huge Berserk Rebel Warthog would probably shit a brick at the thought.

SHE WAS RAISED IN A CONVENT

Sometime in the mid 1950s, when I was still working as an engineering aide, I discovered that radio drama was not dead — at least on one New York FM station. In England, the competition created by TV drama had not reduced radio to endless music and talk shows; they were still doing dramas, and this New York station was rebroadcasting them. Among them was "The Lives of Harry Lime," starring Orson Welles — who, of course, also directed. The Great Round One also occasionally wrote some of the scripts, but a stable of writers did most of the stories and, after a while, I began to notice that the yarns I liked best were attributed to one Arlen Riley.

I thought that had to be a pen-name. It didn't seem likely that anybody could be *that* Irish. Arlen Riley, indeed — why not Paddy Fitz?*

A year or so later I was scheduled to give my first public lecture — on science, pseudo-science and science-fiction — at the New York Academy of the Sciences, sponsored by the New York Society for General Semantics. One day, Jane Heyburn, Secretary of the G.S. Society, phoned me and said that since this was my first public appearance, they would like me to try out the lecture with a small group first.

I had a lot of confidence about the lecture, so I was neither worried nor insulted. "Sure," I said. "I'll do a rehearsal first. Where is this group?"

"They meet at the apartment of a woman named Arlen Riley," Jane said.

Arlen Riley — the name seemed familiar. Then I remembered: "The Lives of Harry Lime."

"You'll like her," Jane said. "I think you have a lot in common. She was raised in a convent."

---

* Pen-name of actor-director Patrick McGoohan —who, oddly enough, co-starred with Orson in a stage production of *Moby-Dick* in London, at the same time this radio show was in production. Americans know McGoohan best as *The Prisoner*.

THE DOG CASTRATOR
OF PALM SPRINGS

After the World Game, I wandered around the World Future Society meeting for a while and then tried the bar. I found two computer crackers I knew from Berkeley. We ordered Moscow Mules and they told me the latest news on the Cyberpunk front: "A guy in San Jose has a virus he says will penetrate IRS. He's still trying to decide whether to have it destroy files selectively or just take out the whole system in one dump."

You always hear that kind of rumor from Bay Area computer people.

The other guy had a bright view of urine testing. "It only screens out the pot-heads and coke-freaks," he said. "They can all go into arts and entertainment — hell, they got the temperament for it, right? But meanwhile, who'll be passing the urine tests and climbing the corporate ladder?"

"The usual alcoholics," I said.

"Well, yeah," he said, "some of them, sure, but dig, baby — the acid-heads, too. There's no urine test for acid. By the year 2000 the top of the pyramid will all be acid-heads. They'll make Tim Leary Secretary of Space and we'll all blast off for the stars."

The first guy interrupted to tell me about the cat killer of Orange County. Cats, evidently, are turning up dead, drained of blood, on lawns all over the Orange suburbs. "Just like the Cattle Mutilations, only now it's aimed right at the kind of people who voted for Reagan and Bush and really worry about Satanism. Real sick humor, huh?"

We had another round of Moscow Mules and the second guy told me about the dog castrator of Palm Springs. "He doesn't kill the mutts, just cuts off their balls. Weird shit."

"Are you sure this isn't just more Right Wing paranoia?" I asked.

"Hell," the first guy said. "NBC did a show about the cats. The Orange County authorities say it's coyotes doing it, but did you ever hear of a coyote that sucks blood and leaves the cadaver behind? Coyotes are like all predators — whatever they kill, they drag off to a safe place, to eat at their leisure. They don't leave bodies lying around on lawns, the way these cats are found."

"I never *dringk*...wine," I said in my Bela Lugosi voice. I wasn't buying any of this.

"This dog castrator has been seen," the first guy said. "He looks like a Mexican, but very short. Almost a dwarf. For some reason he wears thick goggles and a kind of scuba diving suit. And he's got a funny kind of flashlight that paralyzes people if they try to stop him when he's deballing a dog..."

Well, what can you expect in a country where the top officials are Pubic Hair and Vagina?

MORE THAN SYMBOL,
MORE THAN SERMON,
THE BRIDGE PERSISTS

Eight thousand feet above Man and History.
— Note written by Nietzsche in the Alps, 1886

I was in the middle of the Brooklyn Bridge, still contemplating suicide. Around me was a panoramic view — the sky-scrapers of lower Manhattan, the lovely old homes of Brooklyn Heights, the sky so blue it seemed to have been imported from Miami for that special day.

The nearest tower had a plaque on it. I walked over to read it.

The plaque, bronze and bold, had been erected recently, and had the name of the current mayor on it. It was dedicated to Emily Roebling, who supervised the building of the bridge, and her husband, Col. Washington Roebling, who co-supervised, and the Colonel's father, Johann Roebling, who had originally designed the bridge. It had some pious male chauvinist platitude at the end: "Behind every great work of man is the spirit of a woman," I think.

I knew the story of the Roeblings; I had read a book about them. Old Johann, an immigrant from Germany, had invented a type of cable that, he believed, would make it possible to build longer suspension bridges than had ever existed. As is usual with innovators, it took him years to sell the idea, but Manhattan and Brooklyn (separate cities then) finally agreed to put up a bridge he designed. Johann himself was killed in an accident during the first few years of the work.

The old man's son, Col. Washington Roebling, returned from the Civil War and, with a West Point engineering background, took up the job. Spooky, frightening things happened. The men's voices changed in the compression chambers below the water-line, and the superstitious had to be reassured repeatedly. Then, as they went deeper, the men started coming up the surface inexplicably crippled. It took a while before doctors understood what happens when a body comes up from the depths too fast. Eventually, they learned to bring the men up slowly, so they would not be crippled by the rapid change in air pressure.

By then, Col. Roebling had been crippled himself. From his bed, he watched the work with binoculars and Emily, his wife, studying engineering from his books, took on co-responsibility for supervising everything. Eventually, she became the first woman admitted to the American Society of Civil Engineers.

The Brooklyn Bridge was finished 13 years after it was started. The same design was later used for the even longer Golden Gate Bridge linking San Francisco to Marin — designed by a man who had grown up in Brooklyn Heights, looking every day at that stone and steel poem the three Roeblings had created out of Pure Math, tragedy, and sheer persistence.

I suddenly felt all self-pity drain out of me, replaced by absurd optimism. I didn't know why I was so moved, but suddenly I understood that the meek never inherit a damned thing: only the very brave and very stubborn make any impact on the world. The bridge stood there, a miracle in its time, taken for granted today, but an epiphany to me: great things are possible, to those too pig-headed to admit defeat.

Suicide was idiotic, unthinkable. I walked on, toward Brooklyn Heights, enjoying the sky and the sea and the white soaring gulls.

SHE WAS NOT RAISED
IN A CONVENT

I rang the doorbell and waited. The door opened — and there stood the most beautiful red-headed woman I had ever seen.

"Arlen Riley?" I asked.

"Bob Wilson?" she asked.

She let me in, with a mildly irritable complaint about my having arrived early. I lamely explained that I didn't know that part of Manhattan and had started early to be sure I wouldn't be late. She processed that and then said she had to put her face on.

I was alone in the living room. I found a copy of Allen Ginsberg's *Howl*. Hell, I thought, if she's reading that, nothing I have to say about modern literature will be new or surprising to her.

Arlen reappeared with her "face" on. She looked perhaps one percent more beautiful than when she had opened the door, but she seemed more comfortable with herself.

We talked about Korzybski and General Semantics until the study group arrived and then I gave my lecture.

At the end, I was suddenly overcome with anxiety. I was sure nothing I had said had impressed these bright, quick Manhattan intellectuals.

I was astounded when they all seemed to find both me and my talk quite impressive.

I stayed with the group until it broke up around five in the morning. All of us talked and talked and talked and talked. Nobody but me had a working class accent, and some of them even knew how to pronounce words in French.

Before we broke up for the night, I found out that Arlen's youth "in a convent" had been a myth. Jane had misunderstood something.

I rode home on the subway thinking about how wonderful it would be to have an affair with a woman who was really beautiful and wrote scripts for radio shows. It was a gorgeous fantasy, but it didn't seem possible.

WHERE MIND IS NOT

> I think that people want peace so much that one of these
> days government had better get out of their way and let
> them have it.　　　— Dwight David Eisenhower

I was in Maui again, to give a lecture and seminar. A friend named K.C. Chin, who publishes an ecological newspaper, invited me to dinner at a Mexican restaurant in Haiku. We ate outside on the veranda, and I enjoyed the view of the town and the humping green mountains in the distance, with all the wild technicolor Maui trees and shrubs everywhere. It was December 1, 1990 and we were wearing light shirts because December in Maui is like the Garden of Eden.

Every time I looked at those gorgeously colored Maui plants, I thought of Joseph Banks, the first European who ever saw them. He was the Royal Scientific Society's botanist on board Captain Cook's ship, touring the South Pacific and filing-and-indexing its flora. Banks made beautiful, scrupulously accurate color drawings of every new plant he saw, and when he was finished, his book, *Floralegium,* doubled the number of flowers known to Western science. I can't look at the plants in Hawaii without thinking how high Banks must have felt while sketching them: thousands of nature's jewels and spangles never known to Science before. The man must have been on an acid trip without acid. He painted like a Taoist Leonardo.

In the last few years I've been in Maui twice and Berlin about five times. Since these are twelve hours apart on the clock, my reality-tunnel is now half the size of the planet, as contrasted to the one square mile of Irish Catholic culture in which I grew up in Gerrison Beach. It has been a series of quantum jumps, every decade of my life — my model of the world has mutated and changed repeatedly as the Information Explosion continues. The month before Maui had been particularly busy; I had been in New York and Portland, Oregon, and San Jose and Huntington Beach. I am away from home, lecturing, about two week-ends every month, and I have learned to *feel*, as well as think, that I live on Spaceship Earth, as Bucky used to say.

Maui is always a highlight on my travels. I generally enjoy Mexican restaurants, but a Mexican restaurant with all the beauty of Maui around it is a special treat. The joker-god Maui has the same attitude as Ludwig II — you can't have too much loud color and bright contrast, and to hell with critics who want the "understated."

K.C. is a computer freak as well as an Environmentalist. As we ate, he was trying to persuade me to buy a modem and start networking. For a part-time professional Futurist, I am very reactionary about that. I don't want anything attached to my computer that might be a port of entry for viruses. Especially now that World War III seems almost upon us, I think crazies in our own peace movement and Islamic terrorists are going to be doing some very icky and messy things to the networks of banks and military systems and the IRS — *which will also infest any network that interfaces with any of these at any point.*

That lovely evening in Haiku sticks in my memory, because at that time I still did not believe fully in the Horror that was lurking directly ahead of us.

The next morning I heard on the TV that the "defense" department (lovely euphemism!)* had sent 60,000 body-bags to the Persian Gulf. It hit me exactly like the time I was arrested in Yellow Springs: I turned on and tuned in totally, on sheer adrenaline.

For years I have been telling the story of Prince Peter Ouspensky, who in his early years in the Gurdjieff Work did not understand Gurdjieff's insistance that most people are so deeply hypnotized that they act exactly like mechanisms. Then, shortly after World War I started, Ouspensky saw a truck headed for the front, carrying artificial legs. Suddenly, looking at a truck full of artificial legs to replace legs that had not yet been blown off, but would certainly be blown off very soon, Ouspensky understood

---

* From the birth of the Republic on through the reign of Franklin Delano Roosevelt and the end of World War II, we were at least honest enough to call it the War Department.

*that all human behavior on the large, historical scale is so
mechanical that it can be mathematically predicted.*

And, listening to the TV in Maui Meadows, I understood with
the same mathematical certainty that those 60,000 body-bags
meant that war was mechanically ordained. That day, December 2, the peace movement was "strong" and vocal in every city
and even in the pulpits, many in Congress were still opposing the
drift toward Holocaust, nothing seemed "certain" yet, but — I
knew that the men who ordered those 60,000 body bags understood the American people better than I did.

Six weeks passed and the mechanism moved in its predetermined grooves. Wheels and gears: merciless wheels and mindless gears.

Two days before the bombardment of Iraq started on January
16, CNN released a poll showing that 51% of the public still
opposed war. Two days after the killing started, a similar poll
showed that 97% now supported the war. Mark Twain, I remembered, had written about that, long before Gurdjieff, in an essay
called "The War Psychoses." During the build-up to every war,
Twain documented, many speak out in opposition, but once the
killing starts almost everybody goes mad with blood-lust and
very, very few still dare to ask, "What the hell are we doing this
for? Does it make any sense at all?"

Every morning, before I work on this book, I have been looking at CNN to see if there is any reason for hope. I see a few
large and impressive peace protests, here and around the world,
but mostly I see empty robot faces monotonously reciting the
magick incantations, "We must support the President," and "We
must support our troops," both of which mean the killing must
continue.

I was marched to the front of the class after we reconvened,
and punishment was administered. This consisted of being told
to hold out my hand — I knew what was coming, having seen
other boys punished, but I held the hand out anyway, since I had
a nasty suspicion that something even worse would happen if I
refused — and then she whacked me across the knuckles, as hard
as she could, with a steel yardstick, five times.

I felt every eye in the class on me and did not allow myself to cry. My hand cramped and hurt like a bastard for about a day after.

Where Mechanism is and Mind is not, war happens.

G.E.N.I.

June 1989: I was at a seminar on Bucky Fuller's Global Energy Network, at the World Future Society. The speaker was Peter Meisen of Global Energy Network International (G.E.N.I.)

The Fuller network or grid is a simple plan to integrate the electrical systems of the whole planet. Because of the peaks and valleys in electricity usage (caused by the human waking-sleeping cycle) every part of the world could be selling electricity to every other part and also buying from every other part — selling at "night" and buying by "day." (On this giant sphere it is "night" and "day" at the same time, remember?)

This would be very cost-effective for all, Bucky claimed; and indeed the Soviet Academy pronounced the plan "feasible and desirable" back in 1980. I wanted to know if any concrete steps had been taken to actualize the grid.

Peter Meisen spent most of his time explaining the ecological benefits of the world electric network. Sharing electricity means fewer new plants have to be built and hence there will be less pollution. Non-polluting sources of energy (solar, wind) can be integrated into the grid at any point, as they are developed. The Brazilians could pay the interest on their national debt by selling electricity and might not have to cut down so many trees, slowing the Greenhouse effect.

On general humanitarian grounds, the grid is desirable because whenever kilowatt hours increase, birthrate drops and starvation then drops also as more kids have enough to eat. On economic grounds, every nation that joins the World Grid will be able to "do more with less" and reap vast savings.

And, of course, the Grid would educate everybody, in a very concrete way, about how synergetic economics works — how it is possible to advantage everybody without disadvantaging anybody.

I had read most of that in Bucky's books and was impatient for the question period.

When I did have a chance to ask what was happening, Meisen said that the American Society of Mechanical Engineers is now interested in the grid and doing a study, and that there would be a conference in Moscow the following year.

Of course, G.E.N.I. has a hidden pacifist agenda. When the nations of the world "build" the grid (mostly by connecting existing grids) it will be visible to all that nobody has anything to gain by blowing up any part of an energy system that is helping all of us and hurting none of us.

INFORMATION DOUBLES AGAIN

By 1967, information had doubled again, and humanity knew or could access twice as much knowledge about the universe as we knew seven years earlier in 1960.

Two years earlier, a physicist named John S. Bell had published a notable Theorem, which showed that the universe was non-locally "connected" or, perhaps more precisely, non-locally *correlated*. Particles could "influence" each other, or relate to each other, even though there was no mechanical Newtonian or Einsteinian cause-and-effect relationship between them. This was so stunning in its implications that the majority of physicists did not know how to begin thinking about it and the first results of what Bell had discovered did not begin to appear until the 1970s.

Meanwhile, in 1967, the educated minority, all over the world, had heard of Bucky Fuller and his Global Planning by then; most had heard of Marshall McLuhan, who had synthesized, from Fuller and Korzybski, a whole new way of looking at how humans shape and are shaped by the communication technologies they use. More and more serious thinkers were trying to define the mutation the world was undergoing as Industrialism gave way to — what? "Post-Industrial society" was the most popular term, but did not define the situation very precisely; it reminds one of "pre-Celtic" and "not-cheese."

Out of the American civil rights movement and the Third World struggles for liberation from imperialism, something completely new emerged — a worldwide Youth Revolution that nobody could define at the time and nobody has yet defined even today. It was a rebellion against war, and against racism, and against every Elite which greedily hugged its power — but it was also a new style of music, a change in drug habits (alcohol being rejected in favor of pot), a new awareness of ecology, a new variety of the Feminism that had begun with the Industrial Age (and now seemed to have only *partially* succeeded when Female Suffrage was enacted)...

Bucky Fuller said that all the confusing, and sometimes feuding, movements that made up the Youth Revolution had one thing and only one thing in common. *The participants were the first human generation that had been raised on television.* Marshall McLuhan added documentation about how TV produces a reality-tunnel radically different from the purely bookish reality-tunnel of the Gutenberg generations. TV, without preaching it explicitly, McLuhan noted, implicitly trains us to think tribally again, but on a new scale: the Global Village is our home.

In 1967, Caskey, Marshall and Nirenberg showed that the genetic code operates similarly in bacteria, guinea pigs and toads, suggesting that the code is a universal system used by all Life. Telephones introduced direct dialing between the U.S. and Europe. Jocelyn Bell discovered the first pulsar. Probes and Orbiters circled the moon, preparing for the first human landing two years later.

Martin Luther King Jr., who had introduced Gandhi's nonviolent tactics into the U.S. civil rights struggle, finally, after long agonizing, took a public stand against the Vietnam War, thereby allying himself with the Youth Revolution. Senator Robert Kennedy called for a halt in the bombing. U.S. public sentiment was turning against the war, according to the pollsters, but King and Kennedy would both be assassinated within a year — by two of the "deranged lone assassins" who were becoming as common in America then as crushed beer cans on a beach. Even people who were educated (like me) to regard conspiracy theories with acute skepticism were beginning to wonder, a little, about where all those "lone" gunmen came from.

Physician Benjamin Spock, poet Allen Ginsberg and boxing champion Muhammed Ali were all arrested that year for activities in opposition to the war. These were just three prominent names among thousands of cultural leaders who joined the Peace Movement. The U.S. ruling elite for the first time was totally out of favor with the nation's intellectual elite.

One hundred fifty thousand American marched on the Pentagon in protest, and I was among them. It was a nervous day: the "crazies" (as we called them) were now a prominent part of the movement, and nobody knew how many of them were really crazy and how many were *agents provocateur.*

When I got to the steps of the Five Sided Castle somebody was passing around a joint. I took a toke, and thought I would someday tell my grandchildren that I smoked Weed on the steps of the Pentagon.

The next day I was back at my job as Associate Editor of *Playboy*. Nobody there ever told me to inhibit my anti-war activities. They never objected to any of my "eccentricities," although they surely knew I was writing on the side for *The Spark*, a Chicago pacifist magazine. They paid me a higher salary than any other magazine at which I had worked and never expected me to become a conformist or sell my soul in return. I enjoyed my years in the Bunny Empire. I only resigned when I reached 40 and felt I could not live with myself if I didn't make an effort to write full-time at last.

CYBERSPACE & TECHNO-ZEN

New Reality-Tunnels For All

You stand among the ape-people as they circle the Black Monolith; their cries of awe and terror literally surround you. The music comes from all sides, and, as you step forward, you can actually *touch* the Monolith...

Click. You and Toto dance along the Yellow Brick Road and with every step you take, the farmlands on both sides reveal exotic new plants and flowering shrubs...if you turn your head to see them. Suddenly a voice calls out and you turn rapidly, trying to see who spoke. You only see a scarecrow, but then he speaks again.

Click. You step from one brain cell to another. Inside the second cell, you eagerly examine the millions of moving parts. What has happened to Oz and 2001? Evidently you have tuned in on a neuroscience educational channel...

When TV gets replaced by Cyberspace, that might be an ordinary occurrence after dinner, as you sit inside your Cybersuit and look for the alternative world you want to enter that evening.

On April 30, 1990, I had my own first trip to Cyberspace, and the field itself has continued to progress as an accelerated acceleration. "I saw it with my own eyes" and "I touched it with my own hands" will soon become arguments that carry no conviction, in court or out. "I saw a dinosaur looking in the window" or "I have an appointment to fuck Marilyn Monroe tomorrow" will become things you can say without people questioning your sanity. The rules of the Reality Game have changed, and changed utterly.

The San Jose *Mercury News* — not exactly a science-fiction journal — described the Cyberspace office of the near future in an article on May 27, 1990, as follows:

"The user would move down virtual hallways, entering the virtual offices of colleagues, visiting virtual conference rooms and virtual marketing centers where virtual products are displayed, pausing to read virtual bulletin boards, and so forth."

Steve Pruitt of Texas Instruments outlined how such "virtual work spaces" might operate during the first international Cyberspace conference in Austin, TX, in May. Pruitt's vision may sound as "spooky" or "occult" as some student of Cabala "astrally projecting" up and down the "paths" of the Tree of Life, but a good deal of the technology for such virtual offices already exists and brilliant people at M.I.T., Stanford and other places have grants to develop the hardware and software for the creation of all the rest of this ghostly alternative world. Science has stolen magick back from the sorcerers.

One argument for building such virtual offices: if people can conference in this way, without leaving home, we will collectively use less petroleum and hence suffer less air pollution. (We might even escape our compulsion to go to war whenever the oil supply is threatened...)

Another argument: it will save time and money, in the long run, to meet this way instead of assembling all the warm bodies in one physical place on Earth.

At an April 30 conference at New York University, where I appeared with Dr. Timothy Leary and two of the leading Cyberspace designers — Eric Gullichsen and Myron Krueger — one member of the audience asked, "How long will it take to build a holodeck, like the one on *Star Trek?*"

"If somebody gave me the funding," Myron Krueger answered immediately, "I think I could build it starting tomorrow."

Once Virtual Reality systems begin networking, as our computers already do, you can visit your mother in Des Moines without leaving your home in Marin Country. And you can arrange with her that you will both experience the visit as occurring in the best restaurant in Paris.

There's no reason, says Cyberspace designer Jaron Lanier "why somebody in Moscow couldn't dance with somebody in Los Angeles." (*Los Angeles Times,* June 12, 1990).

But let me make this more concrete by describing my own first Trip into Cyberspace. This occurred at the April NYU conference, and I used hardware and software created and/or assembled by Eric Gullichsen. This prototype version employs only a helmet and a glove (we will discuss the full Cyberspace Suit below.) Once you have donned the helmet and glove, you visually enter Cyberspace. Since about 90 percent of our brain's reality-map derives from visual cues, you "feel" Cyberspace as "just as real" as the ordinary space of consensus reality.

Specifically, I experienced myself in a countryside, near a small city. I pointed the glove, as instructed, and began "moving" toward the city. When I turned my head to the right, I "saw" the view in that direction; when I turned to the left, I "saw" that view; when I looked behind me, I "saw" that view.

Entering the city, I did not explore any of the ghost-offices of the Pruitt kind that might exist there. I enjoyed, rather, wandering the streets and checking how "real" the details looked each time I turned my head inside the helmet, and how each street had the same "completeness" (degree of detail) as all the others, even though each individual street had different features than any other.

Then I got interested in a UFO of some sort hovering above the city. An "alien spaceship"? An O'Neill Space City? Some cute joke Gullichsen had included in the software? I pointed the glove upward and "flew" to the orbiting sphere. Alas and goddam, when I got there I could not find any way to enter. Since my time limit was approaching — others, back in consensus reality, awaited their chance to enter Cyberspace — I left the mystery unsolved, knowing I'll get a chance to go back and try again soon. I "flew" back to Earth and explored the city some more, finding an Illuminati pyramid that delighted me so much I "jumped" over it.

My time had run out. Eric removed the helmet and glove and I re-entered consensus reality.

Some people, according to reports, experience nausea or dizziness either on entering Cyberspace or on leaving it and returning to ordinary space. I had no such problem. It seemed exhilarating going in and also coming back out, perhaps because I have had a lot of experience with non-ordinary realities.

Well, that gives you a rough idea of the kind of Virtual Reality available with helmet and glove alone. Jaron Lanier and several others have Cyberspace Suits in development, which will fit you like clothes and give the kinesthetic reinforcement necessary to fill in most of the 10% of our reality-map not based on visual cues. With these suits, if you leap over a pyramid, as I did, your muscles will have the sensations of a high jump to round out the "evidence of your eyes" and complete the brain's sense of having "really" made the leap.

Now, in addition to the entertainment possibilities suggested in my Cyberspace versions of *2001* and *The Wizard of Oz* above, and the obvious educational implications, Virtual Reality suggests some quite awe-inspiring potentials in general brain programming. For instance, after visiting Eric Gullichsen's Euclidean Cyberspace, I immediately thought that I would find it more interesting to go into a non-Euclidean space, especially Reimanian space. I feel sure all physics students will have that opportunity in the near future. It will vastly accelerate the neurological reorganization that we all had to go through in learning what General Relativity means.

But why limit this to physics students? If education ever becomes a serious enterprise again, *all* students should have some experience in curved space, just to break the hypnosis that keeps most people in a Euclidean Virtual Reality and prevents them from even glimpsing the Reimanian Virtual Reality that underlies Einstein's model of the universe.

Or — consider Quantum Cyberspace.

The best artistic expression of quantum logic, in my opinion, appears in the three *Back to the Future* films. You see the same town in 1885, in 1955, two versions of it in 1985 and two or three versions of it in 2035. In the course of this odyssey, the characters, buildings and "objects," which seemed "solid" and particle-like at first, become probability waves as they quantum jump from one eigenstate to another. Billed as entertainment, with no hint of "education" about it, this series nonetheless gives the audience a clearer view of the non-Aristotelian logic of quantum physics than any educational TV show I ever saw.

Now just imagine the Virtual Reality re-make of this trilogy, 20 years or so in the future. The audience, living through this quantum adventure, visually and muscularly, and inter-acting with it, will come out understanding non-Aristotelian logic as deeply, on a gut level, as any Ph.D. in math who has spent years trying to intuit what the quantum equations "really mean."

How about Cyberotica?

Yep, the Evil Genius who designed MacPlaymate has already started work on a Virtual Reality version. Virtual Sex lurks just around the corner — and my whimsy about a Virtual Marilyn Monroe will almost certainly seem like a great idea to some designer (if the perverted bastard hasn't thought of it already, without my help.)

How about Virtual Reality jokes and surprises? Considering some of the weird software available for ordinary computers, we will certainly find some "funny stuff" in Cyberspace. You are walking through a 3D equivalent of the mazes in the computer game, *Scarab of Ra*...or through one of Pruitt's virtual offices, seeking a virtual conference room...or about to slip Behind the Green Door with Marilyn Chambers...or whatever Trip you want that day...when suddenly — *shlunk!* right in your groin — the wet, damp nose of the most horrible dog imagined by anybody since Conan Doyle dreamed up the Curse of the Baskervilles — "That's our dog, Ballsniffer," says George Carlin in your ear, "He's a full-bred Australian Crotch-Hound."

Personally, I see the ultimate implications of cybernetic Virtual Reality as a kind of Techno-Zen. When we can change "realities" as easily as we now change TV channels, the Buddhist "detachment from fixed ideas" will become an intuitively obvious goal for all, and a goal easily attained.

To explain the revolutionary potentials of that seemingly innocent remark, let me say it otherwise. The most important discovery of modern neuroscience, I think, consists in the discovery that every "reality" we perceive/create has emerged from an ocean of more or less random signals, which our brain has edited, organized and orchestrated into what social scientists call "glosses" or "frames" — reality-tunnels, in Leary's language. As Korzybski noted over and over, it is only due to the speed of conditioned reflexes that we do not even *notice* our role as co-creators of these reality-tunnels. (Or, as Nietzsche says, "We are all greater artists than we realize.") Thus, we all have what Buddhists call "fixed ideas" or, in Stirner's lovely phrase, "spooks in our heads." In the terminology I've been using, we are hypnotized by our own B.S. (belief systems.)

Learning a new art or science requires what psychologists call "reframing." Abandoning a fallacious dogma and accepting new facts requires "reframing." The cure of any neuroses or compulsion requires "reframing." To grow means to reframe, or to change reality-tunnels. *But we cannot do this if we have a conditioned attachment to conditioned perceptions and conditioned frames or glosses. We all want "liberation" but we rarely notice how conditioned reflexes make us our own jailers.*

Although everybody in the neurological and social sciences has understood this for at least 40 or 50 years, the known techniques for curing the problem — reframing, deconditioning, getting rid of the spooks, detaching from the fixed ideas — have all had major drawbacks that notoriously prevent popularizing them. *Most of the effective techniques require hard work.* Worse yet, some not only require hard work but come from non-white cultures — from the yogis and shamans of the Third World — and the "mental imperialism" still rampant in our culture makes it impossible for most people to take seriously any discipline that doesn't have "respectable" Caucasian ancestry. (See *The Skeptical Inquirer,* any issue.)

And, of course, the fastest, most dramatic technique for entering alternative realities, not only derives from shamanism but uses psychoactive substances (*drugs!*) and hence appears sinful, Satanic and unthinkable. Huge Berserk Rebel Warthog has declared "war" on those who use this technique of reframing.

None of these prejudices can obstruct the use of Cyberspace. It does not come from a non-white culture, but from the heart of our own technology. It has been proven 100% Acid Free (although not all of its designers are.) It does not require a lot of hard work, like yoga. And yet it clearly teaches the same lesson as all the shamans and yogis since the dawn of time: You create one reality-tunnel at a time out of a phalanx of possible reality-tunnels. You can learn to change your reality-tunnel. You can experience many reality-tunnels.

As a *felt experience,* not just an abstract idea, this "liberation" constitutes what New Agers call Awakening. And Virtual Reality certainly makes this insight a felt experience. The Zen detachment from fixed dogmas and fixed emotions (always based on dogmas) will become available to millions as Cyberspace technology spreads through computer games, through entertainment, through education and business, into every aspect of our society.

The reign of dogmas — first religious dogmas, then political dogmas (ideologies) — has made humanity "prey upon itself like monsters of the deep." The decline of dogma that comes with detachment from conditioned reflexes can only accelerate the peace-making process that seems already afoot on this planet.

Once the fiction of one "reality" dies as a concept, and the operational fact of "realities" (plural) becomes generally recognized, we might all discover that human beings can actually live together without constantly making war over who has the "real" "reality."

"But Why Didn't She Duck?"

On 4 October 1985 Mr. Justice Lynch, after long labor, produced his own brainchild — a final report on the Kerry babies. He ruled, following the forensic evidence, that the Cahiriciveen baby was not the child of Joanne Hayes and the Abbeydorney baby was. He further ruled, contradicting the forensic evidence, that Joanne had strangled the Abbeydorney baby. (The doctors, remember, claimed it was born dead.) The Guards, thus, had not obtained a totally false confession, just a partially false one.

On the numerous other conflicts between the Guards and the Hayes family, Judge Lynch opined that the Guards had "gilded the lily" but the Hayes people were "barefaced liars." He did not recommend prosecution for perjury on either side, and did not recommend prosecution of Joanne for infanticide (perhaps remembering that the forensic evidence contradicted his verdict?) He made no comment on the original issue the Minister of Justice had appointed him to investigate — how the Guards had persuaded six people to confess to stabbing a baby they had never even seen.

In the next week, one (male) member of *Dial hEirann* (the Irish parliament) called for Lynch's impeachment. Dozens of magazine articles and six books have documented, at exhausting length, that the evidence contradicts his verdict in almost all details.

As the cold, dark autumn of 1985 settled in, the statues of Ireland became more sedate and the crowds thinned out at the shrines. Then, in late October, three Protestants from slummy inner city Dublin attacked the Ballinspittle Virgin with a hammer and smashed its face rather badly. They then turned on the small crowd of Catholic worshippers and denounced them as "superstitious idolators."

A joke went around cynical Dublin the next day: "Why didn't She duck?" But then the number of worshippers at the shrine increased again, and more visions were reported, for a while. With winter the really mean Irish cold came down on us, and nobody went to the shrines. The Hayes family, it was reported,

had had bad luck with their crops and were now "on the dole" —
receiving government assistance.

Nobody has ever been arrested for killing the Cahiriciveen
baby, although the Guards got excited about one possible suspect
for a while — a Dutch woman living in Kerry, who had committed suicide during the Hayes Tribunal. Alas, her diary was full of
nothing but terrifying fantasies about nuclear war, and recorded
no sexual affairs, no pregnancy, no infanticide; she had clearly
killed herself out of despair about what she considered the failure
of the Peace Movement.

G. E. N. I.

Throughout 1989 and 1990 I kept myself informed about the progress of the Global Energy Network.

In the USSR, presentation of the grid by Peter Meisen of Global Energy Network International inspired warm support from the Soviet Academy of Sciences. The Grid received nationwide publicity on TV and more than 100,000,000 viewers watched and heard how this simple plan could raise living standards and decrease pollution everywhere. Meisen came home saying there were now more people in Russia aware of the grid than in any other country.

The Grid also received favorable TV coverage in Greece and Zimbabwe.

East and West Germany agreed to connect their grids.

The G.E.N.I. team received an invitation to return to Moscow for further talks on global networking.

A conference is being prepared in Central America on how to link the local grids and begin the process of linking North and South American grids.

In Washington, the Department of Energy finally roused from its dogmatic slumbers and announced that "further analysis" of the grid seems warranted.

I found myself more and more excited by these reports. When the world grid is linked up, it seems to me, that will be a turning point equal to Watt's steam engine or the splitting of the atom: *the practical world-wide demonstration of synergetic "doing more with less" and "advantaging all without disadvantaging any."* Bucky had said repeatedly, between 1960 and his death in 1983, that humanity will soon choose between Utopia and Oblivion. The grid, I thought, would strongly shift the odds toward Utopia.

A Mid-East conference on the grid was scheduled for late 1990. Among the nations that were interested in linking their grids for mutual advantage were Turkey, Syria, Jordan, Iraq, Egypt, Libya and Kuwait.

The conference was scheduled by the Kuwait Institute for Scientific Research and planned for sometime in summer 1990.

Then all Hell and Terror fell on Kuwait. The world tilted dizzily toward Oblivion as the docile masses step by step marched toward World War III without anybody in a leadership position even saying out loud that that was where we were going.

But, like W.H. Auden in September 1939, I do not believe the writer should spread further gloom on a world already seriously wounded; like him, I wish I could "show an affirming flame."

I don't think evolution "is" "blind" or "mechanical." I think the increasing movement toward an information-rich environment contains, as Schrödinger claimed, an anti-entropic vector. We are passing through Chaos but we will not end in Chaos. We still have a starry destiny ahead of us.

An Anonymous Benefactor

After the photographer took our pictures, a deputy led us back downstairs. I looked into the holding cell again. The same Black prisoners slouched in the same Living Dead silence.

"Hold on. Bring 'em out here," the Greene County sheriff yelled, just as the deputy was opening the cage to put us inside.

The deputy took us out to the front office, where the sheriff greeted us in a friendly manner.

"You made bail," he said. "A person who does not wish to be known has posted it for you."

All six of us stared at him the way you might stare at a man with three heads.

"That means you're free to go," he said patiently. "The court will notify you when you have to appear for trial."

We stared at each other, and then we got the hell out of there before another miracle could happen and cancel the bail.

That was 27 years ago and I never did find out who posted bail for us, although I assume it was one of the rich Quakers in Yellow Springs.

Less than a month later, I was offered a job with a new magazine in New York, called *Fact*. I consulted our lawyer and was told that I could legally leave Ohio if I notified the court of my new address.

Six months later, the lawyer wrote to tell me the court had ruled we were not guilty of contempt but only of trespassing, and the fine had been suspended. We were all ordered "to keep the peace," and not trespass in any more public barber shops.

Old man Gegner closed his barber shop (he said his wife couldn't stand any more sit-ins and other excitement) and moved to Kentucky, where he opened a new shop which was totally segregated — and legally so in 1964.

Gegner was not old enough to dodder. He probably lived to face the bitter day when segregation of barber shops became illegal even in Kentucky. I can't imagine what he did then.

AND INFORMATION DOUBLES AGAIN

By 1973, information had doubled again. Nobody could keep track of it, but if you knew where to look you could find, somewhere in the Big Computers, 128 times as much data as Jesus ever saw, 64 times as much as Leonardo had at his disposal... twice as much as we had in our inventory only six years earlier in 1967.

That year computer-coded labels appeared in super-markets.

Konrad Lorenz and Nic Tinbergen received the Nobel Prize for their pioneering work on imprinting in animals. In America, Timothy Leary was in prison, and nobody in the scientific community was talking about his claim that LSD produces imprint vulnerability and the possibility of serial re-imprinting in humans.

The Watergate scandal was sending tremors through Washington as one government lie after another was discovered; the public in general reeled — for the first time they were facing what historians and "intellectuals" and people outside the U.S. had always known: that our government was as crooked as any other. As soon as Nixon resigned, the lesson was forgotten, and the majority returned to their usual habit of believing whatever the government said, just as Catholics believe whatever the Vatican says.

Why not? *The masses were trained for millennia to regard the king as a Sun-God.* Just because some intellectual Freemasons invented Democracy at the dawn of the Industrial Age doesn't mean that thousands of years of conditioning will disappear immediately.

A cease-fire in Vietnam on January 28 began the process of U.S. withdrawal from the war that had divided the country against itself.

Also in 1973, Iraq nationalized oil, causing great anguish to the multi-national oil corporations. The government of Saudi Arabia, the same year, more modestly cut itself in for 25% of the profits on its oil fields and remained on good terms with the Oil Barons.

Curiously, nobody I knew owned a home computer yet — and I had a wide circles of friends.

I was living in San Francisco and had become a member of the Physics/Consciousness Research Group, which at various times included such physicists as Dr. Fred Alan Wolfe (author of *Making the Quantum Leap)*, Dr. Nick Herbert (author of *Quantum Reality)*, Dr. Fritjof Capra (author of *The Tao of Physics)*, Dr. Jack Sarfatti, Dr. Elizabeth Rauscher, Dr. Saul Paul Sirag and Barbara Honegger, who was taking a degree in parapsychology at John F. Kennedy University. I was sort of the science-fiction writer in residence. We spent most of our time talking about the implications of Bell's Theorem, which had recently been tested and seemingly confirmed at UC-Berkeley.

Bell's Theorem demonstrated a connection-or-correlation between systems that are not causally related. That is, it entirely contradicts an assumption which governed science from Newton to Einstein — the assumption that all scientific laws must express a kind of "billiard-ball" model of the world, in which every moving ball is only influenced by the balls with which it collides. Bell's math demonstrated that some sort of non-local "field" or perhaps an "implicate order" controlled the balls even if they had no mechanical connection with each other.

Nick Herbert liked to call this non-local relationship "the Cosmic Glue."

Saul Paul Sirag, another physicist, showed me a paper by Dr. E.H. Walker, "The Compleat Quantum Anthropologist," which argued that mind, like quantum systems, functions non-locally. This made sense to me because all systems that divide mind from matter lead to intractable paradoxes. It also made sense because it gave me, for the first time, a model that could explain some of my more "cosmic" LSD experiences. Dr. Walker's paper started me thinking in terms of a Local Self, inside space-time, and a Non-Local Self, outside space-time. This may have been what the Zen Master, Sensaki, meant when he spoke of Little Mind and Big Mind. Such a model not only accounted for LSD voyages but it also made a good container for all the confusing phenomena which parapsychologists put into separate bags and call ESP, precognition, out of body experience, synchronicity — all the strange "psychic" events that have dogged me all my life

(which I can no longer attribute to the Atheist's God, Mr. Random Chance.)

In terms of Walker's interpretation of Bell's Theorem, all of these non-Newtonian aberrations merely represent sudden information flow from Non-Local Mind to Local Mind.

There are several alternative models of what Bell's math "means" when we try to convert it into worlds. I find them all equally fascinating and have discussed them in my *Schroedinger's Cat* trilogy (Dell, 1978) and in *Quantum Psychology* (New Falcon Publications, 1990). Personally, I like Walker's model best of all, but that does not mean I "believe" it. As Dr. Sarfatti once said, "Belief is an obsolete Aristotelian category."

Parapsychologist Barbara Honegger eventually got her degree, but then left us to take a job in the Reagan White House. What she found there so thoroughly disillusioned her that she now spends most of her time on the lecture circuit and radio talk shows, warning the American people that the Huge Berserk Rebel Warthog team does not mean well by us.

IN MEMORY ...

The good people of Kerry gave the Cahiriciveen baby a Catholic burial and put a tombstone on its nameless grave. The tombstone says:

IN MEMORY OF THE KERRY BABY

ME

SUN-KING SYSTEM RESTORED

Population Barefoot and Illiterate

In 1980, according to Ms. Honegger, George Bush traveled to Paris to arrange a deal whereby the Iranians were bribed with money and promised the first shipment of the guns they later got *via* Colonel Ollie North. According to Honegger, this was at that time by no means a "guns-for-hostages" deal, *but precisely the reverse.*

The condition of the bribe and gun deal was that the Iranians promised *not* to release their American hostages until after the election, so Carter would look ineffectual and Reagan would come into office in an aura of triumph.

According to *COVERUP*, a film by the Empowerment Project, most of the guns for the Contras and other Death Squads in Latin America go though a Costa Rica estate belonging to a former, or allegedly former, CIA officer, John Hull. (Since the film was made, Hull has admitted he is a CIA agent, but denies all other charges.) *COVERUP* has an interview with a pilot who flew several missions to Hull's ranch and says he always brought cocaine back to the States after delivering the guns to the terrorists. The money for all this went through the World Finance Corporation in Miami and hence onward to the Cisalpine Bank in the Bahamas and the rest of the Marcinkus-Calvi-Sindona financial Fun House.

The Costa Rican government has indicted Hull for these guns-and-drugs deals, carried out on their soil. He is back in the U.S. and the Justice Department shows no inclination to let the Costa Ricans extradite him, but the Christic Institute, a public interest law firm, is trying to bring him to trial on a civil complaint, naming Colonel North and General Secord and the other Iran-Contra figures as co-defendants.

We have not seen the end of this story. In Italy, the Puppet Master himself, Licio Gelli, is again waiting trial. He had come back to Switzerland to get at those numbered bank accounts a second time — and the Swiss managed to deliver him to the Italian police without another dramatic jail-break occurring.

The Vatican/CIA/P2 drug laundering system worked beautifully for many years. The Death Squads were efficient. The ordinary people of Latin America would seemingly remain barefoot, illiterate and submissive, on penalty of a bullet in the head if they got uppity. The Vatican and the multinationals were happy. Reagan was happy, and wanted everybody else to become happy, too. The cocaine-money-guns loop had worked very well for over a decade, and all looked rosy for the future. But then — wouldn't you know it? — somebody double-crossed somebody else and Calvi ended up dangling from the bridge and the whole house of cards started to fall, first in Italy, then in Washington.

Mike the Shark died of poison in his cell in Rome. He had been convicted of murdering a bank examiner and was awaiting a second trial on conspiracy charges.

ANAL-EROTICISM IN
THE WHITE HOUSE

"The Old Man Loves My Ass"

Historians will marvel at that era of fun and games — when Nancy was telling us "Just say no" and the CIA was telling its pilots "Just fly low," when Col. North was drafting a plan to suspend the Constitution indefinitely and bragging to friends, "The old man (Reagan) loves my ass," when cocaine and guns and money were flowing like a river in flood through the secret bank accounts of the CIA and its friends, including the P2 faction in Rome and the Vatican. And the CIA was governed by our old friend Mad Bill Casey, of the Knights of Malta, and a man with no qualms about lying to Congress, as Barry Goldwater finally noticed with dismay. "I am really pissed off," Goldwater eventually wrote to Casey, when the full extent of Mad Bill's deceptions began to dawn on the Senate.

Mad Bill, like General Musumeci in Italy, died of natural causes while under investigation. Sometimes I wonder if the artists who, in Beria's words, "arrange" suicides have learned to "arrange" natural deaths.

Looking at the record — which I have been researching ever since Calvi was found hanging from that bridge — I recall an old friend, Alan Watts, Zen philosopher and wit. "The greatest error of historians," Alan once told me, "is the idea that the Roman Empire 'fell.' It never fell. It still runs the Western World, through the Vatican and the Mafia." I didn't believe that when Alan said it; I thought it was one of his jokes. Now I wonder.

And I wonder, too, about the views expressed by Roberto Calvi himself, who certainly knew more about politics and power than Alan Watts ever did. Calvi used to tell friends that *The Godfather* was the greatest novel ever written. "Read it," he would say. "Then you will understand the way the world really works."

And we should consider also, perhaps, the words of Michael Corleone in *Godfather III*. After 15 years of trying to get out of the rackets into "legitimate business," Michael cries out, "The higher I go, the crookeder it gets. Is there no end?"

An alternative view to Mr. Calvi's and Mr. Corleone's was expressed by a philosophical fisherman named Bartolemeo Vanzetti. He said, "The higher of them, the more jack-ass." This assumes, without stating explicitly, the Buddhist view that the pursuit of power is the quest for the unattainable by the unphilosophical through the tactics of the unspeakable.

Vanzetti also said, "[Nicolo Sacco's] name will live in the hearts of the people when you and your false god are a dim memory of a cursed time when man was wolf to the man."

THE MANDELBROT SET?

War is a crime. Ask the infantry. Ask the dead.
— Ernest Hemingway

According to computer scientist Dr. Jacques Vallee, information is now doubling *every 18 months.*

Nearly four *billion* years of evolution to get to the first tool. Almost four *million* years to arrive at the information density of Rome in 1 AD. Only one-and-a-half *thousand* years for information to double and for the West to arrive at Leonardo, the high point of the Renaissance and the dawning of Protestantism. Two-and-a-half *centuries* for the next doubling, the rise of Industrialism, the birth of democracy — and the radical supra-democratic heresies of socialism, anarchism, feminism...

Only six years for the doubling of information between 1967 and 1973.

Even then, nobody I knew personally had a home computer. Today, *everybody* I know has a home computer.

We are in what Toffler calls the Third Wave — Information Civilization. If Vallee is right about information doubling every 18 months, and Gordon is right about fractals increasing where information flow increases, then everything *must* become steadily more unpredictable from here on — more "chaotic" in the mathematical sense.

That "chaos" may be expressed as breakdown and violence, such as we are seeing in the current rumble between Goddam Insane and Huge Berserk Rebel Warthog. In the doubling of information between 1900 and 1950, we went through a World Depression and two World Wars.

The "chaos" may, however, be expressed instead as a rapid acceleration toward a more stable and coherent world. After the Democratic Revolutions of the late 18th Century, Europe settled into peace and steady progress for nearly a hundred years.

The "chaos" is most likely leading us to social transformations that none of us can foresee with more than foggy approximation. I think it will include economic collapse and economic recovery, space colonization, longevity, Bucky's World Energy Grid, and breakthroughs in nanotechnology that will literally make the most advanced scientific gadgets "as cheap as dirt."

Is this information-acceleration a Mandelbrot fractal, as Terence McKenna claims? Will we reach a point in 2012 where information doubles a million times a second?

I don't know. But, just as the Persian Gulf War was an awful shock for those of us who dare to dream of a better world, I think there are other shocks ahead that will be even more disconcerting — to those who think they can still "govern" the world by violence. *In the first **month** of this war there has been more anti-war protest, world-wide, than any **year** of the Vietnam war...*

I don't know; I have no infallible crystal ball — but the day I decided not to jump off the Brooklyn Bridge in 1955, I committed myself to going along for the ride, however rough it gets. I also try, within my limits, to make a contribution that will add to the probability of Utopia and decrease the probability of Oblivion, for all of us.

THE SANGHA ...
LIGHT IN MANIFESTATION

Rev. Yoshikami never said an unkind word about any of the other schools of Buddhism. "Every school is for a certain type of person," he said. "No school is for everybody. You find your own school." Once he added as an example, "Zen is the school for samurais and neurotics."

It took me a while to realize that, since there are no samurais around anymore, the Rev. had rather severely limited the clientele for Zen.

I liked old Yoshikami. His school of Buddhism was Shinran, a variation on Amida Buddhism, which in turn is based on faith in Amida, the Buddha of Boundless Compassion. Amida refused to accept Nirvana until every sentient being could enter that blessed quenched state along with him. Amida Buddhists believe that if you call on Amida just once *with true faith* — saying *"Namu Amida Butsu"* (Japanese for "In the name of Amida Buddha") — you will reach Nirvana eventually, even if you fuck up so much that it takes a couple of hundred thousand incarnations to get you there. Amida never gives up on you. He's like a finance company that way — a reverse finance company that wants to give you Something for Nothing.

Shinran was a 12th Century monk who decided that not everybody was capable of *true faith* in the boundless compassion of Amida. Some people — like me, for instance — will always have a degree of doubt about everything. Are we therefore barred from Nirvana? Does the compassion of Amida — who has vowed to bring the Dharma-light to every sentient being — not reach out to such wretches as us? Shinran decided he couldn't believe that: boundless compassion must not have limits, by definition. His school of Buddhism is based on the teaching that if you call on Amida just once — *"Namu Amida Butsu"* — *with or without true faith,* the infinite mercy of Amida will eventually deliver you from all errors and bring you to the Pure Land of Infinitely Reflected Light.

I like Shinran Buddhism. It seems the most humane of the religions I have sampled in my long career as a gourmet of physical and metaphysical reality-tunnels. When Arlen and I decided to get married, after living together for only six months, I persuaded her we should let the Shinran Buddhists tie the knot. I wanted Amida on my team.

Rev. Yoshikami gave us a lovely ceremony in his tiny church just off Riverside Drive. There were gold ornaments and silk curtains and heavy incense, fat and jolly Buddhas in buttery gold and ebony black, and theta-wave chants in Sanskrit, Japanese and English. There was a Heavy speech by Yoshikami on the Buddhist doctrine of karma — ineluctable causality everywhich-way in time — pointing out that this marriage had been ordained since the Big Bang and the consequences of our union would go on to the final Big Crunch.

Then Yoshikami asked us if we would place our trust in the Buddha, and we said we would. "Buddha" is both a guy who lived in India once and the state of Clear Mind of all and any who attain to what Buddha attained.

He asked if we would place our trust in the Dharma, and we said we would. Dharma is the "law" or perhaps the artistic harmony that places each piece of the space-time jig-saw right where it must go.

And then he asked if we would place our trust in the Sangha, and we looked at him blankly for a second and then said we would. We had never heard of the Sangha.

The ring was passed over an incense burner and then I put it on Arlen's finger and kissed her. She was the Buddha, the Dharma and even the unknown Sangha in my estimation.

The ceremony ended. I bowed to Yoshikami and he bowed to me, I bowed to a few associate priests and they bowed to me, and then Arlen and I were on the street, out of the timeless Buddhist reality-tunnel and surrounded by the New York 1959 reality-tunnel. Traffic. Smog. Curses. Howls. Skids. Noise.

We turned to each other and asked, "What the hell is the Sangha?"

In later years I read enough Buddhism to find the answer. The Sangha is known in many traditions. Sufis call it the Power-house. Catholics call it the Communion of Saints. Gurdjieff called it the Conscious Circle of Humanity. Occultists call it the Illuminati. I prefer to consider it an unbounded net of jewels each of which reflects and contains the reflection of each of the others.

THERE IS NO END

800-666-6666 — the toll-free number of the Beast
2 x 4 x 666 — the lumber of the Beast
666a — the tenant of the Beast
668 — the neighbor of the Beast

— Chuck Hamill

When the first edition of this book appeared, the reviewers almost all commented on its general historical and philosophical notions and entirely ignored the political-criminal revelations it contained. The one exception was a hack in a right wing occult journal called *Gnosis,* who said I had a prejudice against the Catholic Church and the C.I.A. Evidently this custard-head thought that if the evidence implicated the Church of England and British Intelligence, I would not have printed it.

Of course, with my weirdness, if a multi-millionaire banker were found hanging from a bridge with his pockets full of bricks, I would be very curious, even if he belonged to the Church of Connie's Panties and had no connection with any government body but the Department of Street Cleaning.

Now these murky matters are back and perhaps cannot be buried again…

The Calvi case, at one end of the cocaine loop, and the C.I.A. distribution network in the U.S., at the other end, are suddenly bursting into the news again, with new revelations pouring forth as if a very dark closet door suddenly sprang open to let out a thousand dancing skeletons.

In Italy, Calogero Ganci, 34, a member of the Corleone Mafia family,[*] who has been in jail since 1993, suddenly gave a full confession, admitting more than a hundred crimes, including the murder of an anti-Mafia judge. The resulting indictments and new media interest led to more confessions from other Mafiosi in

---

[*] A major player in the Mafia only in the last generation, and not to be confused with the fictitious Corleone family in the *Godfather* films, who were based on the Gambini family.

captivity, including one Franceso di Carlo, 51, who confessed to strangling Roberto Calvi and hanging him from that bridge in London.

The whole P2-Mafia-Vatican web, which had begun to look like a gangster thriller with no climax as the '80s ended, is now filling the European press again. (A good general summary can be found in the London *Times* for 20 June 1996.)

On this side of the pond, the San Jose *Mercury* has published a series of articles alleging hard documentary evidence of the C.I.A.'s roll in the same cocaine trade as Calvi, and even showing concrete details of the C.I.A.'s activities in dumping crack cocaine into the Los Angeles ghetto during the 1980s. (See the *Merc* for September and October 1996, for the unfolding or the revelations.)

The *Mercury* is the best-selling newspaper in the third largest city in California and cannot be ignored, as similar revelations in little mags (or this book) were ignored. Congresswoman Maxine Waters and Senator Diane Feinstein have both called for congressional investigation of this scandal.

Col. North ("the old man loves my ass") is still safe from indictment on a legal technicality (his testimony before Congress was given under immunity) and Mad Bill Casey is still dead, but all the others in this sorry saga may be live meat for the prosecutors very soon. That emphatically includes George Bush and maybe even Ronald Reagan, unless the Alzheimer's he developed when last questioned ("I can't recall... I can't remember...") also grants him immunity.

After years of cynicism I can hardly believe it, but it does appear that there is a real chance that the truth about the cocaine trade may finally escape from the underground media (which told the basic details ten or more years ago) and reach the courts and the major media.

As I write, Bob Dole is running all over the country talking about a minor increase in marijuana use under Clinton (an increase from 5% to 10% of the youth population, for which only the most metaphysical connection to Clinton can be found) to distract attention from the Reagan-Bush regime's full-scale involvement in cocaine.

There is no end to this. In the next volume *(Cosmic Trigger III: My Life After Death)* we will look at the Priory of Sion and UMMO...

TO BE CONTINUED ...

OTHER TITLES FROM NEW FALCON PUBLICATIONS

Prometheus Rising
 By Robert Anton Wilson
Rebels & Devils: The Psychology of Liberation
 Edited by C.S. Hyatt; with William S. Burroughs, et. al.
Undoing Yourself With Energized Meditation
 By Christopher S. Hyatt, Ph.D.
PsyberMagick
 By Peter J. Carroll
Prime Chaos
 By Phil Hine
Info-Psychology
 By Timothy Leary, Ph.D.
Zen Without Zen Masters
 By Camden Benares
The Golden Dawn Audio CDs
 By Israel Regardie
The Infernal Texts
 By Stephen Sennitt
An Insider's Guide to Robert Anton Wilson
 By Eric Wagener
Join My Cult!
 By James Curcio
Ceremonial Magic & The Power of Evocation
 By Joesph Lisiewski, Ph.D.
Virus: The Alien Strain
 By David Jay Brown
Monsters & Magical Sticks
 By Steven Heller, Ph.D.
Changing Ourselves, Changing the World
 By Gary Reiss, LCSW
Speak Out!
 By Dawn Menken, Ph.D.
Labyrinth of Chaos
 By Brian Wallace
Beyond Death
 By Timothy Owe
Bio-Etheric Healing
 By Trudy Lanitis
Fuzzy Sets
 By Constantin Negoita

For the latest information about new titles, availability and
pricing, visit our website at **http://www.newfalcon.com**

FROM ROBERT ANTON WILSON

REALITY IS WHAT YOU CAN GET AWAY WITH

What is Humphrey Bogart doing in a movie with Popeye, George Bush and Elvis Presley? That's what the archaeologists of the future are trying to puzzle out. Now you, too, can inspect this outrageous cinematic fabrication set in a time very like our own …

"A fun romp … the best screen is inside your head, just waiting to have this rollicking adventure projected on it."
—Mike Gunderloy *Factsheet Five*

ISBN 1-56184-080-7

THE WALLS CAME TUMBLING DOWN

"The title refers not only to the walls of Jericho in the Bible fable but also to the tunnel-walls of the labyrinth of Minos in the Greek myth, which hid Theseus and the Monster from each other for a long while before their final confrontation. Of course, I also had in mind the walls of our individual reality-tunnels…"

"With his humorous rapier, Wilson pokes and prods our misconceptions, prejudices and ignorance. A quantum banquet."
—Ray Tuckman, KPFK Radio

ISBN 1-56184-091-2

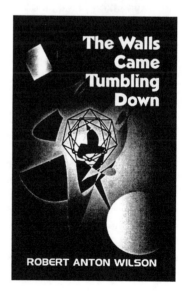

FROM ROBERT ANTON WILSON

COSMIC TRIGGER I
Final Secret of the Illuminati

The book that made it all happen! Explores Sirius, Synchronicities, and Secret Societies. Wilson has been called "One of the leading thinkers of the Modern Age."

"A 21st Century Renaissance Man. ...funny, optimistic and wise..."
—*The Denver Post*

ISBN 1-56184-003-3

COSMIC TRIGGER II
Down to Earth

In this, the second book of the *Cosmic Trigger* trilogy, Wilson explores the incredible Illuminati-based synchronicities that have taken place since his ground-breaking masterpiece was first published.

Second Revised Edition!

"Hilarious... multi-dimensional... a laugh a paragraph."   —*The Los Angeles Times*

ISBN 1-56184-011-4

COSMIC TRIGGER III
My Life After Death

Wilson's observations about the premature announcement of his death, plus religious fanatics, secret societies, quantum physics, black magic, pompous scientists, Orson Welles, Madonna and the Vagina of Nuit.

"A SUPER-GENIUS... He has written everything I was afraid to write."
—Dr. John Lilly, psychologist

ISBN 1-56184-112-9

FROM ROBERT ANTON WILSON

PROMETHEUS RISING

Readers have been known to get angry, cry, laugh, even change their entire lives. Practical techniques to break free of one's 'reality tunnels'. A very important book, now in its *eighth* printing.

"*Prometheus Rising* is one of that rare category of modern works which intuits the next stage of human evolution... Wilson is one of the leading thinkers of the Modern age."
—Barbara Marx Hubbard

ISBN 1-56184-056-4

QUANTUM PSYCHOLOGY
How Brain Software Programs You & Your World

The book for the 21st Century. Picks up where *Prometheus Rising* left off. Some say it's materialistic, others call it scientific and still others insist it's mystical. It's all of these—and none.

Second Revised Edition!

"Here is a Genius with a Gee!"
—Brian Aldiss, *The Guardian*
"What great physicist hides behind the mask of Wilson?"
—*New Scientist*

ISBN 1-56184-071-8

FROM ROBERT ANTON WILSON

ISHTAR RISING
Why the Goddess Went to Hell and What to Expect Now That She's Returning

The Return of the Goddess. Wilson provides a new slant on this provocative topic. Exciting, suggestive, and truly passionate. First published by Playboy Press as *The Book of the Breast*. Updated and revised for the '90s. All new illustrations.

ISBN 1-56184-109-9

SEX, DRUGS & MAGICK
A Journey Beyond Limits

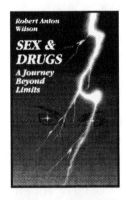

Both Sex and Drugs are fascinating and dangerous subjects in these times. First published by Playboy Press, *Sex and Drugs* is *the* definitive work on this important and controversial topic.

"Wilson pokes and prods our misconceptions, prejudices and ignorance."
— Ray Tuckman, *KPFK Radio*

ISBN 1-56184-001-7

THE NEW INQUISITION
Irrational Rationalism & The Citadel of Science

Wilson dares to confront *the* disease of our time which he calls 'Fundamentalist Materialism'. "I am opposing the Fundamentalism, not the Materialism. The book is deliberately shocking because I do not want its ideas to seem any less stark or startling than they are..."

ISBN 1-56184-002-5

FROM ROBERT ANTON WILSON

WILHELM REICH IN HELL

*Foreword by C. S. Hyatt, Ph.D.
and Donald Holmes, M.D.*

Inspired by the U. S. government seizure and burning of the books and papers of the world famous psychiatrist Dr. Wilhelm Reich. "No President, Academy, Court of Law, Congress, or Senate on this earth has the knowledge or power to decide what will be the knowledge of tomorrow."

"Erudite, witty and genuinely scary…"   *—Publishers Weekly*

ISBN 1-56184-108-0

COINCIDANCE

A Head Test

The spelling of the title is *not* a mistake. *Dance* through Religion for the Hell of It, The Physics of Synchronicity, James Joyce and Finnegan's Wake, The Godfather and the Goddess, The Poet as Early Warning Radar and much much more…

"Wilson managed to reverse every mental polarity in me, as if I had been pulled through infinity."
      —Philip K. Dick, author
            of *Blade Runner*

ISBN 1-56184-004-1

New Falcon Publications

Invites You to Visit Our Website:
http://www.newfalcon.com

At the Falcon website you can:

- Browse the online catalog of all of our great titles
- Find out what's available and what's out of stock
- Get special discounts
- Order our titles through our secure online server
- Find products not available anywhere else including:
  - One of a kind and limited availability products
  - Special packages
  - Special pricing
- Get free gifts
- Join our email list for advance notice of New Releases and Special Offers
- Find out about book signings and author events
- Send email to our authors (including the elusive Dr. Christopher Hyatt!)
- Read excerpts of many of our titles
- Find links to our author's websites
- Discover links to other weird and wonderful sites
- And much, much more

Get online today at http://www.newfalcon.com